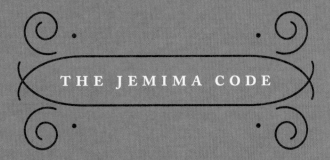

THE JEMIMA CODE

The Jemima Co

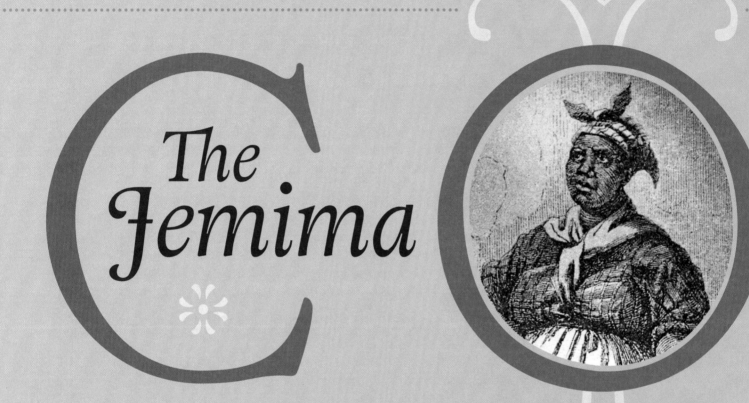

Two Centuries of
African American Cookbooks

Toni Tipton-Martin

FOREWORDS BY
John Egerton and Barbara Haber

University of Texas Press
AUSTIN

Requests for permission to reproduce material
from this work should be sent to:
Permissions
University of Texas Press
P.O. Box 7819
Austin, TX 78713-7819
http://utpress.utexas.edu/index.php/rp-form

The paper used in this book meets the minimum
requirements of ANSI/NISO Z39.48-1992 (R1997)
(Permanence of Paper). ∞

Design by Lindsay Starr

Library of Congress Cataloging-in-Publication Data

Tipton-Martin, Toni, author.
    The Jemima code : two centuries of African
American cookbooks / Toni Tipton-Martin ; forewords
by John Egerton and Barbara Haber . — First edition.
        pages cm
    Includes index.
    ISBN 978-0-292-74548-3 (cloth)
    1. African American cooking. 2. African Americans—
Food—History. 3. African American cooks—History.
I. Title.
    TX715.T598 2015
    641.59'296073—dc23   2014033779

The publication of this book was supported
in part by the University of Texas Press
Advisory Council.

Every effort has been made to trace copyright owners
where necessary. The University of Texas Press will
be happy to hear from any who proved impossible to
contact.

The recipes for tea cakes that appear on page 205 are
from *Colorful Louisiana Cuisine in Black and White* by
Bibby Tate and Ethel Dixon, copyright © 1988 by
Black and White Cuisine. Used by permission of the
licenser, Pelican Publishing Company, Inc.

The recipe for "Sweet Potato Mounds" that appears
on page 209 is an excerpt from *Soul Food*, copyright
© 1989 by Sheila Ferguson. Used by permission of
Grove/Atlantic, Inc.

Frontispiece illustration from
Aspects of Afro-American Cookery.

OR US ALL

The professional cooks of the country were Negroes
and the national cookery came from them.

GAILLARD HUNT, AMERICAN HISTORIAN,
1914

CONTENTS

Miss North Carolina, Miss Betty Jo Ring, says that her favorite cake is Paynie's chocolate cake. She is shown here with Mrs. J. F. Spruill of the Sorosis, in whose home many of the recipes were tested for measurements, with Mrs. Spruill writing down the ingredients as Jessie Payne, right, concocted the various delicacies. (Photo by Leonard Studio)

4

FOREWORD

A Gallery of Great Cooks

JOHN EGERTON

OF ALL THE COOKBOOKS published in the
United States from its birth as a nation
through the end of the twentieth century, only a
small fraction bore the names of African American authors. In that span of over two centuries,
an estimated 100,000 recipe collections made it
into print—but only 200, give or take a few, were
credited to black cooks and writers.

Adding to this curious revelation is the fact
that only four of these "minority cookbooks"
were published before 1900—and all four of
them in the North—whereas most of the others, all twentieth-century volumes, were written
and published in the South. (For the purposes at
hand, "the South" denotes a generalized geo-
graphic region between the Potomac and the
Pedernales, loosely linked by such cultural mark-
ers as music, religion, race, family, and food.)

It is no mere coincidence that the cookery of
the American South is generally regarded as the
most distinctive and varied regional cuisine in
the nation—and has been, through good times
and bad, since the early 1800s. There are numerous reasons for this—climate, culture, the

seasons, the soil—but none of these is as con-
vincing as the cumulative body of evidence to
be gleaned from the long and tangled skein of
southern social history.

Throughout 350 years of slavery, segregation, and legally enforced white primacy, the vast
majority of women of African ancestry in the
South—and many of the women of European
lineage who oversaw their work—lived lives
tightly circumscribed within hailing distance of
the region's domestic kitchens. To them fell the
overarching responsibility for the feeding of the
South, as well as the duty of birthing and nurturing replacement generations. Practically all the
latitude accorded to black women in that society,
and a major share of white women's liberties
as well, were limited to those tasks—cooking,
housekeeping, child rearing.

In hindsight, we might conclude that nothing good and lasting could have come from the
arbitrary confinement of black women and their
white governesses to the southern kitchen (and
the bedroom, but that is another story for another time). And, we might be almost entirely right

about that: nothing good—except the fusion of European and African foodstuffs and culinary skills.

That the domestic encirclement of black and white women down through generations of life in the South has had a positive bearing on the quality and distinction of the region's food is an irony of classic proportions. What evolved over time could well have been called Afro-European cookery; so much of its style and substance, after all, accompanied migrants to the South—some forced, others voluntary—from those two continents. But no one ever called it that. The vaunted American ideal of the melting pot, of *e pluribus unum*, was almost exclusively a Eurocentric notion, and it didn't gain wider application until after World War II, the civil rights movement, and other mid-twentieth-century social upheavals had come to pass.

Nevertheless, the proximity of whites and blacks in the South, their isolation from mainstream America, and the centrality of women to the region's foodways made Afro-European cookery an existential reality almost from the beginning. Long before the South or the nation as a whole got around to debating the deeply fraught social issue of racial integration, the South had thoroughly and indivisibly integrated its food. This was not done with foresight or intention; it simply happened in the prescribed course of events as the black minority did most of the work and the ruling white majority took most of the credit.

From the late 1790s, when the first American cookbooks were published, until the 1960s, when segregation laws were slowly beginning to fade, the cookbooks of the South seldom even hinted at the contributions of African Americans to the region's foodways. It was rare for the books to acknowledge blacks' presence at all, except in mindlessly demeaning caricature, and it was almost unheard-of for recipe books to bear the names of black authors. But in fact, their contributions were enormous—and the more latitude they were given to cook creatively and to manage kitchens, the more their excellence blossomed.

Black cooks (some men, but most of them women) excelled in the kitchens of middle- and upper-class households across the South and beyond, even as they somehow managed also to put food on the table in their own homes. Not every white family in every southern state had a black cook, of course, but from the early nineteenth-century antebellum period until well past World War II, African Americans were commonly close at hand whenever and wherever food was being prepared in the region.

When, in the 1820s, American cookbooks began to appear with some regularity, the South was in the forefront. One of the first and most substantial was *The Virginia House-Wife*, by Mary Randolph, published in Baltimore in 1824. It was intended specifically "for the young inexperienced housekeeper"—that is, newly wedded white women who lacked cooking skills because they had grown up in homes where kitchen labor was delegated to black servants.

It was at about this time—1827, to be precise—that Robert Roberts, the head butler in the Waltham, Massachusetts, home of a wealthy white family, put his byline on *The House Servant's Directory*, a book of general rules (including kitchen management and cooking advice) for the "downstairs" staff in the houses of the social elite. The Roberts volume is now generally cited as the first American cookbook to be published under the name of an African American writer. (That a black male in the North should appear at the head of a chronological list of these books is not indicative of the pattern that evolved, namely, that black women from the South wrote by far most of them.)

It is but one of the many virtues of the volume at hand—*The Jemima Code: Two Centuries of African American Cookbooks*, by Toni Tipton-Martin—that it embraces all the recipe collections of African American cooks known to have been published up to 2011. By drawing on more than a decade of research, Tipton-Martin has assembled an impressive body of information on this long-ignored subset of American culinary publishing. She gives us the provenance of each book, additional annotation on most of them, and historical essays on the most important ones as well as authentic period photographs and cover illustrations from the entire collection. *The Jemima Code* is a rich and comprehensive bibliographical study, the first of its kind—and it is all the more welcome and valuable for being such a long time in coming.

In poring over the most extensive cookbook collections in the country—including the Culinary Archive of the Clements Library at the University of Michigan, the Schlesinger Library at the Radcliffe Institute for Advanced Study at Harvard University, and the David Walker Lupton African-American Cookbook Collection at the University of Alabama—Tipton-Martin read and researched every volume listed herein. As an avid collector, she has acquired a substantial number of these books for her personal library. In addition, she coauthored one of them—*A Taste of Heritage: The New African-American Cuisine*—with the chef Joe Randall of Savannah, Georgia, in 2002. And in 2005, she rescued from obscurity and brought back into print *The Blue Grass Cook Book*, a 1904 volume by a well-to-do Kentucky white woman, Minnie C. Fox, who acknowledged the vital contributions of several black women and men to her culinary work and illustrated the book with photographs of them.

AUNT JEMIMA materialized in the 1880s, a product of commercial advertising inspired by the comic blackface routines of white vaudeville actors. As black women grew more self-assured and instrumental in the culinary arts of the post-bellum South, their white mistresses and masters had to find an explanation for this anomaly; in a culture that considered all blacks to be inferior, there was no room for exceptional intelligence and skill. They needed a female counterpart to the loyal and compliant Uncle Tom—a mythic persona, a caricature for all seasons. She had to be humorous, stout, lighthearted, illiterately magical—stern enough to control the children without threatening them, dependable and loyal enough to assure mothers that the kitchen was in good hands, asexual enough to foreclose any wayward thoughts among the men of the house.

So the stereotypical Aunt Jemima sprang to life: a jolly fat black woman in a do-rag, cooking up a storm, singing while she worked. She was the dominant white majority's response to the prospect of black parity, or even superiority, in the kitchen. The image, the name, the code said it all: it had to be this way, or no way.

Tipton-Martin found the Jemima imagery at every turn in her research. But as she began to uncover and study the twentieth-century cookbooks that African American women (and men) wrote, an altogether different picture took shape: a more humane and realistic composite of talented, experienced, inventive cooks in full command of their kitchens. One by one, these gifted cooks turned writers had quietly broken the Jemima code and taken their rightful place among the best of America's culinary professionals. Inspired by them, Tipton-Martin took on the task of illuminating the work of the trailblazers, hoping in the process to "rescue Aunt Jemima from the image-makers, to transform and redefine her as who she so often truly was: the house commander, the sustainer, the nurturer, the survivor, the teacher, the protector, the rock." And foremost, a superior cook, gifted and creative in her own right.

This book is their collective story, compiled, defined, and explained by Toni Tipton-Martin. The two hundred African American authors of these cookbooks are united for the first time here, in these pages, filling the gaping space previously occupied only by Aunt Jemima. ❧

JOHN EGERTON was a founder of the Southern Foodways Alliance in the Center for the Study of Southern Culture at the University of Mississippi and the author of *Speak Now Against the Day: The Generation Before the Civil Rights Movement in the South*, which won the Robert F. Kennedy Book Award, and *Southern Food: At Home, on the Road, in History*. He died in 2013.

Illustration from *A Date with a Dish: A Cookbook of American Negro Recipes.*

FOREWORD

Why Cookbooks Matter

BARBARA HABER

Now that the field of food studies is well underway, cookbooks are understood to be important resources for the study of history and culture, but their newfound significance raises the question of whose history and whose culture is revealed through these books. A glance at some standard cookbooks thought to reflect U.S. social history illustrates both the absence of African American contributions to this history and misconceptions about this underrepresented group. These gross omissions are finally being corrected, in particular by Toni Tipton-Martin in her valuable book *The Jemima Code: Two Centuries of African American Cookbooks*.

At the beginning of our republic, Americans relied on cookbooks brought over from England and other parts of Europe, suggesting that a national identity regarding food was slow to evolve. Not until 1796, with the publication of Amelia Simmons's *American Cookery*, did a cookbook using such native ingredients as cornmeal and cranberries appear, a sign that Americans were feeling more familiar and comfortable in their

new country. The next landmark cookbook to come along was Mary Randolph's *The Virginia House-Wife* (1824), which describes—presumably for other rich landowners—the responsibilities of running a southern plantation. The book reflects a slave society from the perspective of a highborn southern woman with impressive management skills. At the same time, *The Frugal Housewife* (1829), by the northern abolitionist Lydia Maria Child, was written for a humble audience and for the purpose of raising money to support the author's antislavery cause. Both books, which reflect a critical period in our nation's past, lack any apparent insights from the African Americans whose freedom was at the center of a growing conflict that would eventually lead to America's Civil War.

By the 1840s, a cookbook industry was underway, its volumes written mainly for a general audience of homemakers. Notable among them was Catherine Beecher's *A Treatise on Domestic Economy, for the Use of Young Ladies at Home, and at School* (1841), a title that describes Beecher's mission to prepare women for the responsibilities of skillfully running a household, including the handling of servants. Beecher's approach points to the separate-sphere dogma of the day, which saw women's roles as strictly domestic and men's as providing for a family by working outside the home. This socially constructed doctrine prompted Beecher to uplift the domestic sphere by professionalizing its status, spelling out for a white audience how to handle a home and servants.

Regional American cookbooks, which were appearing regularly by the mid-nineteenth century, focused on parts of the country that we recognize today as having distinct culinary traditions: the South, New England, and even the Midwest; recipes for Hoosier Pickles and Buckeye Dumplings showed up in books published in Indiana and Ohio. The implicit assumption in all these books is that the authors were offering a white audience recipes invented by whites. Although we are somewhat aware of the originality and contributions of African American cooks who worked in southern white homes, their work was rarely acknowledged in cookbooks published before 1900. And if they were, remarks about these cooks were condescending. Two works by African American authors that appeared before the Civil War, Robert Roberts's *The House Servant's Directory* (1827) and Tunis Campbell's *Hotel Keepers, Head Waiters, and Housekeepers' Guide* (1848), make it clear that people of color were seen as living outside the mainstream of American life, their highest expectation being to professionally manage other servants.

Just after the Civil War, a distinctly American form of cookbook writing, the community cookbook—or charity cookbooks, as they sometimes are known—came into being. At first they were compilations of recipes submitted by women to books sold as fund-raisers to help war widows and orphans, but the idea spread as a way to support other nonprofit causes. Such purposeful cookbooks continue to be published, and these days they support institutions, schools, churches, arts programs, and social causes. But because these books are published locally, and because old ones especially are hard to find and collect, we have little knowledge of those that were produced by groups of African Americans.

By the end of the nineteenth century, cooking schools in several American cities had been established, and their founders routinely published cookbooks, the best-known being Fannie Farmer's *The Boston Cooking-School Cook Book* (1896), in its time the standard cookbook found in New England homes. Influenced by the home economics movement, which paid attention to scientific cooking, Farmer's book was notable for its attempt to standardize level measurements for the home cook. Farmer and other female cooking-school teachers were dedicated to educating women for the purpose of running efficient home kitchens that would turn out tasty food. And it should be noted that while most of their courses were designed for a middle-class white audience, others were designed to teach servants, many of them African Americans, who would be doing much of the manual work in the houses of whites. Thus, within the larger separate sphere that separated white women from men, there was a servant class living within its own domestic sphere.

The late nineteenth-century influx of immigrants, mainly from Europe but from other continents as well, transformed America's eating habits by introducing the country to new foodways. While newcomers were learning about an unfamiliar culture, they were adding their own food traditions to the jumble that has evolved into what we think of today as American cuisine. Migrations within the country had a similar effect. From the time of World War I through the 1950s, hundreds of thousands of blacks moved to industrialized cities in the North and West and brought along foodways that have influenced American culture generally.

What becomes clear is that African American voices have largely been missing from what we think of as American culinary history. This major group of Americans has been either rendered invisible or portrayed as passive cooks functioning strictly by instinct. But now, through Toni Tipton-Martin's *The Jemima Code*, visibility is being restored and recognition given to the lost voices and contributions of African Americans.

This major project took root when Tipton-Martin began to collect cookbooks written by African Americans. As she acquired several hundred books, many of them scarce, she gathered evidence that would allow her to reinterpret American food history. She located even more of these books in libraries with major cookbook collections, and then set out to write a unique bibliography. In it, Tipton-Martin is replacing the worn-out stereotype of a happy-go-lucky turbaned black mammy by bringing to light books that prove the proficiency of African Americans as thoughtful and creative cooks and as highly skilled technicians and managers. *The Jemima Code* is going to change forever how we regard the history of cooking in America. ❧

BARBARA HABER is a former curator of books at the Schlesinger Library, Radcliffe Institute for Advanced Study at Harvard University, and the author of *From Hardtack to Home Fries: An Uncommon History of American Cooks and Meals* (2002).

You can't duplicate it in a home-made batter; you don't get it in any other mix . . . the matchless 4-flour flavor of Aunt Jemima Pancakes

The treasured Aunt Jemima recipe combines 4 flours in a special way. Wheat flour for lightness, corn for tenderness, rye for richness, rice for browning quality. This 4-flour blend gives Aunt Jemima pancakes a flavor no others can match.

The Story of Aunt Jemima

Aunt Jemima means far more than pancakes; she is an American tradition. Her story goes back to the days of lavish Old South hospitality on Colonel Higbee's great plantation. There crinolined ladies, from far and near, came in their carriages up the tree-lined drive to taste the delicacy for which Aunt Jemima was famous. That delicacy was pancakes—luscious-light, golden-brown pancakes, which Aunt Jemima prepared from her own secret recipe.

From then on, the fame of her pancakes grew until today Aunt Jemima Pancakes are America's favorites. No other pancake mix has ever been able to give such wonderful flavor and lightness. No other pancakes are such a cherished part of the American way of life.

Page from *Aunt Jemima's Magical Recipes*
(Quaker Oats Company, 1930s).

THE JEMIMA CODE

INTRODUCTION

There are only two lasting bequests we can hope to give to our children: One is roots, the other is wings.

HODDING CARTER

 Y THE TIME I WAS thirty years old, I could count my southern life experiences on one hand. When you grow up in a tiny family in Los Angeles, sheltered by expatriates who left skid marks when they quit the South, it is easy to believe that your family drama does not play east of the San Bernardino Valley. As a child during the civil rights era, I lived in exile—sheltered from the narrow perspective of Negro subservience and "proper place," liberated from the burden of low-class living. My parents built new and improved lives near the Pacific coast.

Not that the social, cultural, and culinary dimensions of southern living were unrecognizable out west. Sweet tea and fresh-squeezed lemonade washed down Aunt Jewel's crisp fried chicken, smoked pork bones seasoned Nannie's Sunday greens, and Mother always baked her cornbread in a big black cast-iron skillet. But that was just dinner; everybody we knew in Baldwin Hills ate that.

I didn't care all that much for pork ribs and became easily nauseated by the potent smell of chitlins, which blasted through the air like a dragon's fiery breath every time our neighbors from Tennessee opened their front door. Perhaps the most obvious evidence of my western upbringing was my unapologetic admission that I sprinkled sugar on my grits. As far as I could tell, precious few of my culinary notions qualified as southern, and it was entirely possible that I could have stumbled blindly through the rest of my life without ever discovering the Jemima living in me—if not for Vera Beck.

Vera called to mind one of those African American matriarchs familiarly thought of as saints—a woman in her twilight years whose culinary expressiveness was like a gift she bestowed on the people she loved. Whenever I think of her—and it is often—I see a proud, generous, loving, tenderhearted, talented, exceptional cook. She made the best biscuits, chowchow, fried green tomatoes, and Mississippi mud cake I have ever tasted. And although she earned her living as my test-kitchen cook in Cleveland, at one of the few major daily newspapers that dared to preserve the tradition, she was a self-taught kitchen genius armed with recipes handed down by word of mouth through generations of rural Alabama cooks. Her talent flowed from a photographic memory and her five senses. Such gifts have all but disappeared from contemporary kitchens.

As I got to know Vera better, she forced me to circle back and confront a personality quirk that Virginia Woolf described as "contrary instincts." I thought I was content—a thirty-something food editor living far away from home on the eastern shore of Lake Erie, enjoying amazing and exotic world cuisine. I had come of age as the daughter of a health-conscious, fitness-crazed cook whose experiments with tofu, juicing, and smoothies predated the fads. Both my mother and my grandmother knew a lot about cooking, but they didn't dispense kitchen wisdom regularly. Vera read my unfamiliarity with her southern-accented fare as a sign of incomplete social conditioning. Later on, I came to see that I was a casualty of the Jemima code.

Merriam-Webster defines a code as "a systematic statement of a body of law; especially one given statutory force; a system of principles or rules (as in moral code); a system of signals or symbols for communication . . . used to represent assigned and often secret meanings." To decode, the dictionary goes on to say, is "to convert (as a coded message) into intelligible form; to recognize and interpret (an electronic signal); to discover the underlying meaning of."

Black codes once defined legal place for former slaves. As Americans, we still live with all sorts of standardizing codes—dress codes, moral codes, codes of conduct, codes of law, bar codes. Recipes are codes.

Historically, the Jemima code was an arrangement of words and images synchronized to classify the character and life's work of our nation's black cooks as insignificant. The encoded message assumes that black chefs, cooks, and cookbook authors—by virtue of their race and gender—are simply born with good kitchen instincts; diminishes knowledge, skills and abilities involved in their work, and portrays them as passive and ignorant laborers incapable of creative culinary artistry.

Throughout the twentieth century, the Aunt Jemima advertising trademark and the mythical mammy figure in southern literature provided a shorthand translation for a subtle message that went something like this: "If slaves can cook, you can too," or "Buy this flour and you'll cook with the same black magic that Jemima put into her pancakes." In short: a sham.

Exposure to this Machiavellian deception begins early in life, like a communicable childhood disease. Negative pictures of black women first invade the subconscious through literature, television, or film. The stereotyped caricature, described succinctly by Rebecca Sharpless as rotund and head-ragged, grinning broadly, speaking in crude dialect, comforting white children, and always putting the needs of other people before her own, is incubated in schools, where written history and its lessons on slavery reinforce and substantiate the dim, demoralizing portraits of black women as "noble savages" managing domestic responsibilities for their white mistresses. This endless cycle ravages self-esteem, identity, sense of belonging, and cultural pride, leaving scars for generations that are invisible but not insignificant—as tuberculosis does.

It is true that black women did much of the cooking in early American kitchens. It is also true that they did so with the art and aptitude of today's trained professionals, transmitting their craft orally. Society has been slow to accept oral history as a legitimate record. But since my ancestors were denied the opportunity to learn to read and write, they transferred important cultural traditions from one generation to another through face-to-face, personal exchanges. They told stories on the front porch, during special occasions, and at celebrations. They transferred cooking techniques while working side by side or sharing a meal together.

"African American children, mostly female, began their cooking apprenticeships at a young age, closely observing older cooks within their family and extended family," the historian Frederick Douglass Opie writes in *Hog and Hominy: Soul Food From Africa to America* (2008). "Over time, adults would assign chores of ever-increasing difficulty to acclimate the child to the art of cooking." Opie's observations come to life in the stories told by former slaves and recorded by the Federal Writers Project (FWP; 1935–1939) of the Works Progress Administration, and in those relayed in Susan Tucker's "artful oral history," *Telling Memories among Southern Women: Domestic Workers and Their Employers in the Segregated South* (1988).

Harriet Barrett told an FWP interviewer in Texas, "Dey put me to cooking when I's a li'l kid and people now says dat Aunt Harriet am de bes' cook in Madisonville." Ella Wilson, who grew up a slave in Arkansas, described the rigors of her culinary education this way: "I had to get up every morning at five when the cook got up and make the coffee and then I had to go in the dining-room and set the table. Then I served breakfast. Then I went into the house and cleaned it up. Then I tended to the white children and served the other meals during the day."

Such routines seem devoid of classic culinary proficiencies until we consider the wide-ranging tasks young apprentices would have observed to get all that food on the table—from mundane acts like fanning away flies from the dining room table, to killing, gutting, and plucking feathers from fowl. After starting out as something like sous-chefs, they matured into exceptional kitchen leaders, evaluating the supplies and ingredients left by the mistress, memorizing the instructions for making dishes, and sometimes fixing supper for their own families after dark with only a "pine knot torch" for light, as a former slave named Betty Powers recalled. Sylvia King, a former slave who was born in Morocco and received culinary training in France, did all these things and then some in Texas—working

in the gardens and orchards, drying fruit, making cider, seasoning hams after curing—but still found herself alternating between field work and the spinning loom.

Respect for this work has been slowly gaining recognition from scholars and independent writers, thanks in part to the Southern Foodways Alliance's oral history project and its mission to preserve and celebrate the American South's complex food history and its unknown artisans. Compelling explorations and analysis by the scholars Psyche Williams-Forson, Rebecca Sharpless, and Anne Bower also are prioritizing African American women's culinary legacies.

Building Houses Out of Chicken Legs: Black Women, Food, and Power (2006), Williams-Forson's thought-provoking study of black women and their relationships with the "gospel bird," turns attention away from the caricatured image of Aunt Jemima and its implication that black women were "worthless figures capable only of menial servitude."

As Rebecca Sharpless explains in *Cooking in Other Women's Kitchens: Domestic Workers in the South, 1865–1960* (2010), kitchen workers seasoned the lives of others and made their existence pleasurable with "elaborate, delectable feasts" created from recipes modified to suit the local climate, available ingredients, the tastes and religious preferences of the household, and other circumstances—with fruits, vegetables, meats, and staples that extended "beyond their ancestral roots." They made do under the most adverse circumstances, providing sustenance for their own loved ones from their employers' leftovers as well as ingredients bought with the cash wages earned with their labor. And they also salved wounds, nurtured spirits, and imparted wisdom over steaming plates of nourishment. "In so doing, they contributed to one of the most noteworthy parts of southern American culture," Sharpless emphasized.

Talented, inventive, nurturing—how is it that these are not the predominant images of African American cooks? Why don't we celebrate their contributions to American culture the way we venerate that of the imaginary Betty Crocker? Why wasn't their true legacy preserved? Can we ever forget the images of ignorant, submissive, selfless, sassy, asexual domestics with inborn culinary gifts? Is it possible to replace the burned-into-our-eyes, mostly unflattering pictures of generous waistlines bent over cast iron skillets? Will we ever believe that strong African American women, who toted wood and built fires before even thinking about kneading bread dough or mixing cakes, left us more than just their formulas for good pancakes?

The jury is still out on these questions.

In the meantime, the cookbook authors introduced in *The Jemima Code* present a new picture, one that replaces the Aunt Jemima asymmetry, granting recognition to a group of people with little traditionally documented history.

IN MY CALIFORNIA YOUTH, before I moved to Cleveland and came under the influence of Vera Beck, several experiences, considered in retrospect, pointed me toward a focus on black cooks and inspired me to become a novice collector of rare cookbooks written by African Americans. In 1985, a few years after graduating from journalism school at the University of Southern California, I got a chance to find my voice as a food writer at the *Los Angeles Times*. By the time that Ruth Reichl came on board as the food editor, I had spent hours standing in our test kitchen across the counter from its director, Donna Deane, watching, listening, smelling, and tasting every dish she prepared. I sorted and organized the cookbooks in our library and, on most days, pored over the A-to-Z recipe files, researching and soaking up everything I could about cooking. The shelves sagged from the weight of recipe books from such faraway lands (and times) as the former Austrian Empire, but few titles mentioned the food of my culture. Even the southern cookbooks were silent on the subject.

I wondered, "Where are all the black cooks?" I decided to find out.

After a long period of thinking and some hand-wringing I realized that precious few of the people I wanted to interview about the techniques that my ancestors had used skillfully in big-house kitchens and had applied creatively to slaveholders' rations were still living. Nonetheless, black cookbooks might confirm their impact on American food, families, and communities.

A cookbook may be informally defined as a collection of directions translated into understandable language so that anyone can make the dish being described. These directions, also known as recipes, range from simple to extremely complex. They usually follow a standardized formula, such as the one outlined by Joan Whitman and Dolores Simon in *Recipes into Type: A Handbook for Cookbook Writers and Editors* (1993): title, headnote, ingredients list, instructions, number of servings, notes, and variations.

Recipes are protected by copyright, but copyright law does not protect ones that are mere listings of ingredients. Changing a single ingredient or step in the method is an accepted way to create a new dish and thereby establish a new claim of ownership. By this standard, a cook who, for example, substitutes lime juice for lemon juice in a published recipe, or changes the language that describes the process for handling pie crust, has created a new, "adapted" recipe, according to the U.S. Copyright Office.

As a result, creations that mixed African and Native American technique with American ingredients and European recipes disappeared into cookbooks written for mainstream white audiences. A cookbook, however, is rarely purely utilitarian.

Historians and scholars recognize recipes and cookbooks as important research tools for understanding women and their work. Janet Theophano's definitive study *Eat My Words: Reading Women's Lives through the Cookbooks They Wrote* (2002), presents myriad ways that women use cookbooks as scrapbooks with recipes—to recount the stories of their lives, encoding images of themselves by using food as a metaphor.

A cookbook author lures the reader into the kitchen through all sorts of tools: portraits, poetry, culinary authority, and the promise of delicious food. She writes in a particular tone, using a specific selection of words arranged according to a particular stylistic mode (such as memoir, journal, community compilation, or souvenir journal). The work opens a window into her community and can impart knowledge about her region, its economy, social divisions, current events, and important personalities. A cookbook author tells stories that preserve history, memories, celebrations, and identity; that advocate for social causes, such as education, suffrage, child welfare, abolition of slavery, eradication of poverty, or improved social welfare; that use highlights of her own life to memorialize her work, her family's favorite recipes, and the secrets of her friends; and finally, that aim for the greater good—as projects of patronage, religious comfort, or preservation of cultural legacy.

This theory seems tailor-made for works written by African American servants. With limited access to other artistic forms of creative expression, preparing and sharing a decadent caramel cake or batch of crisply fried chicken displayed their talent and spread their knowledge, a way to "set the record straight," as the literary scholar Doris Witt explains in her important reading of black women, food and identity, *Black Hunger: Soul Food and America* (1999). Recipe collections could be means of personal and cultural realization: "The cookbook offers both the famous and the anonymous a force through which to create self and history, a means to become a poet, an historian, an ethnographer, and even, as the example of Dick Gregory would suggest, a political satirist."

If black authors were at all like other writers, I thought, their cookbooks would preserve the treasury of dishes prepared and served over the years in the home and in public food establishments of all kinds—"an authentic example of a culture, an expression of the taste, style, and habits of a particular people at a particular time,"

as the cookbook consultants Hays, Rolfes & Associates and Perre Magness explain in their 1986 guide *How to Write and Publish a Classic Cookbook*.

Over time, I uncovered a documentary record that allowed for a reinterpretation of black cooks as professionals with technical, organizational, and managerial core values; Jemima clues, I called them. Their cookbooks substantiate the kind of skills that are taught in the best culinary academies, that I observed in newspaper test kitchens, and that display learned wisdom. These proficiencies include knowledge of fundamentals (food safety, hygiene, and scientific principles); artistic abilities such as food styling, garnishing, and decorating dishes so that they are sensorily pleasing to the eye and the palate; tested methods of cooking with both high-quality and inferior ingredients, or with regional and "exotic" heritage foods; and haute cuisine laced with wine and herbs.

Also hidden in these treasures are important African techniques that slaves brought with them to plantation kitchens—several of them had been theorized in the 1930s by the Brazilian intellectual Gilberto Freyre and were subsequently revisited in a 1971 cookbook by Helen Mendes, *The African Heritage Cookbook: A Chronicle of the Origins of Soul Food Cooking, with 200 Authentic—and Delicious—Recipes*.

Mendes, a social worker, chef, and scholar, had tired of the "implication of white authorities that Black Americans had no culinary past." To establish a legacy beyond homage, she wrote a treatise on an African "cook's education," which began for her when, as a toddler, she walked through the forest lands with her mother and young brother to pick fruits and gather herbs, wild tubers, mushrooms, and edible greens. In her book, she identifies ingredients, utensils, and the cooking fundamentals she practiced—roasting over an open pit, boiling, stewing, steaming, baking, frying, jerking (salt drying), and smoking.

These remembered traditions appear in the pages of black cookbooks in forms that made life easier and saved time and resources. Examples include simple breads mixed with cornmeal and water and cooked over an open flame, battered and fried vegetables (fritters), and stews made ahead in one pot, plus basic tips on keeping muffins from sticking and scalded milk from scorching, and for knowing the best month to pickle onions.

Not long after the revelation that there are cookbooks establishing African American culinary authority, a smallish, plainly packaged Dover paperback appeared in the book giveaway that the *Los Angeles Times* food staff held to thin out the new volumes that flooded the newsroom each year. The *New Orleans CookBook*, by Lena Richard, offered no biographical information about the author—not even her picture. I plucked it from the pile anyway. The way I figured it, a book of Creole recipes might provide some insight. Little did I know that Richard's writings would be the first of many gifts of African American know-how.

My cookbook library grew gradually during my years at the *Times* and the *Cleveland Plain Dealer*. Then, in 2005, the University of Alabama Libraries published a bibliography of the David Walker Lupton African American Cookbook Collection, a "treasure trove of rare and obscure books, many of them self-published, that too often pass 'under the radar,'" curators said at the time. This valuable resource became my shopping list when Doris Witt published it in *Black Hunger*, and I used it to hunt down vintage editions in secondhand shops and Internet bookstores.

Using search engines set up for used, rare, and out-of-print books, I set a monthly schedule, entered the title and author of one of the books on the list, then waited for something obscure to pop up.

The first book that did was *Eliza's Cook Book*, a collection of middle-class recipes curated in 1936 by the Negro Culinary Art Club of Los Angeles. The starting bid: $1. I was ecstatic, and set my watch to the same time on the countdown clock so that an alarm would remind me when the auction was set to end. At the appropriate time, I typed in my maximum bid and then frantically refreshed the page every couple of seconds as the amounts accrued. As the final seconds ticked away, a bidding war escalated the price for *Eliza*: $100, $225, $350. I held my breath and entered $400. And waited. "Congratulations! You've won!" appeared on the screen. The book arrived by mail within a few days.

Life went on like that for several more years. I eventually owned nearly three hundred African American cookbooks, including a few not listed in the Lupton bibliography. Some of the works were trade published. Others came to print on their own. All were dignified, but dwarfed by beautifully photographed hardcover southern cookery books published by food industry luminaries.

These little rays of light organized themselves into the framework of this book and revealed an African American kitchen arsenal, handed down orally between generations by clearheaded, thinking cooks who practiced what the chef Michael Ruhlman described as "mental *mise-en-place*." They understood systems and formulas, and could translate their talent for recipe development into words, even if few of them had the means, time, and resources to do so. Through them, I traveled back to harrowing but simple times when familiar dishes and storytelling about the old ways—grinding corn into meal, roasting wild turkeys, and baking sweet potatoes "so big," Fannie Yarbrough remembered, that cooks would "have to cut 'em with an ax"— beckoned hungry folks to the table.

TO BREAK THE JEMIMA CODE, I wrote 160 critiques of black cookery books published from 1827 through the 2010s, arranging them chronologically and according to the social themes, work ethos, or careers the authors represent. Where possible, I tried to let the authors speak in their own behalf.

In going through these books, I measured each author's writing according to a methodology taught by Barbara Ketchum Wheaton at Radcliffe in the "Reading Historic Cookbooks" seminar. The process involves careful examination of every aspect of a cookbook—the introductory words of the author, the ingredients, methods of preparation, and production elements such as binding, paper choice, coloring, and fonts. Narrowing the focus to fundamentals and culinary techniques shifts the emphasis onto the diverse talents and practical competencies possessed by each author, and diminishes the make-do and "something outta nuthin'" processes behind chitlins, Hoppin' John, and salmon croquettes, which usually preoccupy African American foodways research.

"To read a book in its entirety is like trying to eat dinner in just one bite," Wheaton cautioned on the opening day of class in Cambridge. Similarly, each cookbook in this bibliography exposes a different characteristic of black kitchen workers and offers new ideas that refute the notion encoded in the Aunt Jemima construct, namely, that all black cooks, chefs, and cookbook authors work by natural instinct.

In "Nineteenth-Century Cookbooks," household manuals authored by men during the early nineteenth century introduce the supervision and management priorities required to run fine New England houses, first-class restaurants, and hotel dining rooms. Recipe compilations by two free women of color rebut one of the "key mythologies" promoted by white Reconstruction-era writers about black women cooks—that they cooked by a mysterious voodoo magic. As Doris Witt's essay in *African American Foodways: Explorations of History and Culture* (2007; edited by Anne L. Bower) points out, both these cookbook authors, Malinda Russell and Abby Fisher, acknowledge the influence of southern cooking on their unique culinary styles yet distance themselves from the mammy stereotype. Russell, in fact, explains that she studied "under the tuteledge" of another knowledgeable black cook, stressing the "transcribability" of what is known by experience, testing, and practice, rather than some "culinary aura."

Transcribability is a theme that continued into the late nineteenth century as household workers of all types presented themselves as industrious professionals, crafting award-winning recipes from imagination and limited resources, and according to scientific methodologies, while operating food businesses despite restrictive black codes that in some regions forbade them from selling door-to-door or trading in open markets.

"Surviving Mammyism" covers early twentieth-century cookbooks by chefs and domestic-science educators, shedding light on efforts by the African American upper class to reform the diets of poor African Americans in the South and to inspire cultural pride. In 1902, for example, John B. Goins of Chicago published *The American Colored Waiter*, a manual that, though not a cookbook, represented an attempt to treat service work "intelligently." His copiously illustrated text includes detailed line drawings of carving strategies, place settings, and food presentation, as well as some general recipes. In addition, Goins instructed his contemporaries about practical service rituals while stressing important values and work ethics, including proper dress and punctuality.

In textbooks published between 1900 and 1926, domestic-science educators at historically black colleges spread the "gospel of industry and self-reliance." The emphasis was on the growing preference for a healthier variety of ingredients, on the use of kitchen tools, and on cooking methods that shunned frying or dependence upon fatback for seasoning, as Opie explains in *Hog and Hominy*.

Despite these signs of social progress, advertisers and manufacturers continued to adorn recipe booklets with black faces that reinforced the stereotype of the "docile servant who was always ready to serve," notes Marilyn Kern-Foxworth in *Aunt Jemima, Uncle Ben, and Rastus: Blacks in Advertising, Yesterday, Today, and Tomorrow* (1994). Yet in a surely unintended consequence, the constant association of blacks with the preparation of tasty food affirmed an observation made in 1967 by Arthur Marquette in *Brands, Trademarks, and Goodwill: The Story of the Quaker Oats Company*: "The American Negro has always represented in American life the acme of the culinary arts, respected as in France are the chefs who belong to the Société Gastronomique."

The domestic workers and prominent caterers highlighted in "The Servant Problem" used food and cooking to expand their culinary borders and solidify their middle-class status in the Jim Crow South, despite their "poignant absence" from cookbooks written by southern white women—including those by Jews, as Marcie Cohen Ferris explains in *Matzoh Ball Gumbo: Culinary Tales of the Jewish South*. As "central figures" in synagogues and home kitchens, African American cooks prepared menus for private and family functions, blending African American flavors and cooking methods in what became an integrated kosher style.

The cookbooks written by black authors from the mid-1920s to 1950 demonstrate a multicultural recipe development designed for the taste buds of the upper class—both white and black—who enjoyed fried chicken, sweet potato pies, grits, greens, and barbecue at home with their families and at important social gatherings. These menus "had little to do with the recipes of Africa or the plantation foods of the antebellum South and were inspired by the prevailing taste and ideas of grand dining in Europe," as Jessica B. Harris notes in *High on the Hog: A Culinary Journey From Africa to America* (2011). By mid-century, Harris continues, black cooks had "heralded a new age of African Americans in food"; they "used developing media outlets like *Ebony* magazine and new technology like television to create national and international reputations and to teach the world about the growing scope

and diversity of African American food." These transformations are covered in "Lifting as We Climb."

Unfortunately, the soul era of the 1960s, which enabled civil rights activists, soul food cooks, and artists to proudly claim the improvisational, make-do-style dishes of the ancestors, documented in the soul food cookbooks described in "Soul Food," bound "black cuisine to poverty ingredients composed as an act of the spirit," not the brain, as Adrian Miller points out in *Soul Food: The Surprising Story of an American Cuisine, One Plate at a Time* (2013).

The authors discussed in "Simple Pleasures," who published during the 1970s, tried to unring that bell by embracing the confidence and cultural pride of the black power movement, embellishing and deepening it with African foods, celebrations, and practices. These gutsy "new soul" cooks refused to be defined by the narrow perspective that black food meant only pork parts, greens, and cornbread, establishing permanence for African American heritage cuisine through culinary autobiographies that reflect personal preferences and reclaim ancestral wisdom—whether the food was stamped "southern," "mama's" or "home style." Their books reflect a passionate pursuit of healthy cooking, balanced diets of moderation, vegetarianism, and life without pork. They trace their preferred, wholesome culinary styles to many sources and regions within the African diaspora: Afro-Caribbean, Louisiana Creole, and Lowcountry Gullah peoples as well as the American South generally.

In "Mammy's Makeover," middle-class values, the embrace and practice of classic techniques, and a real sense of nostalgia prove one thing: 1980s authors observed and understood "fusion trends" and "nouveau cuisine" as a mechanism to give soul food the spirited uplift that it should be remembered for.

And with that, black cooks were set free.

It seems natural for this bibliography to end in the 1980s, even though my collection includes works published right up to the present day. Since then, authors have seemed less constrained by narrow themes that once limited their art. We have not yet reached the time when creative recipes by African Americans without southern flair are the norm, but I can tell you that twenty-first-century authors are reinterpreting our culinary lineage with just as much intelligence as slave cooks balancing the plentitude of big-house menus and spartan cabin cooking.

In the 1990s, as described in "Sweet to the Soul," African American cooking was clearly not just soul food. We learned to cook convivially with celebrities and musicians, and conceived of cooking as a gift to others. Dishes for special occasions, swanky parties, church socials, and heart health mingled with those that wed southern cookery to French, English, African, and Caribbean modes.

Books published since 2000 jump-start the imagination and cover such diverse topics as organic and vegan soul, and the breathtaking cookery of an English farmhouse. Dessert anthologies satisfy the sweet tooth with treats collected at church gatherings and fund-raising socials. And the wide range of children's cookbooks provides lessons in patience and self-reliance through smart recipes that hint at the science and chemistry of the craft. (These seem almost like a natural prelude to the "minimalist" trend, with its simple techniques and few ingredients.) Bread baking and grilling charm specialists.

I like to think my collection tells a new African American kitchen story, a culinary autobiography, as Traci Marie Kelley put it, with culinary truths and whispered wisdom that substantiate a heritage of greatness, exemplify culinary freedom for black cooks, and allow everyone to embrace Jemima's bandana.

I believe the written legacy left by these new role models does what black cooks hovering in the shadows have always done: spur everyone on to distinction and instilling confidence, whether that path of culinary excellence leads to business, education, or the sustaining of community.

Finally, I hope that awakening this heritage offers an occasion for doing what a well-traveled and widely popular culinary expert, Duncan Hines, suggested in 1955: "Many southern ladies had Negro cooks to help them; and just how much we owe to their skill I have no way of knowing except that almost all of the finest southern dishes are of their creating or at least bear their special touch and everyone who loves good cookery should thank them from the bottom of their heart" (*Duncan Hines' Food Odyssey*).

Nineteenth-Century

Century

COOKBOOKS

*Breaking
a Stereotype*

NANCY GREEN, a fifty-nine-year-old former slave, had an exclusive contract to play the role of Aunt Jemima, a jovial plantation kitchen cook—singing, grinning, telling stories, cooking, and entertaining crowds at the 1893 World's Fair (Columbian Exposition) in Chicago. Like Hattie McDaniel, the Oscar-winning actress who played Mammy in *Gone with the Wind*, Green had struggled to establish a career outside the domestic sphere. The opportunity to portray a celebrated character liberated her from menial chores of washing dishes, sweeping floors, and "answering bells," but that character, modeled after a fictitious kitchen slave, was a cultural flash point, drawing both praise as a path to economic freedom and fire as a reminder of servitude.

The limelight enjoyed by McDaniel and Green was in stark contrast to the invisibility of all but a few African Americans then laboring unsung and uncelebrated in the culinary world. Aside from a few—pepper pot vendors, vegetable women, hot corn girls, and cala women—who achieved some independence for themselves, practically all black cooks existed in the culinary shadows as far as cookbook writers were concerned. (Calas are fried cakes made mostly of sweetened cooked rice; they were especially popular in New Orleans.) And yet some culinary workers achieved a degree of fame. Four African American authors managed to publish books during the nineteenth century—unsurprisingly, outside the South—with words that say a lot about their kitchen habits and recipes that display American and African accents.

W. E. B. Du Bois drew attention to six prominent food service workers in his 1899 study of life, conditions, and opportunity, *The Philadelphia Negro . . . Together with a Special Report on Domestic Service*. In a section titled "The Guild of the Caterers, 1840–1870," Du Bois traces the evolution of ex-slaves from home service to "more independent and lucrative employment." He paid tribute to six "masters of the

I'd rather make $700 a week playing a maid than $7 a week being a maid.

HATTIE MCDANIEL

gastronomic art"—Robert Bogle, Peter Augustin, James Prosser, Thomas Dorsey, Henry Jones, and Henry Minton—whose lives exemplified the possibility of uplift: "The whole catering business, arising from an evolution shrewdly, persistently and tastefully directed, transformed the Negro cook and waiter into the public caterer and restaurateur, and raised a crowd of underpaid menials to become a set of self-reliant, original business men, who amassed fortunes for themselves and won general respect for their people."

One of these culinary leaders was recognized in a lengthy poem, *Ode to Bogle*, composed by Nicholas Biddle, who praised him as a "distinguished gentleman" who achieved both fame and fortune in food service and "virtually created the business of catering in the city."

And there were others. George Washington Parke Custis, the adopted son of the first president, esteemed Hercules, the chief cook at George Washington's Philadelphia home and at Mount Vernon, "a celebrated *artiste . . .* as highly accomplished and proficient in the culinary art as could be found in the United States" (*Recollections and Private Memoirs of Washington*). James Hemings treated guests at Thomas Jefferson's Monticello to haute cuisine with an African sensibility—okra soup, gumbo thickened with sassafras leaves (filé), and fried chicken served with browned fried cornmeal dumplings and rich cream gravy. Thomas Downing ran a famous oyster house in New York City.

The first published culinary work by an African American was written by Robert Roberts and published in 1827. I already owned a facsimile edition of *The House Servant's Directory* when the New York City cookbook dealer Bonnie Slotnick helped me acquire a first edition. With the explicit instructions that Roberts left behind in the *Directory* as my guide, I got lost in the pulse of life and work in early nineteenth-century New England. I toured the grounds of Gore Place in Waltham, Massachusetts, walking around the dining room and the stone kitchen in the basement of the mansion, and standing

in the room where Roberts composed his opus and recorded his observations. I imagined what it must have been like for Roberts to watch through the tiny window of his study on the upper floor as guests' carriages approached on the main road. I heard Roberts organizing his squad of household employees with a distinctive air of professionalism. It was a transforming achievement. A game changer. My vision for a book about women expanded to include men.

The *Directory* was so popular that later editions were printed in 1828 and 1843. Roberts leaves no category uncovered in his extremely valuable guide. He instructs readers about the proper care and maintenance required to run a fine New England home. The book's page-length subtitle catalogues its contents, including "how to conduct large and small parties with order"; "general directions for placing on table all kinds of joints, fish, and fowl"; "upwards of 100 various and useful receipts"; "full instructions for cleaning plate, brass, steel, glass, mahogany; and likewise all kinds of patent and common lamps." He attends to the virtues that define good cooks, tutors young workers on proper kitchen behavior, and offers "friendly advice to cooks and heads of families" that would secure their "advancement." The "benefit of clean feet" was an unexpected pointer.

Twenty years later, another black author, Tunis Campbell, composed what Jan Longone, adjunct curator of the University of Michigan's Janice Bluestein Longone Culinary Archive, described as "one of the earliest manuals written by any American on the supervision and management of first-class restaurants and hotel dining rooms" (Feeding America Project, http://digital.lib.msu.edu/projects/cookbooks/index.html). In addition to his book, Campbell was an activist and a leader in Georgia politics. And like Roberts's opus, his work rose above mere novelty; it demonstrated practicality and proficiency.

Entrepreneurial values showed up next. Cooks who operated "cookie stands" or devised tools that made work easier, everywhere from

The Jemima Code

Baltimore and Rhode Island to New Orleans, "controlled almost all of the food supply" in the communities in which they lived, observed Cheryl A. Smith in *Market Women: Black Women Entrepreneurs; Past, Present, and Future* (2005). These industrious women exemplified a kind of targeted self-care that emerged time and again despite restrictive slave laws and repressive black codes. For example, Charity Bird sold baked cakes in Texas. Susie Taylor bartered chicken and eggs, and also earned enough capital to finance a school in Savannah. Mary Ellen Pleasant purchased magnificent properties in the San Francisco Bay Area with money brought in by her catering company. A cake baker named Myra Miller was highly regarded in Atlanta for her works of dessert art. Judy Reed invented a dough kneader, and Madeline Turner designed the fruit press.

Still, few African American women broadcast their talents in the stormy years following the Civil War and Reconstruction. Two who did published books for economic reasons, with recipes that reflected diverse experience, not ethnicity. A free woman of color named Malinda Russell wrote what is known to be the first complete African American cookbook, published in Michigan in 1866. *A Domestic Cook Book: Containing a Careful Selection of Useful Receipts for the Kitchen* records the ways that she and her contemporaries used recipes to gain their independence. She and Abby Fisher, who came along some fifteen years later, made their way in the marketplace with the support and endorsement of white women who respected them as cooks and entrepreneurs and who helped them get their collections printed.

We can assume from Russell's success as a caterer, and the appeal of Fisher's cakes and unique brand of pickles and preserves, that the business sense and vision that characterize shopkeepers,

restaurateurs, and modern food merchants were important considerations for them as well. Of course, they had no social media to help them promote their tiny operations. And yet despite her social status, each woman possessed sales and presentation skills in addition to her cooking ability. We can assume that these practices included persuasive speaking; developing a good sales pitch; motivating and inspiring customers to buy; paying attention to customers' buying signals; making eye contact; speaking with authority through charismatic, bold, and forthright marketing of the product; managing inventory; and pricing goods.

While black businesswomen have often been depicted as aggressive and showy, or even guilty of such devious methods as stealing the goods they sold, Russell's and Fisher's positive business attributes continued to appear generations later all over the South. Whether the enterprise involved making and selling tamales in the Mississippi Delta or grinding sassafras leaves into filé, cooks in hidden kitchens and businesses—displaying confident competence with very little fanfare—overcame obstacles that had confined them to domestic work.

I am certain that these four authors did not intend for their work to symbolize the legions of African Americans who used food and commerce for independence. But through them, other invisible cooks were imbued with wisdom and knowledge. Their writing stands in for the experiences of thousands of remarkable unnamed men and women who did not let the limitations society placed upon them determine the outcome of their lives.

Such know-how is noteworthy for its contrast with the performances by McDaniel and Green. Very noteworthy. ❧

The House Servant's Directory

ROBERT ROBERTS

....

Boston: Munroe and Francis, 1827;
    New York, Charles S. Francis, 1827
Facsimile edition, Waltham, Massachusetts:
    Gore Place Society, 1977
180 pages

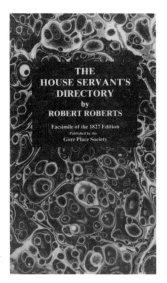

INDEX.

FOR YEARS, the detailed musings of the "outstanding butler" of Gore Place existed primarily in the margins of historic cookery books—mostly because the trade-published compendium is, in form and function, more of a specialized guidebook than a traditional cookbook.

The *Directory* is a comprehensive manual on household management, along with 105 recipes for household remedies, cleaning products, and some dishes. It was the first book of any kind by an African American, that we know of, to be trade published. The book was written by a principled role model who passed along valuable life skills and aspects of character, which he attributes to several sources, in what amounts to a personal letter to friends. His missive weaves pride, dignity, and self-respect among its instructions for properly brushing and folding gentlemen's clothing and making the best ginger beer.

Roberts composed the tome while he served Christopher Gore (lawyer, diplomat, governor, and U.S. senator); his wife, Rebecca; their guests; and members of the social elite in Waltham, Massachusetts, including such visiting dignitaries as Daniel Webster and James Monroe. Readers can expect to be spellbound.

Unlike the diaries and journals of slaveholding families, which recorded daily tasks as perceived by the master, Roberts's philosophical and spiritual messages reveal exactly what a knowledgeable nineteenth-century household manager did throughout the day. We are reminded repeatedly which chores laborers did; common ones included washing and cleaning decanters, polishing silver, and keeping pantries neat and orderly. At a time when few workers left written records of their jobs, this notebook details the exact skills that a supervising servant taught others. The meticulous regulations left behind by Roberts irrevocably reconstruct a host of lost arts.

Ten pages are devoted to setting an elegant table, including instructions on ensuring that the tablecloth overhangs on opposite ends of the table do not differ by more than an eighth

silver, and wash off in hot soap suds, and dry off with hot cloths, which you must have hung before the fire for that purpose ; afterwards polish with your shammy leather.

29.—AN EXCELLENT MASTICK FOR MENDING GLASS, CHINA, &c.

Take whites of eggs, soft curd cheese, and quicklime, of each an equal quantity in weight, then begin and beat them all well together until the mastick becomes quite smooth ; this may be used in most all kinds of ware ; it will cement broken glass, so as to stand fire or hot water without having the smallest effect on the part cemented, but stand like new.

30.—A WASH TO REVIVE OLD DEEDS, OR OTHER WRITINGS.

Boil gall nuts in white wine, and steep a sponge in this solution, then pass it smoothly over the old writings, &c. and they will appear directly as new as when first wrote.

31.—AN EXCELLENT WAY TO PREVENT FLIES FROM SETTLING ON PICTURES, OR MAKING DIRT ON FURNITURE.

Take a large bunch of leeks and soak them in a pail of soft water for 24 hours, then squeeze the leeks out of the water, let it stand for half an hour, then strain it off and bottle for use ; in the fly season take a sponge and wash your pictures

9

of an inch, and a reminder that the bottom of the flower basket faces toward the person at the bottom of the table, and the design faces the top. This section points out that dishes are to be arranged in a straight line, at the appropriate distance from one another, and specifies how to measure the proper space between types of glassware and cutlery.

Tucked alongside lessons such as these are elaborate routines for keeping knives sharp, a condition Roberts calls "*primo bono.*" Instructions for building coal fires, tips for shopping at the market, and directions for carving all sorts of meats and fowl are side by side with Roberts's attitudes about proper behavior and dress and the benefit of rising early. A special section is devoted to kitchen workers, as the author explains: "I have appended a few observations addressed to servants generally, but more especially to the

THE
HOUSE SERVANT'S DIRECTORY,
OR

A MONITOR FOR PRIVATE FAMILIES :

COMPRISING

HINTS ON THE ARRANGEMENT AND PERFORMANCE OF

SERVANTS' WORK,

WITH GENERAL RULES FOR

SETTING OUT TABLES AND SIDEBOARDS

IN FIRST ORDER ;

THE ART OF WAITING

IN ALL ITS BRANCHES ; AND LIKEWISE HOW TO CONDUCT

LARGE AND SMALL PARTIES

WITH ORDER ;

WITH GENERAL DIRECTIONS FOR PLACING ON TABLE
ALL KINDS OF JOINTS, FISH, FOWL, &c.

WITH

FULL INSTRUCTIONS FOR CLEANING

PLATE, BRASS, STEEL, GLASS, MAHOGANY ;

AND LIKEWISE
ALL KINDS OF PATENT AND COMMON LAMPS :

OBSERVATIONS

ON SERVANTS' BEHAVIOUR TO THEIR EMPLOYERS ;

AND UPWARDS OF

100 VARIOUS AND USEFUL RECEIPTS,

CHIEFLY COMPILED
FOR THE USE OF HOUSE SERVANTS ;
AND IDENTICALLY MADE
TO SUIT THE MANNERS AND CUSTOMS OF FAMILIES
IN THE UNITED STATES.

By ROBERT ROBERTS.

WITH

FRIENDLY ADVICE TO COOKS

AND HEADS OF FAMILIES,
AND COMPLETE DIRECTIONS HOW TO BURN

LEHIGH COAL.

BOSTON,
MUNROE AND FRANCIS, 128 WASHINGTON-STREET.
NEW YORK,
CHARLES S. FRANCIS, 189 BROADWAY.
1827.

cook, and assistant cook; and that I might not be thought guilty of presumption, in teaching what it may be thought I may not perfectly understand myself, or, as the old saying is, 'swim beyond my depth,' I shall quote this important part of the work from a most approved author of whose knowledge on these points there can be no doubt."

This section, "A Few Observations to Cooks," is an impressive compilation of characteristics and values designed to produce remarkable manners and improve kitchen deportment even as it comments on commonsense notions like developing the palate. Practical counsel regarding order, cleanliness, and *mise en place* is attributed to *The Cook's Oracle: Containing Receipts for Plain Cookery on the Most Economical Plan for Private Families,* a compendium of sage wisdom published in 1827 by Dr. William Kitchiner. Roberts's section titled "Some Miscellaneous Observations" teaches the best way to store vegetables and bread, the appropriate means for keeping apples fresh and dry, the use of fresh herbs, and a simple way to preserve citrus zest for recipes.

As for the recipes, they too are meticulous. Roberts's formulas are presented in a narrative style designed to make mundane tasks easier.

He includes a few recipes for simple preserves, vinegars, and refreshing beverages, but most of his prescriptions are for household cleaning and polishing products. Recipe 22, for example, tells how to use mutton or suet to remove rust. Recipe 29 offers a useful way to use egg whites and soft-curd cheese to mend broken glass. Recipes 31 and 32 are concoctions that use food for pest management: "An Excellent Way to Prevent Flies from Settling on Pictures, or Making Dirt on Furniture" is an aromatic potion made by soaking leeks; a combination of black pepper, brown sugar, and cream spread on a plate is the recommended solution in "To Remove Flies from Rooms."

Unlike the highly esteemed caterers known throughout the Northeast for their fine dishes, Roberts was no chef. Still, he left a respected, memorable legacy of superior home management and supervisory skills. His provocative cautions to heads of families about the proper treatment of servants display the rapport Roberts must have enjoyed with his employers. And his message was thought so valuable that the *Directory* was among the texts in the library at the Hermitage, President Andrew Jackson's Tennessee home. ❧

Never Let People Be Kept Waiting

A Textbook on Hotel Management

TUNIS G. CAMPBELL

....

Reprint of *Hotel Keepers, Head Waiters, and
 Housekeepers' Guide*

Boston, 1848

Edited and with an introduction by
 Doris Elizabeth King

Raleigh, North Carolina: King Reprints in
 Hospitality History, 1973

126 pages

Tunis G. Campbell

*T*UNIS G. CAMPBELL made a name for
 himself by taking the employee handbook
beyond a list of rules and regulations. He instead
sought to educate his people, instilling in them
a desire to achieve the highest degree of professionalism and pure moral character. His privately
published textbook reveals his invention of an
unusual and innovative plan of service for waiters
in hotel dining rooms, one that pleased guests
with its novelty. He refined a "military-style
dining room 'drill'" system that trained waiters
to serve meals quickly, efficiently, and in perfect
time and step. Then as now, feeding hordes of
hungry travelers could be a logistical nightmare,
and remnants of his doctrine are still visible at
hotel banquets today.

Never Let People Be Kept Waiting was created
in 1973 as part of a doctoral dissertation on the
history of American hotels and public houses.
Because Campbell's book was too fragile to be

reproduced, the Library of Congress provided
a photocopy of the original and a negative of
the engraved portrait of him. The contents were
then retyped for offset printing, the editor's note
explains, and Campbell's wording, spelling, and
punctuation were preserved. The book is illustrated with ten plates that depict the author's
intricate table-waiting "drill," along with such
practical matters as wait stations, the arrangement of dishes on the table, chair placement,
and table locations. An impressive gathering
of 102 "valuable" recipes, grouped by categories and cooking methods (sauces, roasts, stews,
soups, baked goods, desserts, preserves), ensures
that a guest's dining experience is delicious as
well as sensorily pleasing. A treatise on menu
courses and several letters of recommendation
by hoteliers and boarders complete Campbell's
handbook. ❧

A Domestic Cook Book

Containing a Careful Selection of Useful Receipts for the Kitchen

MALINDA RUSSELL

....

Published by the author
Printed by T. O. Ward, Paw Paw, Michigan, 1866
Facsimile edition, Detroit: Inland Press, 2007
40 pages

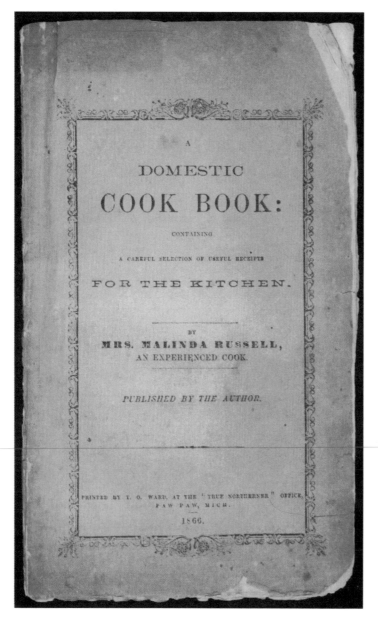

A DOMESTIC COOK BOOK is a self-published fund-raising project written by a free woman of color, "an experienced cook" who tells the reader a great deal about herself, her kitchen credentials, and her priorities, and offers a compelling reason for publishing: she hopes to earn enough from its sale to her former customers to "return home" to Tennessee.

A working mother, cook, and former pastry shop owner, she followed the standard publishing format practiced by white cookbook authors of the era. Her book opens with "A Short History of the Author," which acknowledges everyone who helped develop her talent and bring her project to print. She writes of her apprenticeship under the tutelage of Fanny Steward, a colored cook of Virginia; claims to follow "the plan of *The Virginia House-Wife*"; and as a nod to the domestic-science movement sweeping cookbook publishing, reassures purchasers that she understands the rules and regulations of the kitchen. She writes in a brief introduction: "The kitchen should always be Neat and Clean. The Table, Pastry Boards, Pans, and everything pertaining to Cookery should be well Cleaned."

More than 250 medical remedies, household formulas, and classic pastry shop recipes follow, each one organized into a short narrative composed of a few sentences. Classic formulas for simple southern breads, cakes (including Sally Lunn), and pies, and jumbles dominate the first two-thirds of the book; meats, preserves, cordials, and cures make up the rest. This total is significantly smaller than the prodigious number in *The Kentucky Housewife* (Lettice Bryan, 1839; 1,300 recipes), *The Virginia House-Wife* (Mary Randolph, 1824), or *The Carolina Housewife* (Sarah Rutledge, 1847), but it nonetheless represents a trove of kitchen competencies, particularly where the nuanced and temperamental art of baking is concerned. Salt Rising Bread, Soda Rolls, and Potato Ferment Rolls, for instance, demonstrate her understanding of starches and leavenings. She includes recipes that hint at dishes that will be popular in years to come. Her chicken soup

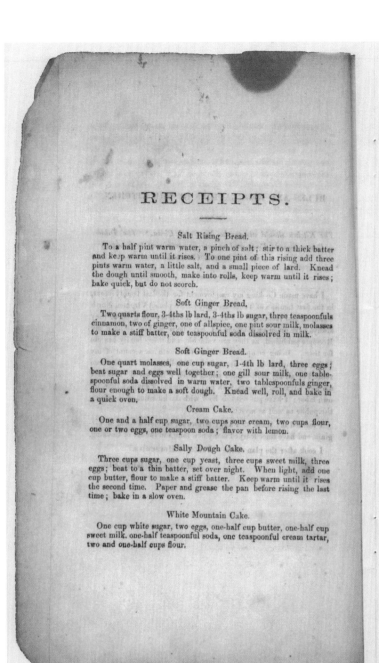

RECEIPTS.

Salt Rising Bread.

To a half pint warm water, a pinch of salt; stir to a thick batter and keep warm until it rises. To one pint of this rising add three pints warm water, a little salt, and a small piece of lard. Knead the dough until smooth, make into rolls, keep warm until it rises; bake quick, but do not scorch.

Soft Ginger Bread.

Two quarts flour, 3-4ths lb lard, 3-4ths lb sugar, three teaspoonfuls cinnamon, two of ginger, one of allspice, one pint sour milk, molasses to make a stiff batter, one teaspoonful soda dissolved in milk.

Soft Ginger Bread.

One quart molasses, one cup sugar, 1-4th lb lard, three eggs; beat sugar and eggs well together; one gill sour milk, one tablespoonful soda dissolved in warm water, two tablespoonfuls ginger, flour enough to make a soft dough. Knead well, roll, and bake in a quick oven.

Cream Cake.

One and a half cup sugar, two cups sour cream, two cups flour, one or two eggs, one teaspoon soda; flavor with lemon.

Sally Dough Cake.

Three cups sugar, one cup yeast, three cups sweet milk, three eggs; beat to a thin batter, set over night. When light, add one cup butter, flour to make a stiff batter. Keep warm until it rises the second time. Paper and grease the pan before rising the last time; bake in a slow oven.

White Mountain Cake.

One cup white sugar, two eggs, one-half cup butter, one-half cup sweet milk, one-half teaspoonful soda, one teaspoonful cream tartar, two and one-half cups flour.

Queen's Party Cake.

One quart sour cream, six lbs sugar, six lbs butter, five lbs raisins, five lbs currants, one and one-half lbs figs, one ounce cloves, one ounce cinnamon, one and one-half nutmeg, extract of lemon or vanilla, whites of eighteen eggs, yelks of ten eggs, one teaspoonful soda, two teaspoonfuls cream tartar, flour to stir quite stiff.

Plain Pound Cake.

One lb sugar, one lb flour, one nutmeg, 3-4ths lb butter, twelve eggs, half gill brandy. Paper and grease your pans well; bake in a moderate oven.

Cork Cake.

Three cups sugar, one cup butter, one cup sour cream, five cups flour, five eggs, one teaspoon soda, one teaspoon cream tartar; flavor with lemon.

Sponge Cake.

One lb sugar, twelve eggs; take out one yelk; ten ounces flour; beat the yelks and sugar together well; beat the whites to a stiff froth; gradually mix together; flavor with lemon; bake with a gradual heat.

Dover Cake.

Two cups sugar, four eggs, one cup butter, one cup sour cream, three cups unsifted flour, one teaspoon cream tartar, one teaspoon soda; flavor to taste.

Washington Cake.

Three cups sugar, six eggs, one cup butter, one cup sour milk, one teaspoon soda, three cups flour, one teaspoon cream tartar; flavor with lemon to your taste.

Bread Dough Cake.

One pint light bread dough, three eggs, two cups sugar, one cup butter, fill with fruit or carraway seeds; stir together well, put in cake pan, let it rise, bake moderately. This cake, if made with fruit and iced, will keep a long time.

Grated Bread Cake.

Grate one quart stale bread, six eggs, one and a half cup butter, three cups sugar, one pint milk, two teaspoons cream tartar, one teaspoon soda, one grated nutmeg, three tablespoons flour; bake in a moderate oven.

Cream Cake.

One cup and a half sugar, two cups sour cream, one teaspoon soda, three cups flour, lightly measured, one grated nutmeg; bake in a moderate oven.

resembles chicken and dumplings; other modern antecedents are smothered steak, bread pudding (called grated bread cake), cornbread, and an onion custard that resembles a modern onion tart.

Elsewhere, the prescriptions can be quirky. Some recipes give ingredients and methods but no amounts. Others list amounts of ingredients but no instructions—the author appears to assume that the reader has some basic kitchen sense (as in bake a cake in the usual way). At other times, when the author deems it necessary, essential steps that ensure success are included. Tips tell the cook whether the oven heat should be moderate or high, when to paper and grease a pan, and which leavening is best for temperamental recipes: soda or cream of tartar mixed with saleratus (potassium or sodium bicarbonate).

She includes some dishes with obvious African roots, such as Burst Up Rice, Graham Cakes, and Ginger Pop Beer. Cosmetics, household remedies, and cures include cologne, made by seasoning alcohol with essential oils; two recipes that cure corns; and Barbers' Shampooing Mixture and Star Hair Oil, aromatic with citronella and lavender. And there are surprises that testify to the book's diversity: novelties such as ice cream; Rice Milk, a thin sort of rice pudding made by soaking rice overnight in an aromatic bath of sweet milk flavored with lemon; Seed Cake, perfumed by caraway; a sweet yeast bread called "Old Maids"; and Sliced Sweet Potato Pie.

Russell was born and raised in eastern Tennessee. When she was nineteen years old, she planned to move to Liberia, but was robbed. To make up her loss, by "hard labor and economy," she "saved a considerable sum of money," and then she was robbed again after the death of her husband. "Hearing that Michigan was the Garden of the west," she moved to the Paw Paw area, where she embarked on this fund-raising project, stating confidently, "I know my book will sell well where I have cooked, and am sure those using my receipts will be well satisfied." ❧

What Mrs. Fisher Knows about Old Southern Cooking, Soups, Pickles, Preserves, Etc.

ABBY FISHER

....

San Francisco: Women's Co-Operative Printing
 Office, 1881
Facsimile edition, with historical notes by Karen Hess,
 Bedford, Massachusetts: Applewood Books, 1995
80 pages

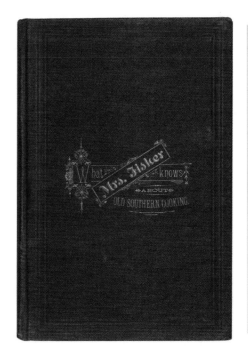

FRIENDS AND CUSTOMERS who appreciated this former slave for her knowledge of southern specialties helped bring this privately printed collection of more than 150 recipes to affluent housekeepers and ladies in the Bay Area, but Fisher's reputation for excellence in business is equally commendable.

Although unschooled, Fisher ran a pickles and preserves manufacturing operation with her husband, Alexander, in San Francisco, and evidently she was no ordinary cook. Her credentials are announced right up front, on the title page: "Awarded Two Medals at the San Francisco Mechanics' Institute Fair, 1880, for best Pickles and Sauces and best assortment of Jellies and Preserves. Diploma Awarded at Sacramento State Fair, 1879." In the preface, she acknowledges that she was reluctant to undertake the project, being unable to read or write, but was persuaded of the value of "a book of [her] knowledge—based on an experience of upwards of thirty-five years—in the art of cooking."

It is a trailblazing cookbook. Like her slave sisters who left an African "thumbprint on every dish they cooked," as Karen Hess puts it, Fisher filled her recipes with African aromas—in dishes eventually characterized as southern, like her "Ochra Gumbo," fried chicken, and croquettes, and in some nonsouthern recipes as well.

Touches of artistic excellence show up in embellished European recipes such as roast venison seasoned with a little green (fresh) or dried thyme; Crab Croquettes and Compound Tomato Sauce (ketchup), spiked with a bit of fine red pepper, "as crabs should be seasoned high to be nice"; Sweet Potato Pie, sweetened with freshly squeezed orange juice and grated zest; and Stuffed Ham, laced with sherry and baked with a sprinkle of nutmeg. Her knowledge of food safety and brining techniques is evident in the detailed preservation and storage instructions.

The "Historical Notes" written for the facsimile edition by Karen Hess explain African terms and culinary practices and tell us a lot about Abby Fisher—her "intelligent handling" of the kitchen range, and the unique and admirable aspects of her baking, canning, and roasting techniques. When the book came to market, this forty-eight-year-old mulatto was living and working as a cook in San Francisco with her husband. It is unclear how, as a former slave and mother of eleven, she made her way west, but one thing is known: she brought culinary flair and an ancestral penchant for okra and black-eyed peas with her. ❧

1900–1925

Surviving

MAMMYISM

Cooking Lessons for
Work & Home

You may talk about the knowledge
Which our farmers' girls have gained
From cooking-schools and cook-books
(Where all modern cooks are trained);
But I would rather know just how,
(Though vainly I have tried)
To prepare, as mother used to,
Apple sauce and chicken fried.
Our modern cooks know how to fix
Their dainty dishes rare.
But, friend, just let me tell you what!—
None of them compare
With what my mother used to fix,
And for which I've often cried,
When I was but a little tot,—
Apple sauce and chicken fried.
Chicken a la Francaise,
Also fricassee,
Served with some new fangled sauce
Is plenty good for me,
Till I get to thinking of the home
Where I used to 'bide
And where I used to eat,—um, my!
Apple sauce and chicken fried.
We always had it once a week,
Sometimes we had it twice;
And I have even known the time
When we have had it thrice.
Our good, yet jolly pastor,
During his circuit's ride
With us once each week gave grateful thanks
For apple sauce and chicken fried.
Why, it seems like I can smell it,
And even taste it, too,
And see it with my natural eyes,
Though of course it can't be true;
And it seems like I'm a child again,
Standing by mother's side
Pulling at her dress and asking
For apple sauce and chicken fried.

EFFIE WALLER SMITH
"Apple Sauce and Chicken Fried,"
1904

 OT MANY PEOPLE know Effie Waller Smith. From 1904 to 1909, she published three volumes of verse, three short stories, and several poems, with titles that expressed her passion for African American traditions. She wrote about everything that was beautiful, good, precious, right, in a religious and romantic collection of poetry that captured her love of her rugged home in the Cumberland Mountains.

What she seems to be longing for, what she wants the whole world to know, is that nothing quite compares to food cooked with the secret ingredient she thought only mama knew: love. And culinary love, she makes clear, results from a combination of oral tradition, astonishing mental kitchen order, and a deep connection to the imagination. Tera Hunter, in *To 'Joy My Freedom*, records one old cook's description of her method: "Everything I does, I does by my head; its all brain work."

Without careful reading, the cook's sentiments and, to a lesser degree, those of Effie Waller Smith justify the stereotype of an illiterate cook: someone competent in the tasks of getting meals on the table but unable to pass that skill beyond the immediate community because he or she could not read or write. But to judge the black cook by a lack of schooling rather than as a miracle of memory and oral transmission is to miss what was truly accomplished: excellence across a range of skills, independence, and social mobility—not to mention the creation of really delicious food.

During the period when Effie Waller Smith was publishing her books, cooking changed, and cooks changed with it. The domestic-science movement that had begun with Catherine Beecher sixty years earlier was running full throttle. Its doyennes established cooking schools, kitchen laboratories, magazines, organizations, and clubs based on the new idea of a business-like home where "husbands were fed and children raised according to scientific principles," as Laura

Shapiro explains in *Perfection Salad: Women and Cooking at the Turn of the Century* (1986). Technological advances such as the gas stove and baking powder made kitchen work easier.

Textbooks, Shapiro goes on to say, designed to "develop respect for the kitchen and bring haphazard cooking methods in line with the operations of a well-regulated office or factory" replaced the regional books authored by housewives. Besides lengthy sections devoted to cookery, these training manuals included hints on household work, table service, napery, medicinal remedies, and useful hints for the home lawyer. "Tested" recipes justified the new priorities of home economics. Cooking was to be transformed from drudgery to a pursuit that possessed "the dignity of an art, of science, and of philosophy," Shapiro concludes.

Black cooks responded just as they always had—with eyes fixed on practical living. Rural folks had the same menial jobs (cooks, laundresses, baby nurses, maids, butlers, chauffeurs, janitors, and train porters) as earlier. But those kitchen workers who were members of the New Negro Movement (founded in 1916–1917) combined culinary advancements with the improvised styles mastered and passed down over the years by the ancestors. Workers organized. Whether as part of the Cook's Union in Georgia or a regional women's club or a national organization, America's servant class dedicated itself to improving working conditions and training one another to achieve distinction.

In 1911, Rufus Estes published the first cookbook by an African American chef: *Good Things to Eat as Suggested by Rufus*. His volume preserves essential recipes crafted by an experienced professional who worked on farms and in a Nashville restaurant, and was selected—for his talent, not his genetics—"to handle all the special parties" as a chef for the Pullman Company.

A year later, *The Kentucky Cook Book: Easy and Simple for Any Cook*, by a "Colored Woman," namely, Mrs. W. T. Hayes, offered further evidence that African Americans learned the art of cooking by cooking. It is a curious collection.

Just four dishes can be associated with the African American "traditional core diet and foodways" described by scholars, including Psyche Williams-Forson—okra salad, Fried Chicken Mrs. E. Hayes, Fricassee of Squirrel, and Sweet Potato Croquettes—and even fewer with Kentuckian overtones. This "colored cook of many years' experience," goes on for forty-five pages, showing off her talent for "experimenting and testing the recipes presented," which she proudly states in the introduction are "simple and easily made, and have proved to be excellent."

But it was the founding of state normal (that is, teachers) and agricultural freedmen's schools that offered the greatest hope for overcoming advertising stereotypes rooted in servitude and "mammyism." From Virginia to Texas, these Negro training schools established domestic-science institutes dedicated to home arts such as cooking and sewing and to educating teachers.

The director of the Home Economics School at the Hampton Normal and Agricultural Institute (in Hampton, Virginia), Carrie Alberta Lyford, wrote several cookbooks, teacher training manuals, and reports, including *A Book of Recipes for the Cooking School*, which emphasized good nutrition. In Austin, Texas, students enrolled at Samuel Huston College learned practical skills in domestic service and household management. In 1902 in Sedalia, North Carolina, Charlotte Hawkins Brown founded the Palmer Memorial Institute, a manual and domestic training school where students grew their own food on a sizable farm. Nannie Burroughs, a nationally recognized educator, church leader, and suffrage supporter, established the National Training School for Women and Girls in Washington, D.C., where classes blended industrial training and the liberal arts with Christian education. And Mary McLeod Bethune's Daytona Educational and Industrial Training School for Negro Girls got underway in Florida with, in a phrase now famously associated with the school, "$1.50, faith in God and five little girls for students." Its classroom motto: "Cease to be a drudge, seek to be an artist."

In the early twentieth century, as the Harlem Renaissance whipped up interest in the music, literature, and food of the "Negro race," domestic-science students established reputations for refined kitchen aptitude and style—no poverty ingredients, no outlook that confined a cook's repertoire to plantation cabin cookery. As black "culinarians," they moved into the middle class with a sensibility that first mastered and then exceeded scientific housewifery. Victor H. Green published *The Negro Motorist Green Book*, a directory of successful boardinghouses, hotels, restaurants, and saloons, to guide blacks traveling in the segregated South to hospitality services and familiar foods. Catering exploded.

Bertha L. Turner's *The Federation Cook Book* exemplified how industrious, make-do methodology could be turned distinctly upscale. The author was eulogized in a California newspaper as "one of the most famous Negro cooks ever

to come out of the Old South." The delicacies she recorded represented the tastes and culinary priorities of black women whose leisure lives had evolved from gossip sessions at the washstand to a network of social clubs that enhanced African American cultural life, as the historian Tera Hunter observed. In her innovative study *To 'Joy My Freedom: Southern Black Women's Lives and Labors after the Civil War* (1997), Hunter recounts an impressive menu put together by an Atlanta hostess: "sumptuous refreshments and delicacies such as oyster soup, Saratoga chips, boiled pompano, wreaths of California grapes, and peppers stuffed with calf's brain."

When I compare this bill of fare to the offerings of white twentieth-century southern cookbook writers, I am reminded of the words of Henry James: "Excellence does not require perfection." Nor does it require paper and pen. ❧

The Federation Cook Book

A Collection of Tested Recipes Contributed by the Colored Women of the State of California

BERTHA L. TURNER

....

1910
Reprint, Bedford, Massachusetts:
 Applewood Books, 2007
95 pages

Dedication

O ye tired and weary house-wives
O ye never-tiring house-wives
Here's a solving, solving, solving,
Of the daily eating problem.
Here's an answer, answer, answer.
To the oft-repeated question
To the quite perplexing question
That confronts us, that annoys us.
What shall we eat? What shall we eat?
Here's a book of tested cooking,
Here's a book of tried proportions
Kindly given by our women,
Thank we them for their donation
Thank them for this little cook book.
Dedicate it to these women
To these helpful, trusty women.
Take it to your friends and neighbors,
May it prove a blessing to you.

YOU CAN TELL FROM the very first pages that this is a book by an author with a message of self-reliance, a woman with class. A state superintendent of domestic science, Bertha L. Turner curated recipes from all over California (and a few from as far away as Indiana), presumably in order to quiet critics who wrongly assumed domestic work to be spadework.

This recipe collection signals a shift from one intended to educate white housewives to one that preserved the culinary values inherited and practiced by the black middle class. A dedication confidently promised to deliver "tested cooking, of tried proportions . . . Kindly given by our women." It is followed by a cheerful poem, composed by a member of the National Association of Colored Women's Clubs.

The dedication suggests that readers purchase the book to express appreciation for those "helpful, trusty" women who cooked in America's kitchens with confidence and skill. After this come about two hundred recipes for simple yet elegant cookery, including numerous ways with lettuce, gelatin, and molds—the "dainty" delights popular among the nation's domestic goddesses at the time—interspersed with more than fifty advertisements for businesses and professionals in and around Pasadena, California.

Common recipes such as American ice cream, cheese straws, and blackberry cobbler mingle with novelties that capture a Southern California flair, such as String Beans a la Creole, made with bacon and spiked with Ortega green chilies; Spanish Rice; and an improvised version of fish cooked in paper (familiar to cooks as *poisson en papillote*), entitled Fish *La Paper Sette*.

A few Africanized dishes survived the trip west with this regal, Kentucky-born matron: croquettes, Okra Gumbo, Creole Dish, Jambalaya, fried okra with ham, spoon bread, biscuits, and cornbread. Recipes for Boston Steak, Duchess Soup, Fish Timbale, and Lobster Cutlets, curated from the author's own collection and from association members, speak to the organization's perception of sophisticated cuisine and entertaining at home. The book includes blank pages where cooks can add their own recipes.

"Take it to your friends and neighbors," Turner urged. "May it prove a blessing to you." ❧

...THE...

Federation Cook Book

.. A Collection of ..
Tested Recipes

.... Contributed by the ....

Colored Women
.... of the ....
State of California

.... By ....
MRS. BERTHA L. TURNER
State Superintendent, Domestic Science
PASADENA, CALIFORNIA

Cookery Jingles

Dedicated to the Federation Cook Book

By Mrs. Katherine D. Tillman, A. M.
Chairman Ways and Means
National Association Colored Women's Clubs

She could draw a little, paint a little,
 Talk about a book.
She could row a boat, ride a horse.
 But alas she couldn't cook.
 She could gown, she could go,
 She could very pretty look
 But her best beau he was poor
 And he couldn't hire a cook.
When he learned the fatal truth
 His flight he quickly took,
And his girl is single still,
 Because she couldn't cook!

 Believe not the love tales
 You find within a book
 Love's fate often turns on,
 The skill of the cook
Before a man marries
 'Tis the gown or the look,
But after the wedding
 He looks for a cook.
 'Tis said to man's heart,
 The shortest route took
 Is reached through the region,
 Controlled by the cook!
Go forth then a blessing,
 You dear little book,
And happiness ever
 Attend the good cook.

Fish, Oysters and Entrees

Baked Fish

Take any good baking fish, make a stuffing of bread crumbs, mix with butter, salt peper and sage. Pour over a little hot water. Bake, basting often.—MRS. B. C. OFFUTT 87 MOUNTAIN ST., First Vice President Sojourner Truth Club.

Jambalaya

Boil rice and set aside. Chop ham in small pieces and fry, add onions and parsley chopped fine, tomatoes and shrimps; season to suit taste; let simmer a few minutes, then mix thoroughly in rice.—MISS ALICE GRIFFIN, BERKELEY.

Creole Dish

Boiled macaroni or spaghetti. Set aside. Take meat (any kind) left over from day before, grind, fry with chopped onions parsley, celery, add tomatoes, season to suit taste and mix in macaroni.—MISS ALICE GRIFFIN, 1626 Russell St., Berkeley.

Tomato Relish

Cut the bread out round and butter. Slice tomatoes to fit bread. Cover with grated Swiss cheese. Put a slice of thin bacon on top and brown in oven. Serve hot.—MISS FLORENCE P. WEIMER, Pasadena.

Tomato and Sardine Appetizer

Cut bread into round slices. Toast and butter. Take small tomatoes of uniform size. Peel and cut off top. Lay 2 small sardines and a half teaspoonful grated cheese on tomato. Make a drawn butter sauce seasoned with Tobasco sauce. Pour over appetizer. Set in oven three minutes and serve.—MRS. BERTHA L. TURNER.

Coquilles of Sweetbread

4 blanched sweetbreads
1 half glass white wine
1 gill veloute sauce
2 truffles
Scant teaspoon pepper

2 tablespoons good cream or 1 half ounce good butter
3 tablespoons mushroom liquor
6 mixed mushrooms
1 tablespoon salt
Half teaspoon nutmeg
Bread crumbs

Cut sweetbreads in small slices and stew them in a saucepan with butter, wine and mushroom liquor. Reduce them for 10 minutes, then add sauce, mushrooms and truffles, cut like mushrooms. Add seasoning and finish by adding 2 tablespoons cream and butter. Fill 6 ramekins with this. Sprinkle them with fresh bread crumbs. Pour a few drops of clarified butter over them and put them in the baking oven. Brown slightly for 6 minutes longer and serve on a hot dish with a folded napkin. Very good.—MRS. R. H. HUNTER, ELEVADO DRIVE, PASADENA.

Fish Timbale

Butter thickly 6 timbale moulds. Have ready some cooked macaroni. Line the moulds with macaroni. Have ready any kind of fish lobster. Fill the moulds with the fish. Take one cup of thin cream, beat thoroughly one egg and mix with the cream, salt and pepper to taste and pour the mixture over the fish then set moulds in boiling water and cook until firm. Turn out on plates and serve with a small sprig of parsley. Serve with any sauce. I use brown butter sauce with the juice of one lemon and one tablespoon Worcester sauce.—MRS. R. H. HUNTER.

Brown Butter Sauce

Two ounces of butter. Put in sauce pan and set on fire and let cook. Be careful not to burn. Put in lemon juice 1 tablespoon Worcester. Put over the timbales and serve hot.—MRS. R. H. HUNTER.

Boiled Halibut With Sauce

2 lbs. of halibut
4 tablespoons vinegar
1 teaspoon salt
A few bay leaves
A dash of cayenne pepper
A little garlic
Put fish on to cook in hot water, add seasoning and boil 30 minutes.

GOOD THINGS TO EAT

SOUPS

ASPARAGUS SOUP—Take three pounds of knuckle of veal and put it to boil in a gallon of water with a couple of bunches of asparagus, boil for three hours, strain, and return the juice to the pot. Add another bunch of asparagus, chopped fine, and boil for twenty minutes, mix a tablespoonful of flour in a cup of milk and add to the soup. Season with salt and pepper, let it come to a boil, and serve at once.

BEAN SOUP—One-half pound or one cup is sufficient for one quart of soup. Soups can be made which use milk or cream as basis. Any kind of green vegetable can be used with them, as creamed celery or creamed cauliflower. The vegetable is cooked and part milk and part water or part milk and part cream are used.

BISQUE OF CLAMS—Place a knuckle of veal, weighing about a pound and one-half, into a soup kettle, with a quart of water, one small onion, a sprig of parsley, a bay leaf, and the liquor drained from the clams, and simmer gradually for an hour and a half, skimming from time to time; strain the soup and again place it in the kettle; rub a couple of tablespoonfuls of butter with an equal amount of flour together and add it to the soup when it is boiling, stirring until again boiling; chop up twenty-five clams very fine, then place them in the soup, season and boil for about five minutes, then add a pint of milk or cream, and remove from the fire immediately, and serve.

BISQUE OF LOBSTER—Remove the meat of the lobster from its shell and cut the tender pieces into quarter-inch dice; put the ends of the claw-meat and any tough portions in a saucepan with the bones of the body and a little cold water and boil for twenty minutes, adding a little water from time to time as may be necessary; put the coral to dry in a moderate oven, and mix a little flour with some cold milk, and stir the milk, which should be boiling, stirring over the fire for ten

Good Things to Eat as Suggested by Rufus

RUFUS ESTES

....

Chicago, 1911
Reprint, Jenks, Oklahoma: Howling
   at the Moon Press, 1999
142 pages

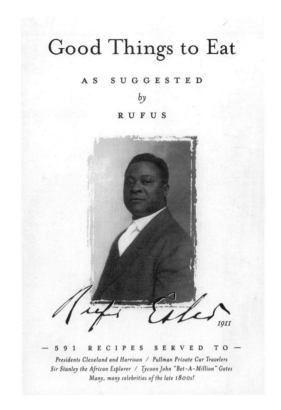

THIS CHEF AND AUTHOR tells us a great deal about his life and the culinary adventures that led him to self-publish just a year after the silent film *Birth of a Nation* pigeonholed African Americans as subservient, irrelevant. In "Sketch of My Life," Estes proudly lays out his journey from apprentice to skilled master chef, confirming learned and perfected proficiencies that distinguish him from Hollywood caricatures. As he asserts in the foreword, "The recipes given in the following pages represent the labor of years. Their worth has been demonstrated, not experimentally, but by actual tests, day by day and month by month, under dissimilar, and, in many instances, not too favorable conditions."

The section "Hints to Kitchen Maids" preaches the importance of a clean kitchen, advance preparation, balanced menus, and scheduling. The bulk of the book—"Good Things to Eat"— contains more than 590 recipes that illustrate a sophisticated and intelligent style. In some respects, Estes does not sound all that different from white twentieth-century cooks in his practice of culinary chemistry, as in salad dressings (emulsions) and pickled vegetables (fermentation). Estes knew classic cooking techniques, too, such as how to prepare a rich veal stock, beurre manié, roux, and reduction sauces.

As one might expect from a chef with a vast repertoire, Africanized interpretations of the foods of the fifth quarter (offal) seep into his repertoire. So do elegant treatments for high-end cuisine. Examples of his fanciful formulas include Chestnut Soup, Turkey Truffles, Tongue Canapes, Squash Flower Omelet, Fried Parsley, Beef Marrow Quenelles, Mashed Parsnip (puree), Green Melon Saute, and a frozen custard dish laced with macaroons and brandy, which Estes calls Glace des Gourmandes.

When the book was completed, a review in the *Chicago Defender* described Estes as one of Chicago's "best known chefs" and announced that an autographed copy of the first book received from the publishers and auctioned to the highest bidder, had been sold. The winning bid: $11. ❧

Bulletin No. 26

*When, What, and How to Can and
Preserve Fruits and Vegetables
in the Home*

1915

Bulletin No. 31

*How to Grow the Peanut and 105 Ways
of Preparing It for Human Consumption*

1925

Bulletin No. 36

*How to Grow the Tomato and 115 Ways
to Prepare It for the Table*

1918; REVISED EDITION, 1925

Bulletin No. 38

*How the Farmer Can Save His Sweet
Potatoes and Ways of Preparing
Them for the Table*

1936

Bulletin No. 43

Nature's Garden for Victory and Peace

1942

....

1942
George W. Carver, M.S. Agr.
Agricultural Research and Experiment Station,
    Tuskegee Normal and Industrial Institute
Tuskegee Institute Press

GEORGE WASHINGTON CARVER published forty-four bulletins during the period 1898–1943 to teach former slaves and sharecroppers practical farming techniques that would help them redirect their hardscrabble lives toward self-sufficiency and conservation. The free brochures included information on crops and cultivation techniques (including fertilizing, composting, and insect and fungus prevention), plus recipes for protein-rich, nutritious meals.

Carver taught that because tomatoes, peanuts, sweet potatoes, soybeans, and cowpeas (black-eyed peas) enriched the soil, they were useful as part of crop rotation practices and furthermore deserved to be part of the weekly diet. His recipes for baking sweet potatoes in ashes, slicing or mashing them to bake with a crust, and serving them with pork and beef were attempts to use African techniques to enliven uninspired menus.

In Africa, for instance, cooks thickened soups and stews with mashed nuts and seeds toasted over an open fire. Carver baked, skinned, and mashed legumes into a paste (peanut butter) and stirred it into consommé, English Peanut Bread, Aunt Nellie's Peanut Brown Bread, cookies, bars, rolls, muffins, doughnuts, cakes, puddings, omelets, macaroni and cheese, patties, timbales, stuffing, and tempeh-like vegetarian treatments called Mock Chicken and Mock Veal Cutlets. To explain the "superior value" of this newly discovered, "muscle-building" food, Carver wrote, "Indeed, I do not know of any one vegetable that has such a wide range of food possibilities either raw or cooked."

If Hollywood's fictional Bubba Blue had been raised on tomatoes instead of shrimp, he might have mesmerized Forrest Gump with Carver's 115 ways with tomatoes. Can't you just hear it: you got your macaroni and tomatoes, tomato goulash, tomato fritters, curried tomatoes, French pickled tomatoes, tomato sauce, tomato ketchup, tomato conserves, tomato jelly, boiled tomatoes, tomato souffle . . . ❧

The Jemima Code

stock to make a puree; heat again and season with salt, pepper, and lemon juice.

NO. 38, MOCK CHICKEN

Blanch and grind a sufficient number of peanuts until they are quite oily; stir in one well-beaten egg; if too thin, thicken with rolled bread crumbs or cracker dust; stir in a little salt. Boil some sweet potatoes until done; peel and cut in thin slices; spread generously with the peanut mixture; dip in white of egg; fry to a chicken brown; serve hot.

NO. 39, MOCK VEAL CUTLETS

Wash one cup of lentils, and soak over night; in the morning strain and parboil in fresh boiling water for 30 minutes; drain again and cook until soft in sufficient boiling water to cover them; rub through a sieve and to the puree add ¼ cup of melted butter, 1 cup of fine Graham bread crumbs, 1 cup of strained tomatoes to which a speck of soda has been added, 1 cup of blanched and chopped peanuts, 1 tablespoon each of grated celery and minced onions; season with ¼ teaspoon of mixed herbs, salt and pepper; blend all thoroughly together, and form into cutlets; dip these into egg and then in fine bread-crumbs; place in a well-greased baking pan, and brown in quick oven; arrange around a mound of well seasoned mashed potatoes, and serve with brown sauce.

NO. 40, PEANUT PATTIES

     1 pint toasted bread crumbs rolled fine
     1 pint of mashed potatoes (white or sweet)
     2 teaspoons baking powder dissolved in the yolks of two eggs.

Season with salt, pepper, sage, and mace; heat all together; form into small cakes; dip each cake into the whites of the eggs, then into peanut meal, and brown lightly in a frying pan containing a little pork fat, not deep fat; turn and brown on both sides.

NO. 41, BROWN SAUCE

Mix thoroughly 1 teaspoon of peanut butter and 2 tablespoons browned flour with 1 tablespoon cream; add gradually 2 cups hot milk, and stir and cook until the mixture thickens; just before serving add 4 tablespoons strained tomatoes, and a little salt and pepper.

NO. 42, PEANUT SAUSAGE

Grind ½ pound of roasted peanuts, ½ pound pecans, 1 ounce hickory nuts, and ½ pound walnut meats. Mix with six very ripe bananas; pack in a mould, and steam continuously for two hours; when done remove from lid of kettle or mould, and when mixture is cold turn out and serve the same as roast meat sliced thin for sandwiches, or with cold tomato sauce or other sauce.

The Southern Cookbook

*A Manual of Cooking and List of Menus,
Including Recipes Used by Noted Colored
Cooks and Prominent Caterers*

S. THOMAS BIVINS

*Principal, Chester Domestic Training Institute,
Chester, Pennsylvania*

....

Hampton, Virginia: Press of the Hampton Institute, 1912
Reprint, Kessinger, 2010
239 pages

MENU

Abraham Lincoln Dinner, 1861.

Soup

Terrapin   Brunoise

Fish

English Salmon á la Hollandaise
Smelts fried, á l'Anglaise

Relieves

Tenderloin of Beef   Sauce Perigord
Turkey a la Richelieu
Saddle of Venison with Currant Jelly

Relishes

French Mustard, Spanish Olives
Horseradish, Assorted Pickles
Sardines Apple Sauce Celery

Entrees

Sweet Bread Larded, with Green Peas

Venison Chops, Sauce Cherreiul
Croquets of Chicken a la Royal

Vol au Vent Financiere
Saline of Partridges a la Chasseur

Roasts

English Capons   Canvas Back Ducks

Grouse Larded Quails Larded
Chicken Salade   Fried Oysters

Pastry and Confectionery

English Plum Pudding
Charlottte Russe au Panneir
Gelve vin de Champagne, garne d'Orange
Blanc Mange a la Rose

Maccaroons   Fancy Kisses
Biscuit Anglais an Gelee
Gateau au Chocolate
Cassette d'Amande Sugared Almonds
Vanilla Ice Cream

Dessert

Almonds, Figs, Apples, Walnuts, Raisins, Dates, Filberts,
Prunes   Oranges
Coffee

No 1.

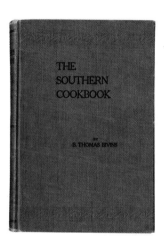

THIS BREEZY OPUS is quite possibly the *Joy of Cooking* of its time. It is obvious that the author intends for his students to succeed in business quickly without spending year after year on the job perfecting kitchen fundamentals and developing recipes. In twenty-two thoughtfully composed menus, advice on dining room etiquette, and more than 620 expertly written recipes, which for the most part give ingredients in specific amounts with clear preparation and cooking techniques, Bivins offers proof that his generation had mastered the scientific cooking methodology of the era.

Pigeons are broiled, pickled, potted, roasted, stewed, baked in a pie, or served under a sheath of jelly. There is a chapter on home brewing and one on foods for the sick. The mass of recipes includes fourteen ways to deal with a haunch of mutton, a section devoted to oysters, and roughly sixty recipes for sweet and savory puddings.

"The writer of this book has one object in view in preparing and sending out to the world the treatise here published," wrote Bivins.

He has labored at the same time to produce a manual which the family and hotel proprietors can take in hand with a certainty of finding directions and assistance in most of the doubts and perplexities which beset their daily life: a book to aid in choosing choice dishes and delicacies for private and public functions and to guide them in the selection of such dishes as will be most desirable—a book which, if studied and followed, will render them sagacious, able, well informed, ready, cheerful and accomplished in whatever makes the table the dearest comfort and the fountain of purest delight.

Listen to the voice of a cooking-school teacher writing in a composed, compassionate, and constructive manner:

"Parsley put in the belly will help to keep it [wild hare] fresh."

"A paste around the dish makes all puddings look better, but it is not necessary."

"Lemon peel should be pared very thin, and with a little sugar beaten in a marble mortar to a paste, and then mixed with a little wine or cream, so as to divide easily among the other [cake] ingredients." ❧

The Farmer Jones Cook Book

FORT SCOTT SORGHUM
SYRUP COMPANY

....

Kansas, 1914
26 pages

THIS MANUFACTURER'S BOOKLET features nearly one hundred recipes for cakes, breads, meats, breakfast foods, and confections—all made with Fort Scott sorghum syrup. During the Depression, when sugar and other goods, including flour, bacon and oil, were scarce, African American ways with sorghum were promoted as an inexpensive substitute for sugar.

"The picture on the front cover is reproduced from life," says the front material. "'Mary' is employed in the family of the Manager of the Fort Scott Sorghum Syrup Co." Pork Cake, a dense loaf made from minced salt pork, spices, and dried fruits, but no eggs or dairy; Rye Drop Cakes, a fried batter comparable to doughnut holes or fritters; Spiced Tongue; Baked Ham; Catsup; and a fruit-leather-like concoction "for constipation," called Senna and Fig Paste, are among her practical surprises. ❧

A Book of Recipes for the Cooking School

CARRIE ALBERTA LYFORD

....

Hampton, Virginia: Press of the Hampton Normal
    and Agricultural Institute, 1921
299 pages

*H*ERE IS A TEXTBOOK designed to educate Negro college students in fundamental cookery and housekeeping skills while they were learning simple academics. This is the first black cookbook that includes a table of contents. Its lessons reflect the educational mission and social uplift goals at the Hampton Normal and Agricultural School as defined by Brigadier General Samuel Armstrong, who founded the school: "To train selected Negro youth who should go out and teach and lead their people first by example . . . to teach respect for labor, to replace stupid drudgery with skilled hands, and in this way to build up an industrial system for the sake not only of self-support and intelligent labor, but also for the sake of character."

For Lyford's students, her clearly written recipes and suggestions must have been like a beacon directing a ship through a thick foggy night. With an eye toward process and formula uniformity, predictability, familiarity, and standardization, her textbook explains what educators considered important practices, which paralleled the course work at elite cooking schools. Lessons include a wide array of basic and advanced culinary skills: meal planning, marketing, cooking, garnishing, serving, and removing courses. There are instructions in the social aspects of conversation—plus page after page of simple advice emphasizing cleanliness, order, discipline, intelligence, freshness, seasonality, and quality.

The author organizes fundamental recipes into standard chapters, some with narrow subcategories such as omelets, soufflés, oysters, croquettes, scalloped dishes, candies, and frozen dishes. There also are formulas organized by cooking method, such as food preservation, cooking in fats, batters and doughs, and "garnishings."

Lyford also published leaflets and reports, such as *A Study of Home-Economics Education in Teacher-Training Institutions for Negroes*, which promoted practical cookery, producing a few unexpected results too. She taught that steaming vegetables was preferred to boiling in order to retain nutritive value, advocated beans as a good meat substitute, and encouraged cooks to serve tomatoes raw, washed, and skinned, without scalding.

A few iconic southern classics such as Hominy Grits, Cornmeal Mush, and Hopping John are in the *Book of Recipes* too, but collards, while "valuable for their bulk and for the mineral matter they contain," are not boiled to death in the usual manner. The recipe, like the college's founding principles, is prudent and nutritionally sensible—a break from the expected that shows a preference for tender, farm-fresh vegetables: "After washing collards thoroughly, add to a large amount of rapidly boiling water, and boil for 15 or 20 minutes or until perfectly tender. Season with salt, pepper, and butter or serve with white sauce." ❧

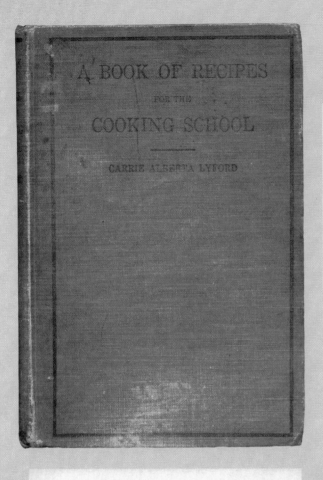

hot oven until the crumbs are a golden brown, about 20 minutes. Serves 6 to 8. (See scalloped dishes).

CELERY

Separate the pieces of celery from the root and wash each piece thoroughly. Remove any discolored portions with a knife. Cut off the leaves and keep them for garnishing or for soup. Reserve coarse or broken pieces, leaves, and roots for cooking. Serve all the delicate, crisp pieces uncooked with salt or use them in salads.

Creamed Celery

3 stalks celery   1 recipe medium white sauce

Wash and scrape the celery, cut in ½ inch pieces, cover with boiling water, and cook until tender (20-30 minutes), drain and serve with a white sauce, using the water in which the celery has been cooked as stock in the sauce. Serves 6.

COLLARDS

In those parts of the country where collards grow readily they are among the most valuable greens and give a much needed variety to the diet. They belong to the cabbage family and are valuable for their bulk and for the mineral matter they contain.

After washing collards thoroughly, add to a large amount of rapidly boiling water, and boil for 15 or 20 minutes or until perfectly tender. Season with salt, pepper, and butter or serve with white sauce.

CORN

Green corn is a valuable table vegetable, both fresh and canned, because of its agreeable flavor and the cellulose which provides necessary bulk to the diet.

Fresh corn should be used on the table or for canning as

INTRODUCTION

A BOOK OF RECIPES FOR THE COOKING SCHOOL

This book of recipes is prepared for the use of the many teachers and students of cooking who feel the need of standard recipes for the every-day dishes with directions simply and concisely stated.

The book represents a compilation of recipes that have been in use in cooking schools of the country for many years. It is not designed for the use of experienced cooks who are seeking a wider variety and a greater elaboration of recipes but for the young cook who desires to prepare simple dishes well. Each recipe has been carefully tested and every care has been taken to state the directions definitely. In every class which has used the recipes and with every teacher with whom the compiler has worked, suggestions, criticisms, and improvements have been made, so that the book represents the combined labors of many students of cooking. The chapter on Food Preservation contains the material used in a Hampton leaflet prepared with the aid of Miss Alma Kruse whose faithful labors made its completion possible.

To all who have thus aided in the preparation of the recipes sincerest gratitude is hereby expressed, and the compiler hopes that this publication will be the means of extending to young teachers the benefits of practices that have proved of value in many schools of cooking.

In sweet memories of a happy childhood spent in the atmosphere of the plantations and cabins of Virginia under the benign influence of my Dear Old Southern Mammy, Aunt Caroline, this volume is affectionately dedicated.

William McKinney

Breads
VIRGINIA BEATEN BISCUIT
One quart flour,
One teaspoonful of salt,
One tablespoon of lard.
Work lard lightly into the flour and salt, mix with iced water and then beat dough with rolling pin until it blisters. Cut into biscuits and bake in quick oven.

SOUTHERN SWEET-POTATO BISCUITS
Two cups flour,
One cup of mashed boiled sweet potatoes,
Two tablespoonsful of lard,
One teaspoonful of salt,
One and one-half teaspoonfuls of baking powder,
One-half teaspoonful of soda.
Enough buttermilk to make soft dough. Mix flour, salt, soda and baking powder together. Add sweet potatoes and work the lard in lightly. Mix with milk to make soft dough, roll thin cut into biscuits and bake in quick oven.

JOHNNY REB CAKE
2 cupsful of flour,
1 cupful of yellow meal,
4 tablespoonsful of sugar,
⅓ teaspoonful of salt,
1 teaspoonful of Cream of Tartar,
½ teaspoonful of soda,
        or,
2 teaspoonsful of baking-powder.
Add enough milk or water to make a thin batter, and bake.

CONTENTS

Aunt Caroline's Dixieland Recipes

A Rare Collection of Choice Southern Dishes

COMPILED BY EMMA AND
WILLIAM MCKINNEY

············

Chicago: Laird and Lee, 1922
147 pages

*E*MMA AND WILLIAM MCKINNEY compiled and edited more than two hundred of Caroline Pickett's classic southern masterpieces into a collection of "attractive and economical" recipes—a hardcover book designed to satisfy the "exacting tastes of the most pronounced epicure."

The book represents a good example of culinary segregation. By that, I mean that the McKinneys attributed specific formulas to the cook, mammy, or other "aunt" or "uncle." These dishes, with rare exception, limited Caroline's repertoire to narrowly defined ethnic recipes made from poverty ingredients. Dishes that represent the standard southern diet are not labeled at all.

Caroline's ghettoized recipe list reads like a menu for modern soul food: Mammy's Graham Muffins, Aunt Caroline's Corn Bread, Uncle Remus Mint Julep, Pickaninny Cookies (thin sugar cookies), Aunt Sug's Nut Cookies, Mammy's Peanut Candy, Uncle Remus Omelette, Aunt Caroline's Beef Loaf, Mammy's Chicken Patties, Massa's Cheese Croquettes, Mammy's Veal Loaf, Aunt Caroline's Own Pickle, Aunt Jemima's Lemon Pie, Mammy's Sweet Potato Pudding, Mammy's Dressing, Aunt Caroline's Porridge, Aunt Katy's Macaroni (macaroni and cheese), and Mammy's Candied Sweet Potatoes.

The format telegraphs a confusing, up-and-coming publishing practice in which the authors lavish a wise black cook with praise for creating an entire batch of recipes while denigrating her with words or pictures at the same time.

William grew up under the "benign influence of my Dear Old Southern Mammy, Aunt Caroline," a woman who, coincidentally, he wrote, was the perfect helpmate to fulfill Emma's desire to see her name in print.

"In the art of cooking, the 'Old Southern Mammy' has few equals and recognizes no peers," the McKinneys state in their foreword. "The following recipes have, with great patience and kindly perseverance, been drawn from the treasured memories of Aunt Caroline Pickett, a famous old Virginia cook, the 'pinch of this' and 'just a smacker of that' so wonderfully and mysteriously combined by the culinary masters of the Southland have been carefully and scientifically analyzed and recorded in this volume," and given a practical test.

This seems like a contradictory endorsement to me. ❧

1926–1950

The Servant

PROBLEM

Dual Messages

She does not know
her beauty,
she thinks her brown body
has no glory.

If she could dance
naked
under palm trees
and see her image in the river,
she would know.

But there are no palm trees
on the street,
and dish water gives back
no Images.

WILLIAM WARING CUNEY,
"No Images" (1926)

WHEN I FIRST encountered *The Picayune Creole Cook Book*, I thought it masterfully illustrated the sentiments expressed by this young, eighteen-year-old poet living in Washington, D.C., in post–World War I America.

This popular catalogue remained in print through fourteen editions, many with the same frontispiece, a photographic illustration of an antebellum hearth kitchen and romanticized recipes that " your mother used, and her mother and her grandmother, and the grandmother caught [them] from the old-time 'Mammy' who could work all kinds of magic in that black-raftered kitchen of the long ago."

The Picayune Creole Cook Book was created "to assist the good housewives of the present day and to preserve to future generations the many excellent and matchless recipes of the New Orleans cuisine by gathering up from the old Creole cooks and the old housekeepers the best of Creole cookery." It presented an amalgamated cuisine, created when French chefs and the best cooks of Spain shared ideas that New World cooks adapted "to their needs and to the materials they had at hand," for a result that was "beyond speech."

The book perpetuated the stilted reasoning that she who owns the cook owns the recipes, yet simultaneously imparted a measure of visibility to ignored cooks. It exposed the frustration felt by a growing number of white employers who found it impossible to separate their contempt for black servants from their dependence upon them, and it forecast a coming practice by mainstream cookbook authors—one that opened a crack in what David M. Katzman described as "southern caste etiquette," which dictated that blacks not appear to be in control. Ever.

In *Seven Days a Week: Women and Domestic Service in Industrializing America* (1978), a pioneering study of domestic relationships, Katzman tells the story of a northern mistress, Antoinette Hervey, trying to follow a delicious cookie recipe as told by her servant, "big black Katherine." Hervey recorded Katherine's recipe in vernacular language that was hard to follow. Katherine's mouth-watering treat "came from experience, not from any cooking manual . . . handed down from her mother or a close relative," Katzman explained. "Creativity in cooking was part of a folk tradition shared by many black women. And cooking was part of an oral or practical tradition, not a written one. Rather than reflecting ignorance—the point of Hervey's retelling the story—the anecdote [*sic*] revealed Katherine's mastery of the kitchen arts. . . . But her Northern mistress had little understanding of this Southern folk system."

No matter; the door opened.

Although Katherine possessed the knowledge of a specialist, Hervey and a generation of southern ladies set in place a harsh and false impression that misled the public: the black cook may have cooked excellently, but she was too ignorant to translate that experience into scientific formulas, much less into print.

While the *Better Homes and Gardens Cook Book* (1st ed., 1930) and *The Boston Cooking-School Cook Book* (1st ed., 1896) offered wordy details and sometimes lengthy cooking instructions for inexperienced cooks, southern cookbook authors representing the plantation style asserted their authority racially—by repeatedly resorting to condescending language and disparaging images when mentioning black women, whom previous designers had simply ignored.

Everywhere I looked— Nathalie Scott's composite cook, Mandy; Mary Moore Bremer's "negro woman"; the "colored cooks" described by Harriet Ross Colquitt; and the bandana-headed women whose faces graced the covers of manufacturers' recipe pamphlets and brochures—mid-twentieth-century mainstream cookbook authors in both the North and the South froze black food workers in trophy-like portraits of antebellum characters: the fruit vendor, the potato man, the ground-nut vendor, and the honey man. In commentary that both praised and ridiculed the

cook, these authors inadvertently introduced us to black cooks who understood the nuances of regional cooking.

As late as 1941, respected writers such as Marion Flexner exaggerated their "scientific approach to cooking" by juxtaposing illustrations of elegant plantation scenes against cabin hearth cooking done by black women in head rags. And she was far from the only one. *The Southern Cookbook: 322 Old Dixie Recipes* (1939), compiled by Lillie S. Lustig, S. Claire Sondheim, and Sarah Rensel, has become a perennial favorite with Internet booksellers on eBay. It mingles classic southern recipes, demoralizing etchings of slaves at work, vernacular language, and lyrics from spirituals and hymns.

In their lavishly illustrated *200 Years of Charleston Cooking* (1931), Blanche S. Rhett and Lettie Gay applaud black cooks for their "famed" regional dishes. Crab Soup, Shrimp and Hominy (Grits), Fish Soufflé, Stuffed Crabs and Mushrooms, Fried Chicken with Corn Cakes, and Sweet Potato Croquettes are attributed to a butler named William Deas, "one of the great cooks of the world." Sally Washington, whose "cooking was of a kind to make one speculate as to whether she was a genius in her own right or whether Charleston was gifted by the gods," is credited for her recipe for Red Rice.

Harriet Ross Colquitt made her confused prejudices known through plantation sketches laced with bitter complaints about the near impossibility of procuring recipes for her *Savannah Cook Book: A Collection of Old Fashioned Receipts from Colonial Kitchens* (1933).

We have had so many requests for receipts for rice dishes, and for shrimp and crab concoctions which are peculiar to our locality, that I have concentrated on those indigenous to our soil, as it were, begging them from housekeepers, and trying to tack our elusive cooks down to some definite idea of what goes into the making of the good dishes they turn out. Getting directions from colored cooks is rather like trying to write down the music to the spirituals which they sing—for all good old-timers . . . cook "by ear" and it is hard to bring them down to earth when they begin to improvise.

Eleanor Ott's hyperbolic recipe collection, *Plantation Cookery of Old Louisiana*, boasts wistful reminiscences of the charm of antebellum cuisine and wows readers with the vast number of servants on her grandmother's "culinary plant." At the same time, she revered the cooks for their "Intelligence, Industry, and Art." Kitty Mammy, the plantation doctor and nurse who supervised the herb garden, and Becky Mammy, the high priestess of the milk house, both were honored simply: "Genius, sheer, breathtaking Genius."

A few African American authors manage to self-publish remarkable recipe collections of their own between World War I and the dawning of the civil rights movement. Their collections stand in the gap for the mammy, the Cream of Wheat Man, and the procession of colored maids in Hollywood films. But more than that, these writers can be seen as predecessors of modern celebrity chefs who press through publishing favoritism and prejudice, boost spirits, and cheer on the next generation, all while championing middle-class American cooking.

The delicacies and grace rendered by *Eliza's Cook Book: Favorite Recipes Compiled by Negro Culinary Art Club of Los Angeles*, Lena Richard's wise entrepreneurship, Lucille Bishop Smith's empowering spirit, and Freda DeKnight's global kitchen existed in the shadows of pervasive and perverse debasements. These authors understood the work of the kitchen, and they used that knowledge to untether their foodways from distorted representations.

In the same way, Idella Parker stared down jocular characterizations of domestic servitude and ushered in an era of culinary liberation with her account of life in the household of the Pulitzer Prize–winning novelist Marjorie Kinnan Rawlings. Though little was written elsewhere to accurately credit black cooks as experts, this former domestic, teacher, and cook accepts her life of service as the renowned author's "Perfect Maid," without drowning in that murky dishwater. Her memoir does not contain recipes in the traditional sense, and it wasn't published until fifty years after Rawlings wrote *Cross Creek Cookery*, a book of classic southern dishes. Parker does, however, present an insightful look into the complex relations between a black cook and her white employer. "Marjorie Kinnan Rawlings called me 'the perfect maid' in her book *Cross Creek*," Parker writes in the preface to *Idella: Marjorie Rawlings' Perfect Maid*. "I am not perfect and neither was Mrs. Rawlings, and this book will make that clear to anyone who reads it."

As the story of their life together unfolds, Parker provides a believable, poised, and fair account of how it felt to be underpaid and overworked. Naturally, she was frustrated. After months spent together in the kitchen testing recipes for *Cross Creek Cookery*, including many that Parker claimed were hers, such as the chocolate pie, Rawlings credits her on just three. Still, Parker's courage accomplishes something unique and wonderful: it draws everyone into the kitchen, inviting folks to cook for one another and to persevere through awkward race conversations.

This truth would have been a sight for the sore eyes of Cuney's domestics and the authors on the following pages, who invented regional, cultural, and ethnic specialties when they left their own kitchens to manage someone else's. 🌿

Mammy's Cook Book

KATHARIN BELL

....

1927
160 pages

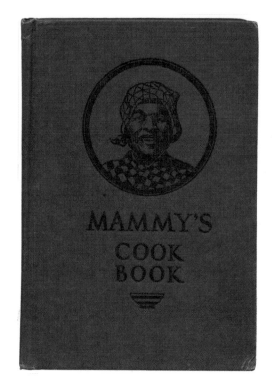

IT IS SURPRISING that a book with "Mammy" in the title has only one or two of the classic stereotypes you would expect. As a matter of fact, this self-published book offers a selection of dishes that capture the full and wonderful array of recipes prepared by an admired black cook for her "white folks," with unique and classic period pieces sprinkled throughout.

When Bell credited these recipes to Sallie Miller, she strayed from the publishing trend of plantation-style cookbooks written by white southern belles claiming to record family history. Instead, her homage unwittingly affirmed the case for African American intellectual property rights.

The cover features an illustration of a grinning black woman wearing a headscarf and a checkered top. The foreword explains why Bell gathered more than 450 standard recipes from the cook and caretaker of her childhood—her mammy. In these ways alone it is representative of its time—an era when William Faulkner and Zora Neale Hurston were painting adoring portraits of black women and black life, and Al Jolson sang of mammy: "God made her a woman and love made her a mother."

Otherwise, there are no caricatures. The usual colloquialisms and vernacular language of the "slave street" are absent. The recipe titles don't directly attribute the formula to a woman named Mammy or even Aunt So-and-so. Curiously, there are only a handful of the recipes traditionally associated with black cookery—croquettes, greens, gumbo, and okra. Bell adds a teaspoon of sugar to Miller's southern cornbread, a practice often observed in black cornbread recipes. The author obviously witnessed the brilliance of the cook in her midst.

Miller's accomplished cookery is organized alphabetically by category: from beverages and breads to soups, special dishes, and vegetables. A section called "Things Worth Knowing" is a gem, chock-full of useful kitchen tips that would be considered standard knowledge today, and a refreshing contrast to the caricatures that dominated cookbook publishing during this era.

Inspired dishes such as Tipsy Pudding (a kind of tiramisu), shirred eggs on toast (called Golden Rain), and several frozen salads made with tomatoes, cucumbers, or cream cheese and served like ice cream demonstrate that the cook understood the secrets of cooking delicate egg custards, and these dishes stand alongside the whips, fools, and goofy gelatin salads so popular back then. ❧

FOREWORD

With the dying out of the black mammies of the South, much that was good and beautiful has gone out of life, and in this little volume I have sought to preserve the memory and the culinary lore of my Mammy, Sallie Miller, who in her day was a famous cook. She possessed moreover, all those qualities of loyalty and devotion which have enshrined her and her kind, in the loving hearts of their "White Folks," to whom they were faithful, through every vicissitude and change of fortune.

Most of these recipes were Mammy's, reduced in quantity to meet the needs of small families, and the high price conditions of the present day. All of them have been tried out, and I have given full details, hoping, even the most inexperienced cook can use them. I have always felt the need of having under one cover, instructions for making the plain every day things, as well as the so-called, fancy dishes. In this book I have endeavored to assemble both, and I hope that it may prove a help and inspiration to all who possess it.

KATHARIN BELL.

3

A Recipe to Cure the Blues

When everything looks dark and drear
    And nothing seems worthwhile,
Just read and try this recipe
    And soon you'll begin to smile.

Take a dash into your garden,
    Fill your lungs with God's fresh air,
Mix the earth around your flowers,
    Dissolve in it your care.

Stir in happiness for someone,
    Add to it a task undone,
Measure out a lot of work
    And a little play and fun.

Soon you'll find your heart uplifted,
    And your lips will sing a song,
As you count your many blessings,
    You'll find your worries gone.

5

Roquefort and Tomato Salad

Rub ⅔ cup of Roquefort cheese to a cream with 1 tb. of butter and roll into six even sized balls. Peel six tomatoes and scoop out center, placing a cheese ball in each and cover with a mixture of ½ cupful of chopped green pepper and 1 cup chopped tender celery. Place on lettuce and pour a lemon French dressing over it and serve cold.

Tomato Surprise

Scoop out tomatoes and fill with chicken salad and garnish with mayonnaise and serve on lettuce.

Shrimp and Tomato Salad

Chop shrimps and tomatoes together with a little celery and mayonnaise and serve on lettuce leaves.

Summer Combination Salad

Use hearts of lettuce for a foundation. Cut up tomatoes, add chopped celery, green onions, sliced cucumbers, radishes and small string beans and serve ice cold with French dressing.

Frozen Tomato Salad

¾ cup ground celery	2 t. salt
1 medium sized green pepper, ground	6 tomatoes
	½ t. onion juice

Cut top off six tomatoes, scoop out all the insides. Put this and celery and pepper through meat grinder, using only tender stalks of celery. Season with salt and onion juice and a little cayenne pepper and leave all the juice, as it should be very thin. Mix in plenty of mayonnaise and freeze as ice cream. When ready to serve fill tomato hulls full and serve on lettuce leaces.

Frozen Cucumber Salad

| 4 large cucumbers | 1 stalk celery |
| 1 green pepper | 1 small onion |

Cut cucumbers in halves lengthwise, scrape out insides into a pulp, taking out as many seeds as possible.

101

BEVERAGES

Oriental Punch

½ pound tea	1 large jar orange marmalade
3 quarts boiling water	1 tablespoon preserved ginger
2 pounds sugar	2 tablespoon ginger sirup
Juice of 2 dozen lemons	5 gallons ice water
1 can grated pineapple	

Pour two quarts boiling water over tea, cover and let stand five minutes. Strain and add sugar, which has been dissolved in remaining quart of boiling water and boiled two minutes. Cool and add remaining materials, allow to stand several hours to ripen. Pour over ice in a punch bowl just before serving. Part of the water may be charged water if desired. Sufficient for seventy-five to a hundred guests.

Hot Chocolate

Dissolve 3 tbsp. of grated chocolate in 1 pint boiling water; boil 10 minutes; add 1 pint rich milk. Let come to boil, sweeten to taste and serve hot.

Punch

Juice of 3 lemons	1 cup sugar
1 orange	1 cup water
1 pint grape juice	1 pint apple juice

Mix all together and strain. Add large piece of ice.

E. Monroe, Ridgewood, N. J.

Lemonade

Juice of 2 lemons	¼ cup cherry juice
2 large cups sugar	2 quarts water

More sugar can be added if desired.

Cherry Juice

To 1 pint cherry juice add juice of 1 lemon, 1 pint of water, sugar to taste.

Harvest Drink

This is the drink that is relished in the hay-field. Take ¼ cup vinegar, 1 cup molasses with 10 cups water. Add level tbsps. of ginger, more or less, according to the fondness for the taste. Serve very cold.

Ginger Water

1 cup sugar	2 tbsp. ginger
1 tbsp. Jamaica ginger or	¼ cup vinegar

Mix all together and add ½ gallon cold water. Lemon juice may be added, also cracked ice.

Dixie Punch

Juice of 6 lemons	1 pint crushed strawberries
Juice of 2 oranges	1 gallon water
1 lb. sugar	

Mix all together and chill with ice.

Pineapple Lemonade

Juice of 3 lemons	2 cups water
1 cup sugar	1 can grated pineapple

Cool, strain and add ice water.

Cocoa

Use 1 rounding tsp. of cocoa and 1½ tsp. of sugar to each cup of milk. Put cocoa and sugar into ½ cup of cream and bring to the boiling point, stirring constantly. Put milk in double boiler. Then stir cocoa into it and if desired add ½ tsp. of vanilla. Serve with tsp. of whipped cream in each cup.

Grape Juice

12 lbs. grapes	3 quarts water

Crush grapes and boil 15 minutes. Strain and add 3 lbs. white sugar. When sugar is dissolved strain thru a cloth and heat to boiling point. Seal.

Cook Book "Work and Serve the Home"

COMPILED BY MAMIE COOK

chairman of Ways and Means Department,
New Jersey State Federation of Colored Women's Clubs

....

Ridgewood, New Jersey, 1928
35 pages

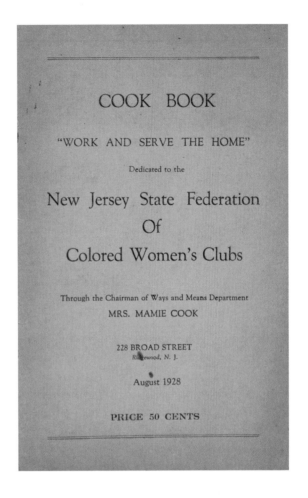

COOK BOOK

"WORK AND SERVE THE HOME"

Dedicated to the

New Jersey State Federation
Of
Colored Women's Clubs

Through the Chairman of Ways and Means Department
MRS. MAMIE COOK

228 BROAD STREET
Ridgewood, N. J.

August 1928

PRICE 50 CENTS

I CANNOT LIE: this is a charming little stapled booklet appreciated for a unique dish or two, some useful shopping tips, and a long list of household hints and remedies, but it is a mess. You have to forgive the typos, misspellings, peculiar arrangement, and missing elements. One recipe lists an ingredient upside down. You could categorize the work as a cook's stream of consciousness—her favorite dishes written down for friends. In this sense, the collection represents a pure record of black cookery without white involvement.

The opening page features two poems, entitled "Merry Jungles," which probably was a corruption of the word "Jingles." What follows is a hodgepodge of chapters and recipes gathered from communities of women in Newark, Jersey City, Ridgewood, Roselle, and Plainfield, plus one from Chicago. Some contributors signed their dishes. For others, the hometown was left off. The rest were anonymous or attributed to the compiler, Mamie Cook. The recipes are printed so tightly on the page that it is often impossible to tell where one dish ends and another begins.

The compiler made other goofs, too. Salads don't always appear in the salads section. The "Sandwiches and Fillings" section is interrupted by a recipe for Shrimps a la Creole, three shopping tips, some oyster recipes, and the formula for making Creole Tripe. There are no page numbers.

Despite all the disarray, two tonics are worth remembering. Harvest Drink and Ginger Water may record early versions of the popular soul beverage red drink. ❧

Aunt Priscilla In the Kitchen

A Collection of Winter-Time Recipes, Seasonable Menus, and Suggestions for Afternoon Teas and Special Holiday Parties

AUNT PRISCILLA

....

Baltimore: Aunt Priscilla Publishing, 1929
176 pages

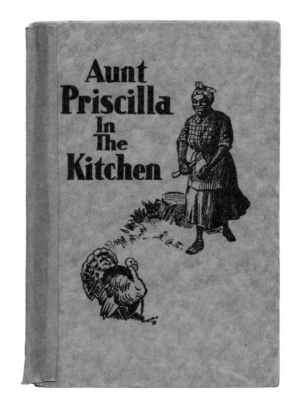

THIS IS A shocking selection of traditional southern recipes, published during the 1930s, presumably for white housewives and written almost entirely in dialect. What I like about it is that Aunt Priscilla was a media expert, and in a way she was the first black food writer at a major newspaper, the *Baltimore Sun*.

Every day, Aunt Priscilla answered reader requests. Every day a recipe in the narrative style followed a brief statement of her culinary wisdom. Dishes could be sweet or savory, simple or complex. On some days, she offered ideas for variations; on other days she shared make-ahead secrets. But always she spoke in pernicious slave dialect. A Jemima-like illustration accompanied her columns. For example: "I'se bery glad to gib you de crab recipes Miss Katie, speshully as serbil mo' ladies done ast fo' de same. Try yo' crab cakes dis way." This was an odd sort of communication coming from a black woman so intelligent that a major metropolitan newspaper featured her recipes. Obviously, Aunt Priscilla was a fictitious character.

Alice Furlaud told NPR audiences that it was Eleanor Purcell, the Anglo secretary of one of the *Sun*'s most distinguished writers, Frank Kent, who posed as the spurious Aunt Priscilla, and she is the one who answered reader requests for everything from divinity to chili con carne. Nevertheless, this work was authored by "Aunt Priscilla, herself." And it is a tidy little recipe collection—a stunning departure from the publishing traditions of previous generations, which co-opted the recipes of black cooks without attribution. By giving Aunt Priscilla her own cookbook, the *Sun* memorialized the practice of giving credit to black women for their kitchen mastery.

Aunt Priscilla planned menus, suggested flavor combinations, explained quantity cooking for a crowd, and recommended compatible decorations. She made stock, cautioned readers not to rush when making roux for thickening soups and sauces, and taught the method for determining proper frying temperatures. The year after Aunt Priscilla's book came out, Betty Benton Patterson, a Houston food journalist, adopted the format when she penned an identical project, *Mammy Lou's Cookbook.* ❧

Aunt Jemima's Magical Recipes

QUAKER OATS COMPANY, 1930S

....

26 pages

WHILE READING the introduction to this booklet, I wondered what could be learned from a mythical figure besides her recipe for great pancakes. Quaker's palm-sized corporate marketing tool posed a practical question for eager housewives integrating packaged foods into their menus: how many inventive ways can we cook with Pancake Mix? The answer: a bunch.

This copious selection of pancakery confirms the company's objective, stated on the last page of the booklet, "Aunt Jemima means far more than pancakes; she is an American tradition": "Buckwheats. Deluxe. Ham. Cheese. Corn. Sausage. Poached Eggs on top. Half-and-Half.

Buttermilk. Anima. Polk-a-dot. Bacon Strip. Pancake-Sausage Roll-Ups. Asparagus. Chicken Roll-Ups. Cherry Roll-Ups. Ice Cream Roll-Ups. Apple Pancakes with Sour Cream. Adirondack. Strawberry. French. Hawaiian. Banana. Apple Ring."

And that doesn't include the waffles, dumplings, fritters, cookies, bars, cake rolls, and other foods that are coated with the pancake batter and fried. Or the toppings that accessorize Aunt Jemima's ubiquitous pancakes: Brown sugar syrup. Honey Butter. Orange Marmalade syrup. Frosty Whipped Butter. Sausage Ball Syrup. Praline Sauce. 🐟

Aunt Julia's Cook Book

AUNT JULIA AND AUNT LEOLA

....

Esso (Standard Oil Company of Pennsylvania), 1934
33 pages

Aunt Julia and Aunt Leola Compare **Notes**.

THE STANDARD OIL COMPANY relied upon African American culinary expertise to promote this brief assemblage of southern dishes—including beaten biscuits, hoecakes, Brunswick stew, and watermelon rind pickles. When it was published in the early 1930s, Rice Muffins, Chicken Pilau, Hopping John, and Red Rice furnished regional Carolina flavor, and two black cooks, Aunt Julia and Aunt Leola, supplied authenticity.

The pamphlet is a bizarre combination of recipes tucked alongside advertisements for car batteries, petroleum products, pesticides, motor oil, tires, and car engine accessories. Presumably, it was given away at gas stations—hence all the automotive-related material. Two useful charts provide postal rates and kitchen measures, plus there is a listing of important rules of the road to remember, and some helpful suggestions for house cleaning.

We learn nothing, however, about its two co-authors. The photograph on the inside cover contains the only mention of their names, and curiously, there are no headnotes accompanying the forty-nine short recipes to give any hint about their roles and responsibilities. What a shame. ❧

Eliza's Cook Book

Favorite Recipes Compiled by Negro Culinary Art Club of Los Angeles

BEATRICE HIGHTOWER CATES

....

Los Angeles: Wetzel, 1936
101 pages

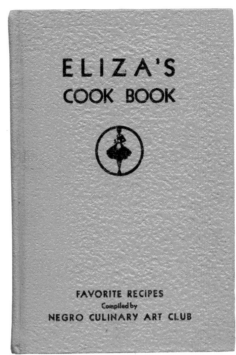

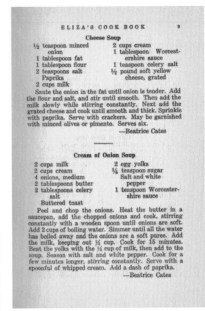

THIS IS A SOPHISTICATED GEM—a miraculous and lovely example of African American flair in the ever-present asymmetry of the Jemima cliché. During the years when Hollywood confined black actresses to roles spoken in broken black dialect or to portraying sassy maids, these upscale recipes of the black middle class showed that there was another side to black female cooks: a sophisticated side.

Amid all the resources women had for cooking with scientific principles and healthful meal planning, the members of the Negro Culinary Art Club obviously noticed a void. Their extensive catalogue of "ladies' luncheon" and light dinner dishes is "Dedicated to the mothers of the members of the Culinary Art Club," women who probably were former slaves. And yet the recipes were decidedly upscale.

Cultural influences are evident, too, in Hispanic-inspired dishes such as Spanish Canapés and Tripe, Adobe Steak, Baked Oysters Mexican-Style, Enchiladas, and Hot Tamale Pie. Gumbo Veal and a slow-roasted dish of lamb and squab carry the Creole banner. Soups are anything but ordinary; black beans, cheese, chicken giblets, oysters, and lobster simmered into thick and creamy brews. Salads are abundant and diverse, dressed with gelatin, cream cheese, rich homemade mayonnaise, sour cream, assorted vinaigrettes, and marshmallows. They bind together fruits, vegetables, and meats in mixtures that the contributors served chilled, whipped, and frozen. In addition, the ladies allocated a separate section for nearly two dozen special dressings. An intriguing recipe for Carrot Wine and an oatmeal cookie invention called Rocks, which predates the modern oatmeal cookie formula, round out this comprehensive collection.

The Negro Culinary Art Club offered some standard southern emblems, too—cornbread and spoon bread, buttermilk biscuits, potato rolls, a version of johnnycake called Johnny Bread, cracklin' bread, chowchow, and a few regional specialties such as Carolina Pilau and Rarebit.

Collectors and historians will appreciate the business advertisements on the concluding pages. ❧

Emma Jane's Souvenir Cook Book and Some Old Virginia Recipes

COMPILED BY
BLANCHE ELBERT MONCURE

....

Williamsburg, Virginia, 1937
85 pages

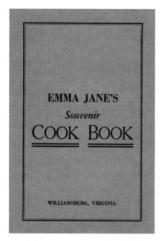

THIS CLASSIC stapled and folded book of 150 standard recipes collected by a white woman on behalf of her black cook is the best example of the worst practice in cookbook publishing—mocking the cook. The frontispiece displays a portrait of Emma Jane Jackson Beauregard Jefferson Davis Lincoln Christian, her brief biography, and a fanciful tale about how she was named by three Civil War soldiers. Then, in a dialect as thick as mud, Emma Jane speaks her mind, ruminating on culinary theory and practice for Miss Sally, a bride to be. It will remind some of the way that authors of early British cookbooks, like Meg Dods, disparaged their Irish maids.

Emma Jane clearly understands kitchen fundamentals. She rambles through eight pages of cooking secrets that she has been practicing for fifty years. Her insightful and practical wisdom covers such weighty topics as how to make sure the table is attractive and hospitable, set with a centerpiece (a single flower stem will do); the proper course for making biscuits; her preference for barnyard turkey over store-bought; how to choose and prepare a fine ham; the secret to perfect sweet potato pie; and her favorite ways with fruitcake, hot bread, and Christmas eggnog.

Above all, Emma Jane believes that there is one important measure to every good cook: gumption. "Yes Sar! 'Gumption.' Fur, dat is a seasning you is got to put in ev'y dish you cook, an' no mistake! Does 'ceats,' as you calls 'em may tell you what to put in, an' what to leave out, but effen you don't use your 'gumption,' you gwine to be leff in de lerch sometime when 'tis pretty unhandy."

Strangely, after delivering so much wisdom, the book concludes with an unspectacular series of breads, meats, vegetables, desserts, candies, preserves and beverages, presented in traditional cookbook language (ingredients list followed by the method)—some with a Virginia flair. There are instructions for preparing Old Country or Smithfield Ham, Emma Jane's Way of Cooking a Ham Other than a Smithfield One, Hominy of Roanoke or Great Hominy, several versions of plum pudding, and Old Virginia Punch. But in a collection supposedly printed on behalf of the cook, a horrible, politically incorrect recipe title, headnote, and tagline awkwardly attribute the formula for the cake in the sidebar to Emma Jane.

See for yourself. 🐝

CAKES AND DESSERTS

"Fool-Nigger-Proof" Cake

As I has said, menny a time, I ain't no fancy cake maker, but here is a re-ceet dat "Ole Miss" taught me. She called it one-two-three-four cake. I tole her effen I made a *suc*-cess of de makin' of it *I* would name it "De Fool-Nigger-Proof Cake"—so dat's what it's been to *me*, ever since. Jes take:

1 cup butter	1 cup milk
2 cups sugar	4 eggs
3 cups flour	3 pilin' teaspoons baking powder

My "Ole Miss" allers said to beat de whites of de aigs an' de yallers *separate*. De yallers in de bowl, an' de whites in de big platter—no mater what any written *re-ceept* told you to do.

So cream yo' butter, po' in yo' sugar, an' mix dat good. Drap in de yallers an' beat some mo'.

Den, arter you has sifted yo' flour twice wid yo' bakin' powder, stir *dat* in, not bein' sparin' wid de el-bow grease, none whatsome-ever. Den drap in de seasonin' jes what ever you happen to have mos' on de shelf, whether it be lemon extraction, vanilla, or both mixed together. Den de last thing, fold in de whites of de aigs dainty laike, put in a quick oven an' bake.

You kin make de layer cake outten of dis mixtures, or jes de muffin ones, jis' whichever you wish mos', at de present time.

—EMMA JANE.

Recipes and Domestic Service

The Mahammitt School of Cookery

HELEN T. MAHAMMITT

············

Omaha, Nebraska, 1939
150 pages

*T*HIS TEXTBOOK of basic instruction is well organized and easy to read. Its layout is attractive and thoughtfully arranged, with a variety of typefaces, inviting recipe titles, and tips for novices that encourage as well as inform. The author does not seem to be motivated to improve the reputations of domestic servants. The objective is simple: she wants to fill the world with wonderful cooks and successful entrepreneurs.

After thirty years of catering and teaching cooking, Mahammitt published this manual of tested recipes for advanced cooks, rules and guidelines for domestics, and instructions for general catering, "in the hope that it will prove beneficial to all whom it may reach."

The spiral-bound hardcover book is divided into four parts, each with chapters that include recipes or general instruction. Book One: Novice Cooks teaches facts that every cook should know, plus recipes for basic dishes. Book Two: Advanced Recipes covers the same topics but adds more variety, flavors, and complex techniques. For example, in Book One, the cook learns just two ways with veal: roast and cutlets. The advanced cook learns to prepare Ragout of Veal and a breaded and braised dish called Veal Birds. Book Three: Domestic Service instructs on the decorum and personal appearance of a maid and describes three kinds of service recommendations for presenting formal dinners: Russian, English, and Combination. The author explains as well how to present informal meals, such as the club luncheon, bridge luncheon, and afternoon tea. Book Four: Catering presents Mahammitt's thoughts on proper etiquette and a dozen essentials for budding caterers. ✤

Lena Richard's Cook Book

LENA RICHARD

....

New Orleans, 1939

New Orleans Cook Book

LENA RICHARD

....

Boston: Houghton Mifflin, 1940

New Orleans Cook Book

LENA RICHARD

....

New York: Dover, 1985
146 pages

LENA RICHARD wrote and self-published her cookbook in 1939 in order "to put the culinary art within the reach of every housewife and homemaker." The book featured the "secrets of Creole cooking which have been kept for years by the old French chef." Court Bouillon, Crawfish Bisque, Grillade a la Creole, Vol-Au-Vent, Calas Tout Chauds, Shrimp Remoulade, Pain Perdu, and Creole Chicory Coffee are just a few of the mysteries she shares to give everyone the opportunity to excel in the food industry.

She breads Creole Fried Chicken in a mixture of seasoned flour and cracker crumbs, and the Holy Trinity (celery, onion, and green pepper) seasoned Creole Red Beans, Jumbalaya (jambalaya), and a creamed oyster-and-shrimp filling for puff pastry shells she calls Oyster *Poulet*. Her caterer's eye for presentation is evident in Lena's Watermelon Ice Cream, a three-layer sherbet treat set in a round mold to resemble a whole melon. A few casual and formal menus are recommended, and she includes a section of miscellaneous culinary techniques that include roux making, mixing standard cakes, and measuring how-tos.

Before Julia Child ever appeared on television, Richard hosted a weekly cooking show on New Orleans's first television station, WDSU, teaching viewers a thing or two about how to make gumbo. She was a well-seasoned cook, quietly achieving the kind of professional swagger celebrity chefs demonstrate today. She ran a catering company, served as head chef at restaurants in New York and Virginia, packaged and sold her famous Shrimp Soup Louisiane by mail order, and owned and operated her own restaurant and a cooking school in New Orleans.

When the father of American gourmet cuisine, James Beard, and the food editor Clementine Paddleford learned of Richard's noteworthy accomplishments, they lobbied the trade to republish her book, despite her race. Houghton Mifflin agreed to do so, with a subtle reminder to the author that she was an outlier. The ladylike portrait that radiated in the frontispiece of her self-published edition was removed and the title changed. ❧

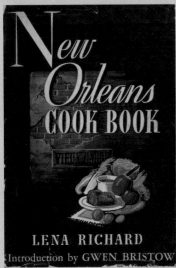

ICE CREAMS AND SHERBETS

LENA'S WATERMELON ICE CREAM

1½ pints whipping cream
½ cup raisins
Green coloring
½ cup sugar

5 cups or 1¼ quarts strawberry sherbert or other sherbert of reddish color

Whip cream until stiff, add sugar, and color one-half green. Line inside of mold with layer of the green cream to simulate the watermelon rind. Put in a layer of white cream next to the green. In center put layer of 3 cups of sherbet, sprinkling this with raisins. Fill mold with remaining two cups sherbet. Place wax paper over all. Put cover on mold, pack in equal parts ice and salt, let stand for four hours.

To serve: Remove mold from ice and wipe thoroughly to get rid of all salt. Take off top of mold and invert mold on a large platter. Cover mold with a hot towel until the cream leaves the sides of the mold.

OLD-FASHIONED CUSTARD ICE CREAM

1 quart milk
6 eggs
1 pint cream

1½ cups sugar
1 vanilla bean

Beat eggs until light, and add sugar. Heat milk to boiling point, add egg and sugar mixture. Cook until slightly thickened. Remove from fire and let cool. Whip the cream and then add to the first mixture. Split vanilla bean, scrape inside and then add hean and scraping. Freeze with equal parts of ice and salt. When frozen, remove dasher and pack. Set aside until ready to serve.

[121]

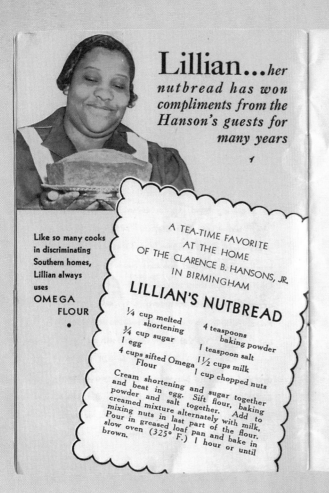

Lillian...*her nutbread has won compliments from the Hanson's guests for many years*

1

Like so many cooks in discriminating Southern homes, Lillian always uses OMEGA FLOUR

•

A TEA-TIME FAVORITE
AT THE HOME
OF THE CLARENCE B. HANSONS, JR.
IN BIRMINGHAM

LILLIAN'S NUTBREAD

¼ cup melted shortening
¾ cup sugar
1 egg
4 cups sifted Omega Flour
4 teaspoons baking powder
1 teaspoon salt
1½ cups milk
1 cup chopped nuts

Cream shortening and sugar together and beat in egg. Sift flour, baking powder and salt together. Add to creamed mixture alternately with milk, mixing nuts in last part of the flour. Pour in greased loaf pan and bake in slow oven (325° F.) 1 hour or until brown.

RICH CHOCOLATE CAKE

1 cup boiled water
4 squares chocolate
½ cup of butter or substitute
2½ cups sifted OMEGA flour
2 cups sugar
1½ teaspoons soda
½ cup sour cream
½ teaspoon salt
2 eggs beaten together
1 teaspoon vanilla

In a pan boil one cup 1 of water, remove from heat, add four squares chocolate and one-half cup ½ butter. Allow to stand until butter melts. Resift two and one-half cups 2½ OMEGA flour with two cups 2 sugar, one and one-half teaspoons 1½ soda and one-half teaspoon ½ salt. Put dry ingredients into dissolved chocolate mixture, add one-half cup ½ sour cream, two beaten eggs 2 and one teaspoon 1 vanilla. Bake in two greased and lightly floured nine-inch cake pans in a moderate oven (350° F.) for about thirty-five minutes.

5

The Home of Mr. and Mrs. Douglas A. Lee, Shreveport

...whose Friends envy them their

Eva...*Like other cooks for the South's first families she uses OMEGA flour!*

EVA'S ORANGE ROLLS

1 cake compressed yeast
1 cup milk, scalded
¼ cup sugar
1 teaspoon salt
1 egg, beaten
4½ cups sifted Omega Flour
¼ cup softened shortening

Soften yeast in the milk which has been cooled to lukewarm. Stir in sugar and salt; then the egg. Add the flour, mixing to form a soft dough. Work in the shortening. Turn out on a lightly floured board and knead gently until smooth. Form into a ball and place in a well-greased bowl. Cover and let stand in a lukewarm place until doubled in bulk. Roll out in a rectangular sheet ½ inch thick and spread with Orange Filling. Roll jelly-roll fashion and cut in 1-inch slices. Place, cut side down, in well-greased cake pans or muffin pans and let rise until doubled in bulk. Bake in moderately hot oven (400° F.) 5 minutes then at 375° F. 15 minutes or until brown. Invert but do not remove pans for several minutes. Yield: 2 dozen rolls.

See page 9 for Orange Filling Recipe

PRIDE OF THE SOUTH BISCUITS

2 cups sifted OMEGA flour
2 teaspoons baking powder
½ teaspoon salt
2 tablespoons lard
⅔ cup milk

Into a mixing bowl sift two cups 2 of sifted OMEGA flour again with two teaspoons 2 of baking powder and one-half teaspoon ½ of salt. Cut in the two tablespoons 2 of lard, then add two-thirds cup ⅔ of milk which must be very cold. Mix quickly, then turn on a lightly floured board. Roll the dough to about one-fourth of an inch thick and brush melted butter over the top. Fold the dough over and cut in biscuit rounds through the double thickness. Brush the tops with a little milk to give a glaze. Set in a warm place about half an hour to rise slightly and bake in a hot oven (450° F.) ten to twelve minutes, or until brown. This makes about three dozen one-inch biscuits.

17

Omega Flour

Tested Recipes for Cakes, Pastries and Hot Breads

OMEGA FLOUR MILLS

....

Chester, Illinois, 1940s
24 pages

THE OMEGA FLOUR COMPANY, established in 1839, published several advertising booklets containing recipes meant to help housewives understand and use the company's products. The pocket-size guides promoted the idea that Omega's recipes were "pre-tested and especially prepared . . . to eliminate the possibility of baking failure." And who better to provide testimonials than the black domestics who were doing the cooking and baking in America's kitchens?

Recipes by black servants introduce each section, which includes a photo of the cook, the estate where she works, or both. The cover illustration is classic early to mid-twentieth-century product trademark—a caricatured mammy demonstrating her culinary skill in order to sell merchandise. But this one contains an eerie element. The picture of an enthralled white female under the tutelage of a grinning, bandana-headed baking expert on the cover is nearly identical to a bloated image in Marion Flexner's *Dixie Dishes*, a 1941 book of southern recipes. In both cases, a giant black cook towers over a novice housewife made to look like a little girl. ❧

LUCILLE'S TREASURE CHEST OF FINE FOODS
(Fourth Edition)

This publication is the result of a long and practical experience in Catering and Professional service. For 12 years I served as teacher-co-ordinator of Vocational Education in the Fort Worth Public Schools; 23 summers as pastry cook and assistant dietitian at Camp Waldemar, Hunt, Texas, where my recipes are still in use to nourish, and make happy, the hundreds of fine girls, counsellors and guests. Fifteen years prior to this time, I was public Catress and Food Demonstrator.

I was employed for 5 years as Teacher Trainer of Industrial Education in charge of Household Service Training in Texas, with headquarters at Prairie View State College. During that time, I compiled 5 Household Service Manuals which were approved by the University of Texas, and the State Department of Industrial Education and were used as Vocational Texts throughout the State.

My most recent creations were "Lucille's Hot Roll Mix" that was a leader in the packaged food commodities; and during the past 6 years, I set up and helped put into successful operation The Commercial Food Technology Training and apprenticeship program at Prairie View A & M College, training cooks, dietitians, food managers, bakers, caterers, and chefs who will, not only continue to raise the standards in the food service industry, but project my services into fields where I can no longer serve.

Copyright 1941-45-47-60

LUCILLE B. SMITH
966 E. Terrell Avenue

Fort Worth 4, Texas

Salad Dressings **Sauces** **Vegetables**
Miscellaneous **Salad** **Sandwiches**
Hot Desserts **Meat Substitutes** **Pies, Pastry**
Eggs **Frozen Desserts**
Candy **Cold Desserts** **Cookies**
Beverages **Breads**

Recipe For A Good Life
LUCILLE'S TREASURE CHEST OF FINE FOODS

Take equal parts of kindness, unselfishness
and thoughtfulness; mix in an atmosphere of
love; add the spice of usefulness; scatter a
few grains of cheerfulness; season with smiles;
stir in a hearty laugh, and

Dispense to EVERY MEMBER OF YOUR FAMILY.

"Reprinted from the Pittsburgh Courier."

Appetizers   (Dips, Spreads and Pick-Ups)
LUCILLE'S TREASURE CHEST OF FINE FOODS

1. Canapes Mephista
2. Cheese Ball
3. Cocktail Chicken Livers
4. Chili Conqueso
5. Cheese Roll
6. Cheese Squares
7. Chili Biscuits
8. Chili for Chili Biscuits

9. Cheese
10. Clam
11. Gua
12. Oy
13.
14.

12.

OYSTER TURNOVERS   Party Pick-Ups

Chop - 1 lb. small oysters very fine. Drain
Season with - 1 t. salt, ½ t. pepper, 1 t. A-1 sauce,
1 t. onion juice and 2 T. Parmesan Cheese.
Mix and add - 1 beaten egg yolk, mixed with
¼ c. melted butter. Add a dash of Tabasco and
1 T. accent. Mix and chill.
Make Danish pastry (see card in pastry block.) Roll to
1/8" thickness. Cut with 1½" cutter. Place 1 t. oyster
on one half. Brush edge with cold water, fold other
half of round over oyster mix. Seal with fork tines.
Prick with fork twice. Brush with egg wash sprinkle
with Paprika. Bake at 425 degrees F. 10 minutes or
until light brown. Cool and refrigerate. Serve hot.
Makes 5 dozen.

Lucille's Treasure Chest of Fine Foods

LUCILLE BISHOP SMITH

....

Fourth edition
Fort Worth, Texas, 1941

I N MORE THAN 200 simple recipes organized to "lift culinary art from the commonplace," this precious receptacle—literally, a box of recipe cards—lays out the author's "long and practical experience in catering and professional service." It is easy to imagine Smith standing at the stove, gently coaching young African American cooks toward culinary proficiency while referring to her numbered and titled recipe cards, each one typed single-space and tucked into a well-organized cardboard box. "Wah-ka-mo'-lay": she indicated the pronunciation on the card for Guacamole Ring, an avocado salad shaped in a mold.

There are eight categories for sweet treats, including cold, frozen, and hot desserts. The set includes recipes for a few iconic southern specialties, such as hush puppies, spoon bread, fried chicken, hominy casserole, and barbecue. But no mention of organ meats or greens. She bakes breads with healthy, whole grain flour and bran, spices poultry with Creole seasonings, and delivers what may be the first published recipe for "Japanese" Bean Pie (favored by black Muslims). Baked fish is dressed with bread or mushroom forcemeats.

But she contributed much more to the food industry than just the recipe cards in this box. A baby blue card from the front of the deck, entitled "Recipe for a Good Life," epitomizes Smith's ambition to empower others by using food as a tool of social uplift.

She lived productively, embracing a job that was one of the few trades considered "appropriate" for a woman of color—perfecting her craft for more than forty years before the first edition of this compilation was assembled. During that time, she raised funds for service projects, fought to raise standards in slums, developed culinary vocational programs in Texas, conducted itinerant teacher-training classes, established the Commercial Cooking and Baking Department at Prairie View A&M University (a historically black college near Houston), compiled five manuals for the state Department of Industrial Education, served as food editor for *Sepia* magazine, and brought the first packaged Hot Roll Mix to market. ❧

Rebecca's Cookbook

REBECCA WEST

....

Washington, D.C., 1942
69 pages

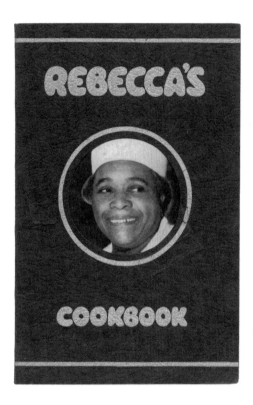

IN 1942, while the world was at war, this author was traveling the country with her "lady," amassing a treasure trove of avant-garde recipes, recording her escapades in a weekly newspaper column, and modeling professionalism for other domestics to match. In what appears to be an early culinary memoir, that "lady," identified by the initials E.P., helped West record ingredients and preparation instructions for dozens of dishes, plus childhood recollections of visits to South Carolina and ruminations about the Bahamas.

An online cookbook dealer sent me a note about the mysterious E.P. and her relationship to this cook. "It turns out that West was the cook in the employ of Eleanor 'Cissy' Patterson, the first woman newspaper publisher and owner of a major city daily newspaper, the old *Washington Herald*," wrote Bill Holland, a former journalist and the owner of CookbookBazaar.com. "Patterson was rich, and owned several mansions. It was she who arranged to have the cookbook published, but was kind enough to give the copyright to West. Before Patterson hired West, she also got recipes for her paper from another African American cook."

Patterson did not resort to the demeaning Jemima stereotype when she transcribed West's thoughts and unconventional recipes. Yes, West speaks in broken English that is evidence of a rural upbringing, but her voice is not represented by the maliciously exaggerated speech common in the black Americana literature being published at the time. Nor does E.P. express elitism or veiled pride. She respected West for her talent and expertise, and the cook beams in eight photographs that capture her as she beats eggs, sifts flour, tastes and corrects the seasoning in her sauce pot, and trims the edges off of pie crust.

The introduction, written by E.P., is primarily the story of how the two met, told mostly in West's voice. E.P. provides the closing paragraphs for perspective. "Perhaps now you know a bit about Rebecca," she writes. "From now on, with wisdom, with humor, with kindness, and a rare dramatic instinct, Rebecca will speak for herself."

And that she does.

In addition to the usual chapters, West devotes five pages and thirty-nine recipes to cocktails and canapés. Terrapin has a separate section all its own. There are fewer than a half-dozen old-fashioned southern specialties with African overtones, including Cheese Croquettes, Pigeon Peas, and Gumbo. West's treatment of fifth-quarter meats such as sweetbreads, brains, liver, kidneys, and tongue is light-years from standard soul food. Her offal is stewed with mushrooms, wine, and cream; chopped into pancakes; skewered onto brochettes; or smoked and served with currant jelly. And if that weren't enough, her way with Picnic Deviled Eggs is unique and intelligent: after filling the egg whites, she presses the

Photo by Jack Wilson

"'Deed it's fun to trim a pie!"

two halves together and wraps them in a square of oiled paper, twisting the ends to keep the halves in place during transport.

Each chapter begins with a tale told by West to explain the origins of her recipes. She weaves yarns about her childhood and the intimate experiences she shared with her employer in the kitchen.

The tale introducing the fish section, which is especially entertaining, provides an exceptional view into the mind of an early American cook. It is followed by imaginative recipes for red snapper fillets sautéed in olive oil, herbs and shallots, then braised in a tomato cream sauce; stuffed baked black bass; kippered herring; baked Spanish mackerel, and scalloped oysters.

FISH

One night when my lady was out to dinner (she went out a lot, but she said it wasn't because she was tired of my cookin) the butler came runnin downstairs all out of breath.

He said, "The lady said she had the best fish tonight at dinner that she ever had an she wants you to try to fix somethin like it." I says, "Now, wait a minute, wait a minute. How does she know it was fish she was eatin?"

He says, "She said she could only see the tail of the fish stickin up out of a cream sauce an she don know what kind of fish it was, but it was good. You better figure out what it was, Rebecca."

So, I got to figurin. Sometimes them dishes is all fixed up to look like somethin they aint, but I says to myself, as a good cook, I can't be put in a hole like that. I know the lady who does the cookin where my lady was havin dinner, so I says to the butler, "Joe, you skip over there an ask her will she oblige me with the recipe for the little fish with cream sauce they had for dinner tonight."

Well, sir, he come back with the whole cook book. An my lady heard about it. She says that's a terrible thing to do, go askin people how they make food. "But," she says, "long as you have done such a thing, copy that receipt for the little fish an then take the book right back."

Jus as I expected, the dish wasn't made of little fish at all. It was ham. My lady was so surprised when I told her. She says, "That's what comes of dinin by candlelight."

Anyways heres some receipts which is really fish:

Red Snapper

Have the fish split and boned. Heat 2 tablespoonfuls of olive oil in a large frying pan, add 1 green pepper finely minced and 6 small shallots, and cook a couple of minutes, turning constantly. To this add 1 tablespoonful of minced parsley and 1 of chives. Lay the fish on the vegetables, season with salt, add ½ cup of tomato sauce and ½ cup of cream. Cover pan and let simmer over low flame for two or three minutes, then set pan in hot oven and bake for 20 minutes. Pour contents of pan over fish after removing it to serving platter. Garnish with parsley or chervil and slices of lemon.

Broiled Pompano

Split the fish, brush with olive oil, season with salt and pepper and broil 10 minutes. Dust with

[18]

The Chef

Colored Girls' Receiving Home

COMPILED AND EDITED BY
FRANCES W. ROSTON

....

Tulsa, Oklahoma: Brix Printing for the City Federation
of Colored Women's Clubs, 1944
59 pages

WITH "PRIDE AND PLEASURE," the City Federation of Colored Women's Clubs presented more than 200 prudent recipes in this combination souvenir journal, recipe booklet, and city directory. The service group offered "this excellent Cook Book to the Women of Tulsa, and the entire State," as a fund-raising project to pay off a debt they incurred while establishing a clubhouse for underprivileged girls.

On May 31, 1921, approximately forty blocks in a thriving black community in Tulsa, Oklahoma, were destroyed, and an estimated 300 people perished, in a race riot that the *New York Times* described as perhaps "the deadliest occurrence of racial violence in United States history." Twelve years later, fearing the possible mistreatment of neglected, abandoned, and delinquent minors at the hands of law enforcement officers, the City Federation of Colored Women's Clubs began a project designed to protect them from being detained in the city jail and to minimize the "unwholesome influence which might affect the entire life of a child so handled."

The sanctuary provided food and medical care for Negro girls, a community recreation center, and a meeting place for small parties and groups. By 1944, the federation had paid off most of its creditors. Proceeds from the recipe book were used to settle the remaining $2,000 in mortgage debt.

Nearly a dozen recipes using ground meat or tuna represent classic family-style cooking sensitive to wartime economizing. Hints on preserving the nutrients in cooked leafy greens and vegetables, tips on making sandwich fillings, general instructions for safe and proper canning, and a few household formulas surely appealed to frugal housewives. Neither exotic ingredients nor fancy techniques were required. And advertisements from dozens of local businesses, churches, individual police officers, and people from as far away as Dallas punctuate nearly every page. ❧

Bess Gant's Cook Book

Over 600 Original Recipes

BESSIE M. GANT

....

Third edition
Culver City, California: Murray and Gee, 1947
79 pages

BESSIE GANT didn't leave a preface, introduction, or headnotes to tell us where she was born or what motivated her to cook. We learn nothing about the kitchens where she must have worked throughout the years. We don't even know why she originally wrote this book, in the early 1940s. But we do know that Gant was a caterer who left behind an articulate collection of plain and fancy dishes, including recipes supplied by Hollywood stars. She was a clever writer, crafting titles for her formulas that were intelligent, straightforward, and ornamental all at the same time.

At the end of Katharine Hepburn's Favorite Prune Nut Cake, Gant offers baking and serving advice from "Miss Hepburn." Gant reports that the child star Peggy Ann Garner served a sauced frankfurter dish and ham sandwich rolls for her teenage friends. Disney Studios provided Walt Disney's Make Mine Music Salad with Mickey Mouse Dressing. Carmen Miranda's Favorite Brazilian Dessert is one of the few recipes with headnotes, along with a quotation from Miranda.

There are dishes by Gant that sound delicious, such as Shrimp Soufflé, French Game Pie, Brandied Kidney Beans, Sherry Wine Sweet Potatoes, Rum Shortbread, and five fried chicken upgrades—"Italian," breaded with bread crumbs and Parmesan cheese; "Bess," floured, dipped in batter, and fried; "Southern," dredged lightly in seasoned flour; "a la Nebraska," battered, rolled in cracker meal and flour, then fried; and "Chicken Smoothie," fried chicken simmered with a splash of dry white wine.

The compilation concludes with a section of random household tips called "Things Worth Knowing" and one that spells out numerous menus for special occasions and casual gatherings, such as children's birthday and tea parties, St. Patrick's Day, Easter dinner, Thanksgiving dinner, bridge parties, and wedding luncheons.

Here are a few of my favorite recipe titles:

Unexpected Guest Dish—canned salmon in a mushroom white sauce served over rice.

A Mealinone Dinner—reminiscent of shepherd's pie.

Sweetbreads Imperium—creamed and served in patty shells.

Le Poulet Familliale (Family Chicken)—boned and baked with bacon, truffles, and mushrooms.

Sweet Yam Delic—a sweet layered casserole.

Albuquerque Rice—rice cooked in tomato juice with chopped aromatic vegetables.

Tomato Magic Rolls—yeast bread laced with tomato juice.

Blushing Bride Salad—pear-flavored gelatine.

Herma's Hot Water Sponge Cake and New Way Pound Cake—traditional ingredients, unusual technique. ❧

A Date with a Dish

A Cook Book of American
Negro Recipes

FREDA DE KNIGHT

....

New York: Hermitage Press, 1948

The Ebony Cookbook

A Date with a Dish

FREDA DE KNIGHT

....

Revised edition
Chicago: Johnson Publishing, 1962, 1973
Nineteenth printing, 1996
384 pages

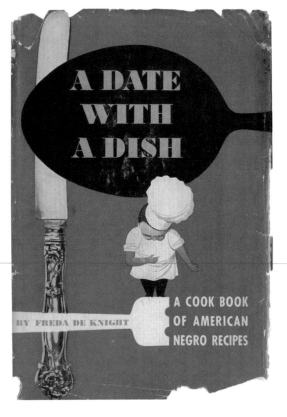

D ATE DIDN'T JUST TEACH readers how to cook—it made them want to do it.

Containing more than a thousand recipes, menus, and cooking hints collected from and by Negro chefs, caterers, celebrities, country folks, housewives, and gourmet cooks from all over America over a period of twenty years, this well-organized treasury built a strong case for the versatility, ingenuity, and adeptness of African American cooks, dispelling the myth of black food as "peasant food" for white readers and attracting blacks to the food industry by celebrating the economic achievements of ancestral professionals and entrepreneurs.

DeKnight's skill as a recipe developer for food manufacturers and her experience as a food editor in the media helped her document African American culinary history as it was practiced nationwide, not as it had been portrayed—to set the record straight, Janet Theophano wrote in her study of the book.

With the help of her assistant, a fictitious literary device called the Little Brown Chef, DeKnight intentionally undertook the retelling of black cooks' lives, providing multiple variations of traditional dishes (for example, cream of tartar biscuits, honey butter biscuits, lemon biscuits, beaten biscuits, tea biscuits, sour milk biscuits, sour cream biscuits, southern yeast biscuits, buttermilk biscuits) and asserting confidence in the ancestors' creative accomplishments, their "natural ingenuity" and "love for good food," without trampling on their legacy. "Those old cooks possessed vivid imaginations, keen sense of taste, and creative ability in the culinary art without the aid of book learning," DeKnight wrote with dignity. Elsewhere, a more relaxed salute to invention in the face of limited resources revisits the theme: "Don't shun ham hocks as poor folks' food . . .'cause they ain't! However, they can do a terrific job in budget slashing."

Delightful chapter introductions and recipe headnotes imparted tips, insight, and wisdom at a time when modern packaged convenience foods and TV dinners minimized a housewife's

There's Magic in a Cookbook

CONFIRMED COLLECTORS OF RECIPES are eternally on the prowl for new treasures to add to their cooking lore. Ten minutes or ten thousand miles from home, there's no telling when or where a prize may be found. And of this choice company is Freda De Knight. She boasts, with not the slightest humility, of having assiduously collected over a thousand wonderful recipes from Negro sources, during the last twenty years.

At seven, she started her schooling in Salem, South Dakota, but she spent her summers cutting out recipes and playing cook instead of cutting out paper dolls and playing house. I feel a great kinship with those youthful culinary pursuits of Freda De Knight's. When I was eight years old, it was my special privilege to prepare the mid-day lunch during the summer holidays. I remembered that I loved gravy. So there was gravy every day, often strange of hue and texture; mostly so thick it could be cut like a pudding! I doted on tomatoes. Day after day we had them fried and baked and stewed and sliced and es-calloped. I wonder now how the family survived.

But young Freda was different—by the time she was five, she was able to bake her first loaf of bread, garnish plates, make biscuits and generally make herself useful. Even at the tender age of five, Freda's efforts smacked of

encounters with real food. *Date*'s recipes were universal, global, and diverse. There are "scrumptious soups made from costly delicacies," such as Crab and Tomato Bisque or Cream of Asparagus Soup, and "breathtakingly good" dishes like ham patties, composed of "leftovers by the poor." Spanish Rice displays African technique (stir-frying rice before steaming) as well as international flair. Ground black walnuts take piecrust from ordinary to unforgettable.

DeKnight is a charming storyteller, too, finding culinary inspiration wherever she can find it—from the old southern cook who "threw in" a few mushrooms and produced a wonderful dish when she wanted to make something special, to Louis Armstrong and his particular way with ham hocks and red beans—a little tale called "The Man, the Horn, and Red Beans."

2.

Enjoy Your Meals

SIMPLICITY, ORDER AND A SUNNY APPROACH MAKE THE PLAIN meal an enjoyable experience. One then eats not merely of necessity, but because the food has been made tempting and appealing.

This type of meal adds a special something to your family happiness, and is a pertinent factor in the training of your children. The home influence forms an everlasting imprint on their minds. Pleasant, jolly meals mean that the family feels free, and will most certainly be proud to bring company home to dinner because "Mother is so regular."

Don't put on company manners for guests; merely be yourself, and in so doing your guests are put at ease, giving them a chance to enjoy your culinary efforts.

The secret of the family table is neither costly, nor a production requiring day-long preparation, but a simple way of doing the correct thing. The "Do's and Don't" of table service are to be found in the comfort and courtesy due those seated at your table. When the prescribed rules do not en-

6

The section titled "A Guide for the House-wife" provides aspiring cooks with important kitchen fundamentals, including a glossary of cooking terms, a temperature guide to heating and frying, a table of equivalents and measurements, a buying guide for canned foods, and an expansive primer on herbs and spices, which offers invaluable tips and recommends flavor and spice additions to enliven and spark imaginative cooking of every kind. Among the hints: the best brands of paprika, "a sweet red pepper which is fired and ground after seeds and stem are removed," are Spanish and Hungarian. Marjoram, a fragrant annual of the mint family, is dried and used whole or powdered to flavor soups, salads, stuffings, meats, and sausages—French-grown is preferred.

DeKnight's self-assured aphorisms are meant to uplift cooks of all backgrounds:

It is a fallacy, long disproved, that Negro cooks, chefs, caterers and homemakers can adapt themselves only to the standard southern dishes, such as fried chicken, greens, corn pone and hot breads. Like other Americans living in various sections of the country they have naturally shown a desire to become versatile in the preparation of any dish, whether it is Spanish, Italian, French, Balinese or East Indian in origin.

"A Date With a Dish" has been written to help you! So make the most of it and plan your menus so that they will be worthy of praise and give your efforts the professional touch. Then you will enjoy to the fullest the meaning of "Culinary Art." ❧

Favorite Carnation Recipes

FREDA DEKNIGHT

....

Los Angeles: Carnation Company, 1950
23 pages

THE INTRODUCTION to this artsy little manufacturer's recipe booklet describes the author as the kind of woman Winston Churchill might have labeled "Tri-phibious"—and what sportswriters call a "triple threat man." Let's just call her superstar.

DeKnight was a home economist, cook, and writer who also gathered more than a thousand African American recipes for *A Date with a Dish*. Then, as if compiling a wide-ranging repertoire of classic cookery were not enough, she extended her reputation, as an ambassador for evaporated milk. She promoted a wide assortment of dishes—soups, sauces, entrees, side dishes, and desserts. And although aware that black cooks were typecast as poverty cooks, she undermined that contention with these sophisticated recipes and countless household tips. 🦢

Sauces

Carnation White Sauce is an all-purpose cooking sauce made by thoroughly blending butter and flour, and gradually adding Carnation Evaporated Milk. Due to the double-richness of Carnation, this sauce has a much smoother, creamier texture and richer flavor than ordinary white sauce. Once you've made white sauce with Carnation, you'll know how much more creamy and rich it can be than when made with ordinary milk.

CARNATION WHITE SAUCE			
Ingredients for:	Thin White Sauce	Medium White Sauce	Heavy White Sauce
All-purpose flour	1 tablespoon	1 tablespoon	3 tablespoons
Butter	1 tablespoon	1 tablespoon	2 tablespoons
Salt	½ teaspoon	½ teaspoon	½ teaspoon
Carnation Evaporated Milk	½ cup	1 cup	1 cup
Water	½ cup	None	None
Makes:	About 1 cup	About 1 cup	About 1½ cups
Uses:	To cream vegetables, meat, eggs, and other foods served over toast, or for cheese rarebit.	For creamed and scalloped dishes. For meat sauce and meat gravies.	For use in making croquettes and souffles.

Method: Blend flour, butter and salt over hot water or *low* heat, stirring constantly. Gradually add Carnation to butter-flour mixture. Continue stirring until thickened (about 10 to 15 minutes).

- Thorough blending of fat and flour mixture with Carnation Milk is the key to lumpless white sauce.
- A wooden spoon is first choice for stirring any milk mixture—is a definite aid in blending white sauce.
- To keep sauce warm, cover tightly and place over hot water.
- White sauce can be dressed up by many little tricks. For instance, paprika adds that rosy glow, chopped pimentos a real festive look. Parsley, green olives, green onion tops, and celery can also be effectively used. An egg yolk will lend a rich golden hue for special occasions. You can change the white sauce for each menu as you would your hat to match each outfit!

4

1951–1960

Lifting as We

CLIMB

Tea Cakes, Finger Sandwiches,
Community Service &
Civil Rights

Benevolence is essentially an altruistic virtue. Self-sacrifice is an inalienable co-efficient of Negro blood.

KELLY MILLER,
circa 1912

EORGIA GILMORE was a courageous cook who stopped riding the bus to work and walked a mile each day to protest unfair treatment on public transit, alongside other maids and cooks who were members of the Montgomery Improvement Association. When she was fired from her job, this buxom woman, whom Martin Luther King called "Tiny," looked for guidance to her ancestors who fed runaway slaves. She set up a restaurant in her living room, where she secretly nourished King and the leaders of the civil rights movement with southern staples: pork chops, stuffed peppers, and chitlins.

She also amassed up to $200 each week from that secret kitchen by selling pies, cakes, and cookies in beauty shops, an enterprise she called the "club from nowhere." The proceeds supported mass meetings and a carpool that provided transportation during the Montgomery bus boycott.

Gilmore wasn't the only woman to use food as an activist's tool, but she is the best known. She and the authors who published cookbooks at the dawn of the civil rights movement embodied principles of King's Beloved Community even before he outlined his six steps of nonviolent social change in 1967. Their unique acts of defiance emboldened everyday folks to do something powerful in the face of adversity: cook. When recalling the early years of the direct action campaign and the women who sacrificed their time, talents, and treasures to support the bus boycotts, sit-ins, freedom rides, and marches across the Deep South, one naturally thinks of iconic figures such as Diane Nash, Ella Baker, and Jo Ann Robinson as well as of obscure citizens like the unwed pregnant teenager Claudette Colvin or the impoverished country girl Mary Louise Smith.

Mention activist cooks and what do you get? Crickets.

But black culinary workers championed their neighbors' economic, social, and political priorities during the civil rights movement in the same way that the Colored Female's Free Produce Society organized women in the 1830s to boycott products produced by slave labor and to "overthrow the economic power of slavery, one bolt of cotton and one teaspoon of sugar at a time," as Susan A. Taylor documented in an essay included in the first volume of *Black Women in America*.

Activist cooks expanded on the work of the Freemasons and biblically based benevolence or secret societies dedicated to humanitarian efforts, including the Tuskegee Club, which held picnics for kids, cooking and sewing classes, and taught women how to buy land and build homes. These culinary community advocates "bore little resemblance to the smiling, subservient, plump fictional mammies projected in advertising and on film, not only liberating black women from the backs of buses but also from white kitchens," as Patricia Turner observed in *Ceramic Uncles and Celluloid Mammies* (1994). And they took their recipes with them.

Reading through the cookbooks they published during this violent era, I was reminded of the paranoia caused by domestic workers' resistance endeavors—and the simultaneous fortitude such struggles revealed. For instance, an FBI report filed in 1942 alleged that a group of communist domestic workers in Jackson, Tennessee, had organized the Eleanor Roosevelt Club of Negro Women to end segregation under the banner "not a cook in the kitchen by Christmas." A year later, the Washington, D.C., FBI office made a similar report, but the clubs' existence was never substantiated.

Black activist cooks, including authors, stabilized their communities in the late 1950s, leaving marks on cookbooks and literature, and in secret kitchens that operated in the face of fire hoses, ferocious dogs, bombs, police nightsticks, and spittle. They promoted democracy, celebrated cultural and culinary achievement, and expressed their humanitarian spirit, giving whatever special ingredients they had. Sometimes that meant making sandwiches in off-the-grid outlets—Sallie Smiley's café in Montgomery, Eva Russell's table in Birmingham, or Annie Lee Stewart's in Grenada, Mississippi. Sometimes it meant

teaching food safety and preservation as county extension agents. Or toting pans of fried chicken, macaroni and cheese, greens, and cornbread to clandestine meetings in church basements, where tired civil rights leaders and Project C ("confrontation") youngsters were hungry for a taste of home.

It has taken nearly sixty-five years for us to learn their names, but we can now count Harry Hart, Jessie Payne, Clementine Hunter, Lessie Bowers, and Dorothy Height among the determined change agents whose hospitality and persevering spirit also nourished a people under siege.

Hart kept athletes healthy, well fed, and strong at Williams College, leaving a blueprint for future generations as one of the handful of black male authors published by a white institution. Hunter painted the black culinary universe on canvas, expanding the boundaries of African American cooking beyond "common gumbo" while allowing consumers to reimagine the plantation through an artist's eyes. The caterer Jessie Payne achieved celebrity status for scratch cooking at a time when society as a whole was celebrating freedom from "slaving in the kitchen," thanks to the flood of shelf-stable products like margarine, cake mix, refrigerated biscuits, TV dinners, and Cheez Whiz. Lessie Bowers, a celebrated "lady in the kitchen," showed off her agile mind by building a school and owning and operating a restaurant in Virginia. Dorothy Height, former head of the National Council of Negro Women, legendary civil rights activist, and diplomatic counselor, contributed a foreword to *The Historical Cookbook of the American Negro*, which celebrated black social achievement and promoted "diversity and democracy" by transforming prejudiced opinions about African Americans and their cookery.

By the time the last of these kitchen testimonies was published, black cooks everywhere were plugging into the electricity of the moral, economic, psychological, and political powers of a new generation. Unyoked from Jim Crow, the emerging African American gastronomical attitude revealed self-assurance. Cooks spread their culinary wings and took possession of a cooking style all their own. Community-minded cookbook writers marched toward the culinary promised land, invigorated by "dignity and confidence" that had been acquired, as Rebecca Sharpless notes in *Cooking in Other Women's Kitchens*, "along with their hard-won rights." 🐝

Harry H. Hart's Favorite Recipes of Williams College with Training Table Records, Notes and Menus

HARRY H. HART

....

Williamstown, Massachusetts, 1951
176 pages

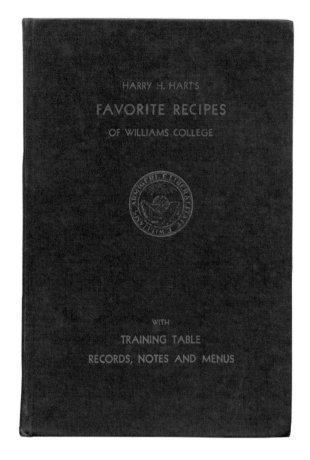

HARRY HART was a local Williamstown hero who dedicated this part yearbook, part recipe book to the Williams men and athletes, in the hope that his role in keeping them fit and conditioned would be a blueprint for other schools. His health-conscious volume included a "Weight Scale of Players," which listed varsity players and their weight before and after football practice—a snapshot that validated the wisdom of his "controlled diet" and demonstrated its "amazing" results, he said.

"Training Table Menus" followed, accompanied by the healthy faces of the college's sports teams (from baseball to lacrosse) in September 1950. A glossary of cooking definitions, a "Table of Standard Measurements," and "Entree Suggestions" were included as helps for readers. The author's "famous" recipes came next—canapés, cocktails, hors d'oeuvres, dinner (meat, poultry, fish), breads, salads, cakes, sauces, and fraternity sandwiches—all enclosed in cloth-covered boards that proudly sported the school color, purple, and the Williams College insignia emblazoned in gilt lettering.

These were hefty bills of fare, featuring solid, family-style cooking. High-protein breakfasts, lunches, and dinners were all accented with parsley, which, Hart explained, was "almost constantly served, as this is rich in iron."

Hart had good reason for such confidence. The foreword, written by the football coach Len Watters, applauded Hart for doing an "exceptionally fine job" of preparing and serving balanced meals that "played a major role in the conditioning of our football squads." Hart was a local hero for more than his work with college sports teams. He received the Carnegie medal for saving a gas company employee from electrocution, was honored by the Williamstown Rotary Club for saving a six-year-old girl from drowning, and rescued a man from a watery grave near New Jersey. ❧

Jesse's Book of Creole and Deep South Recipes

EDITH (BALLARD) AND JOHN WATTS

....

New York: Viking, 1954
184 pages

JESSE WILLIS LEWIS cooked Creole dishes and Gulf Coast specialties that he had learned at his mother's knee in the Ballard home in Bay St. Louis, Mississippi. This book is the authors' compilation of more than 340 of his classic recipes—written in a first-person, conversational style that gives Jesse's tips, instructions, serving suggestions, yields, and history through stories that recall wonderful wisdom and hospitality, sometimes all in one recipe.

The ruminations and recollections by a loquacious cook make the recipes for "Jesse's masterpieces" quite lengthy—many extending to two pages; Vol-au-Vent of Chicken occupies over five. But what is mind-blowing is that these authors observe and record the true finesse possessed by one of history's disregarded cooks, providing details without degradation. It made me want to cook every dish.

Consider just this one paragraph taken from the method for making puff pastry. ❧

> The basic trick of Vol-au-Vent is *not to allow the dough, especially the shortening in it, to get warm.* If the shortening gets warm during the mixing, the grease will melt through the flour instead of staying in lumps or flakes. Cold, hard shortening flakes and lumps are an absolute *must* for successful puff paste. Therefore, Vol-au-Vent is best reserved for cool weather, unless you make it, as so many modern Orleanians do nowadays, in pastry shells prepared by a bakery that specializes in puff paste (or, to use a better-known term, patty shells).

Paynie's Parties

A Collection of Party Recipes from
Mrs. Jessie Hargrave Payne of Lexington,
N.C., Tested and Proven

JESSIE PAYNE

Compiled by Mrs. J. F. Spruill and Mrs. Stokes Adderton
of the Sorosis Club

. . . .

Lexington, North Carolina: Fred O. Sink Printing, 1955
42 pages

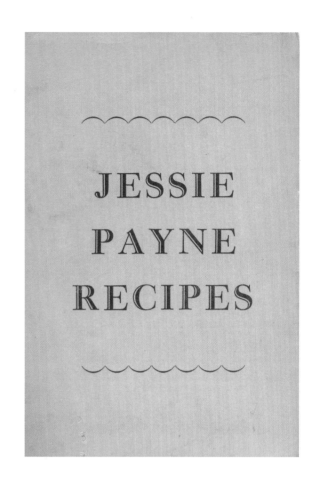

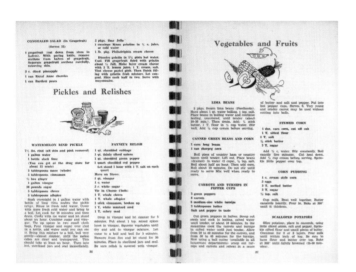

Jessie Hargrave Payne as a young woman had already become famous for her cooking. Recipes for party food are published herein.

O F ALL THE fanciful words in the foreword about Jessie Payne's upbringing, marriage, and employment history, and of all the recipes for "delicacies" assembled, transcribed, and tested on her behalf for this book club project, the most meaningful remarks praise the "magic" of Paynie's wonderful menus and her elaborate and painstakingly crafted banquet foods.

In truth, the collection demonstrates the artistry that happens when time-strapped cooks have access to time-saving convenience foods, which, being already prepared, allow extra time for creativity. Crisco replaced handcrafted lard, cream of mushroom soup was a one-step alternative to making the roux-based mushroom sauce that traditionally accompanied chicken croquettes, canned and frozen crab meat replaced fresh in deviled crabs, and canned fruit, frozen lemonade concentrate, flavored Jell-O, and Bar le Duc (imported currant jelly) gave a flourish to salads.

Paynie shaped food decoratively. Her ornamental collection presented molded and congealed salads (Bunny Salad), fruits and vegetables covered by a blanket of aspic, carrots and turnip balls scooped and served in bell pepper cups, sweet potatoes in orange halves or apple cups, and a variety of garnishes, such as pineapple flowers, jellied ginger ale cubes, radish roses, and a watermelon bowl, all in easy-to-follow, step-by-step directions that any housewife or her cook could master. ❧

Melrose Plantation Cookbook

CLEMENTINE HUNTER AND
FRANCOIS MIGNON

....

Natchitoches, Louisiana: Baker Printing and
Office Supply, 1956

30 pages

Francois Mignon   Clementine Hunter

Melrose Plantation Cookbook

T HERE IS A BIG difference between the
recipes created and compiled on this Cane
River plantation—built by free people of color—
and those published in earlier years by black
authors cooking for the southern aristocracy:
French flair. Fresh vegetables dressed with a
thick, creamy blend of vinegar, oil, and mustard,
and beef or chicken layered with seasoned forcemeats and then baked in a rich pastry dough had
long been part of the black repertoire. But their
creations went by humble names: mayonnaise
rather than an emulsion, beef pie rather than
tourtière. In this cookbook, the culinary artist
making salad dressings, quenelles, pâtés, sausages, and terrines was bold enough to say so.

In just thirty-one recipes, the book captures
an artist's aesthetic. The recipe for each painstakingly described dish fits on one page, floating
elegantly, bathed in white space and light. One
can almost hear Hunter as she directs kitchen
helpers in the language spoken by early American hearth cooks: "dash in the rice" and "boil
the gravy for a pair of minutes." Mignon, who
had observed that expressive style, embellished
Hunter's handiwork with delicate typefaces and
curvy scripts as if to overstate the point, remind-
ing readers of much earlier times and in def-
erence to the proud legacy of the plantation's
founding family.

A fusion of French technique, African finesse,
and native ingredients had dissolved naturally
over generations into the cosmopolitan culinary landscape, resulting in creolized dishes that
show up here with seductive titles such as Beef
Bamboula, Bass à la Brin, and Tomato Robeline.
The authors commingle charming Old World
measures such as an egg-sized piece of butter, a
blade of mace, and a wineglass of brandy with
standard and precise quantities. Common dishes
that provide mere sustenance, such as the "Coon
Gumbo that appeared monthly on many local
tables," were intentionally left out of this selection of fine cuisine, the authors explain.

In addition, Hunter experimented with oil
paints, small brushes, and heavy cardboard boxes
left at the plantation by visiting artists. She won
critical acclaim for her "primitive" paintings, and
in 1943 received a grant from the Rosenwald
Fund to refine her talent. She was honored in
1956 by *Holiday* magazine in its tenth anniversary issue.

That same year, she and Mignon delivered a
tasteful book that includes photographs of the
Melrose Plantation Big House, where Hunter,
"the cook," created culinary art, and the African
House, where Clementine, "the artist," painted
murals depicting scenes of plantation life. ❧

The Historical Cookbook of the American Negro

COMPILED AND EDITED BY
SUE BAILEY THURMAN

*chairman, National Council of Negro Women's
Archives and Museum Department*

....

Washington, D.C.: Corporate Press, 1958
Reprint edition, with a foreword by Dorothy I. Height
    and an introduction by Anne L. Bower
Boston: Beacon Press, 2000
166 pages

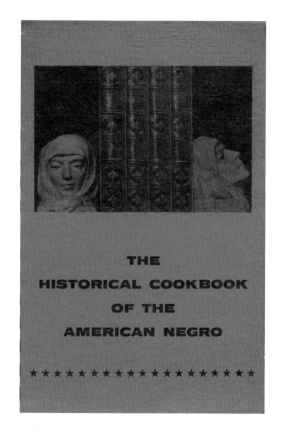

THIS GROUNDBREAKING, unconventional book was a project by the National Council of Negro Women to promote "diversity and democracy," celebrate black achievement, entertain, and educate. It foreshadowed the notion of "black pride" for up-and-coming authors, but surprisingly, amid all the historic intelligence conveyed, the book was not constructed to give a full history of African and African American culinary traditions. The backstory relating African foodstuffs, African American foodways, and the culinary history of more than 250 middle-class recipes occurred only peripherally.

Mary McLeod Bethune founded the National Council of Negro Women in 1935 "to educate, encourage and effect the participation of Negro women in civic, political, economic, and educational activities and institutions" and to "emphasize the important role of African-American women in the creation of a better society."

For eighteen years, a committee of researchers studied archives from Colorado to Washington, D.C., in search of elements to include in a global collection that would present "a new, unique and 'palatable' approach to history" and "honor the great spirits of the past." They gathered biographical sketches of world figures, accounts of cultural heritage, photographs of historic places, and important dates in order to tell the story of the African American middle class.

NCNW members representing seven regional councils contributed their favorite ways with meats, breads, vegetables, fish, fowl, and desserts. The recipes are not organized in traditional chapters for ease of use by a cook. Instead, an unusual (at the time) arrangement categorizes recipes according to the calendar year, linking dishes with famous people, places, African American traditions, and historical events in an obvious expression of the hope that readers would be "nourished by history as much as by food." Drawings, song lyrics, advertisements, speeches, brief biographies, and historic news articles provide additional enlightenment.

The Historical Cookbook of the American Negro

The classic yearlong celebration of black heritage from Emancipation Proclamation Breakfast Cake to Wandering Pilgrim's Stew

National Council of Negro Women, Inc.

authors of

The Black Family Reunion Cookbook

January features recipes suited for New Year celebrations, such as Southern Hopping John, Pecan Turkey Stuffing, and California-New-Year-Fruit Punch. A "Peanut Festival" honoring George Washington Carver Commemoration Day on January 5 is composed of Peanut Bread, Peanut Cake with Molasses, Peanut Sausages, Peanut Macaroni, Peanut Salad, and Peanut Ice Cream.

Honey-Orange Bread for the Poet, which honors James Weldon Johnson, composer of the Negro anthem "Lift Every Voice and Sing," appears in the June chapter in recognition of his birthday on the 17th. The menu for the Ghana's Independence Day Celebration (March 6) includes Stewed Beef or Chicken, Rice and Beans, Stuffed Chicken Middle East Style, and Prawn

and Tomato Curry. International dishes from Italy, England, and Mexico represent United Nations Day, October 24. November remembers Sojourner Truth's last days, W. C. Handy's birthday, old regional recipes for Thanksgiving pies, and Phillis Wheatley.

The reprint edition features an introduction by Anne Bower, associate professor of English at Ohio State University, who points out how this book addressed the problem of misinformation, lack of information, and educational gaps that limit our knowledge of African and African American history:

> The history crafted by Thurman and her collaborators for *The Historical Cookbook* is a blend of information that would have been widely known and other material that was not as familiar . . . It documents well-known events and artifacts like the Civil War, the Declaration of Independence, and the Gettysburg Address. But history here also includes personal stories and observations . . . As part of a cookbook, this redefined history would most likely have been first read and shared among women and then imparted by them to husbands, brothers, sons, fathers, and male friends. In a way, I see this assumption about the transmission of historical knowledge as very much in line with assumptions made by earlier women about their role as moral educators within the home—a theme of community cookbooks from their inception.

Bower added a recipe index and user's guide to steer modern readers through misleading spellings and any cooking instructions that may have been omitted in the first edition. ❧

Plantation Recipes

LESSIE BOWERS

············

New York: Speller and Sons, 1959
194 pages

D ON'T LET THE TITLE or the engraving of a plantation big house on the cover fool you. This is not a collection of cabin cookin' and make-do recipes. It was brought to market by a publishing house known for producing a diverse catalogue of scholarship (primarily European and military history, and some works on classical music), and the publisher's preface acclaims Bowers as a trained professional whose book was the result of "long practical experience, a lively curiosity, and a real love for cookery," adding "The gourmet will find innumerable suggestions to spur her (or him) on."

There is good reason for all of this legitimizing. Bowers studied dietetics in South Carolina and New York. With the aid of the Rosenwald Fund, she proposed, planned, and oversaw building of a school before opening her own restaurant, The Virginian Restaurant, in what is now an affluent suburb, Bronxville, New York. Over the years, patrons clamored for the recipes on her catering and dining room menus—revered dishes such as Virginian Holiday Pie, which was so rich, expensive, and time consuming that it could be prepared and served only two or three times each year.

This recipe and dozens more pay tribute to Bowers and her unique style in chapters covering traditional southern fare, including breads, soups, casseroles, beverages, and delicious-sounding desserts such as Lemon Bisque and Coffee Soufflé. It is not fussy food, but you can't call it poverty cooking either—though some economical cuts of meat, such as liver and sweetbreads, are there.

Conservative Casserole for Low Cost Entertaining might remind some of the packaged, Hamburger Helper–type one-pot dishes made with leftover meat, rice, and tomato soup. And Bowers provides four toppings for thin spaghetti: a sauce with anchovy, a meat sauce, Spanish flavorings, and a marinara. But mostly, this was a polished survey of foods found in southern dining rooms: pecan, and oysters in turkey dressing, creamed lobster, crab, and shrimp.

The book is easy to read, with a comprehensive selection of recipes that are well spaced and plainly organized. Variations on a theme have numbers (as in Chicken Purlo No. 1 and No. 2) so that novices will not be confused. Serving sizes, temperatures, types of equipment needed, storage instructions, and a glossary of common cooking terms are helpful.

The publisher's advertisement describes Bowers and her cookery this way: "the grandchild of slaves" and "a true lady in the kitchen," she was devoted to good health and good food, raised in a family that produced its own meat, vegetables, and fruit, which were prepared "to preserve, not destroy, that farm-firm flavor and texture . . . beautiful to look at and celestial to taste." ❦

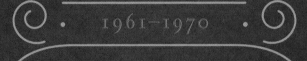

1961–1970

Soul
FOOD

Mama's Cooking Leaves
Home for the City

It seemed to me while certain foods have been labeled "soul food" and associated with Afro-Americans, Afro-Americans could be associated with all foods.

VERTAMAE GROSVENOR, 1970

ITH THE SAME hidden passion that enabled their ancestors to enliven monotonous plantation diets, southern cooks who migrated North and West improvised and made do with whatever was in the cupboard and on the shelves of the corner store. They did what European immigrants had done: establish their ethnic identity around the symbols of their rural culture, cooking country food as a way to satisfy a longing for home. Their menus appealed to city folks, too, showing up in juke joints, chicken shacks, and barbecue stands. "The very things that made them [migrants] most visibly ethnic, allowed them, paradoxically to integrate into the urban consumer economy," Tracy Poe explained in her pioneering study "The Origins of Soul Food in Black Urban Identity: Chicago, 1915–1947." In 1961, for instance, Sylvia Woods opened a restaurant in Harlem, featuring a home-style menu of fried chicken, barbecue ribs, grits, black-eyed peas, collard greens, sweet potatoes, cornbread, and sweet potato pie. In urban areas from New York to Chicago, restaurateurs like her achieved prosperity and a modicum of fame by serving inexpensive food that once was considered backward and country.

They called it soul food.

By 1968, the word "soul" had become the cultural identifier symbolizing this type of black expression: soul music, soul dance, soul food. "Soul" became shorthand for black dignity and pride. In his autobiography, the Nation of Islam leader Malcolm X remembered the soul food fixed by his landlady. The poet and writer Amiri Baraka went so far as to list soul foods in his 1966 book *Home: Social Essays*. "He [Baraka] insisted that hog maws, chitlins, sweet potato pie, barbecued ribs, hopping John, hush puppies, fried fish, hoe cakes, biscuits, salt pork, dumplings, and gumbo all came directly out of the black belt region of the South and represented the best of African American cookery," wrote Frederick Douglass Opie in his exhaustive exploration of African American cookery, *Hog and Hominy: Soul Food from Africa to America*.

The first soul food cookbooks began to appear in the late 1960s. They struggled to define the improvisational aspects that characterized dishes prepared with soul against the rigid requirements of scientific cooking. At the time, white culinary and nutrition "experts" were gushing over haute cuisine made by innovative chefs, promoting the exotic flavors of immigrant cuisines, and building up health foods. African American cooking could be just as innovative, exotic, and healthful, but black authors secured their place at the publishing table by glorifying and translating their mysterious foodways into codified formulas that sought to distinguish their dishes from those cooked by southern white people.

Jim Harwood wrote in *Soul Food Cook Book* (1969): "Soul food takes its name from a feeling of kinship among Blacks. In that sense, it's like 'Soul Brother' and 'Soul Music'—impossible to define but recognizable among those who have it. But there's nothing secret or exclusive about Soul Food." In the same year and in a book with the same title, Bob Jeffries expanded the idea, contending that the catalogue of soul food dishes is long and varied, distinguished from other southern food primarily by race:

> Like jazz, [soul food] was created in the South by American Negroes, and although it can safely be said that almost all typically southern food is soul (up until World War II nearly all the better cooks in the South were Negro), the word soul, when applied to food, means only those foods that Negroes grew up eating in their own homes; food that was cooked with care and love—with soul—by and for themselves, their families, and friends. This, of course, included much of what is now termed traditional southern fare, dishes such as Deep-Fried Chicken, Spareribs, and Country Ham, but it was also much more.

The problem entangling Harwood, Jeffries, and other early "ideologues of soul food," Opie says, is that their books "failed to embrace and incorporate cuisines of other peoples of African descent migrating to the United States from the Caribbean after the turn of the century." They forgot other stuff too.

Soul food had its roots in southern cuisine, and southern cuisine was a rich culinary tradition. But the soul food roster omitted the aspects of country cooking on farms, where dishes were based on fresh fruits and vegetables from the garden or fresh buttermilk courtesy of the family cow.

As a result, soul food became a signifier for "slumming," reenergizing a long-standing debate that had quietly raged about black foodways as a demarcation line between the middle and lower classes. For example, the National Council of Negro Women had skewered the previous generation's black cooks who esteemed their make-do skills and proudly claimed, "We are 'taste cooks' not controlled by the book." The novelist Ralph Ellison associated southern black food with the backward class. And the *Chicago Defender* discouraged stereotypes of black southern migrants and their soul food, urging readers to assimilate by preparing "fashionable white women's foods" in an article entitled "The Housekeeper."

At soul food's apex, the Mobile native Eugene Walters weighed in, affirming African American foodways as being broader than pig parts and greens, in a highly personal account published by Time-Life Books entitled *American Cooking: Southern Style*. Walters's chapter on black cookery, "The South's Great Gift of Soul Food," rightly explains that the term "soul food" came into vogue in the 1960s as African Americans migrating from country to city turned to comforting classic dishes that satisfied their longing for a taste of home. Aunt Fanny Williams of Aunt Fanny's Cabin in Atlanta was called a "true virtuoso of the kitchen" whose "biscuit recipe still produces a triumph." Mary Branch, owner and chief cook at Mary's Place in Coden, Alabama, starred in a full-page spread for her prized delicacy, baked crabs.

He explained the cuisine's origins at length:

[Soul food] was not brought over from Africa, but Africans had contributed their ingenuity and resourcefulness, turning "unpromising" foods that were available to them into a highly distinctive cuisine; was created by women who earned high praise for their artistry in plantation records; includes pork in all its ramifications, chicken fried in every way and everything on earth that can be made with cornmeal; encompasses catfish, black-eyed peas, beans, sweet potatoes and a wide variety of greens, as well as molasses and the spices originally brought over from Africa; and also includes the magic potion known as "pot likker," the rich, nourishing liquid that remains after the greens and a slab of pork have been cooked together. Soul food was the food of the poor South, dishes that became familiar and popular after the South's Civil War defeat—"everybody's food."

As a result, Walters did not isolate southern recipes from those cooked with soul. Roast Loin of Pork with Sweet Potatoes and Apples is followed by Barbecued Spareribs, Spiced Beef Round, Mobile Thyme Tongue, Country Ham Stuffed with Greens, Chitterlings, Ham Hocks and Greens, Ham Hocks and Black-eyed Peas, and Baked Ham. The difference between southern and soul cooking, according to Walters, came down to three "indispensable" ingredients: "imagination, laughter and love."

A report by the American Dietetic Association, *Ethnic and Regional Food Practices: Soul and Traditional Southern Food Practices, Customs, and Holidays*, tried to uncouple the two this way: "Having its origins on Southern plantations and remaining a core component of the dietary intake of African Americans as well as other Southerners, soul food has gradually entered the mainstream. The migration of African Americans and other Southerners to the North and West contributed to the spread of these food practices. Although soul food has certain easily recognized core elements, the components may vary from region to region. Also, improved socioeconomic conditions have influenced African American practices."

When I am asked—and it is often—what I think is the difference between southern and soul food, I defer to the restaurateur and author Leah Chase, who, very early in my career, gave the simplest distinction of all: "Ours just tastes better." ❧

Christmas Gif'

An Anthology of Christmas Poems,
Songs, and Stories, Written by
and about Negroes

COMPILED BY
CHARLEMAE ROLLINS

....

Chicago: Follett, 1963
127 pages

The Black Madonna

Not as the white nations
know thee
O Mother!

But swarthy of cheek
and full-lipped as the
child races are.

THE POETRY OF Langston Hughes. Slave stories by Frederick Douglass, Zora Neale Hurston, Booker T. Washington, Paul Laurence Dunbar, and Julia Peterkin. Recipes handed down through generations from the plantation big house and slave street. These are some of the compositions commemorating the Christmas season that the author collected from her childhood and her experience as a librarian. This anthology sets off the soul food era by instilling pride in African American traditions formerly known as necessities.

Rollins selected recipes for dishes that were easy to make and share: assorted cakes (Scripture Cake, Salt Pork Cake, Stack Cake), tea cakes, several traditional southern pies, Sweet Potato Pone, Molasses Taffy, Sweet Potato Candy, Beaten Biscuits, Johnnycake, and Hog's-Head Cheese. Graceful line drawings depict the Christmas hearth, joyful children at play, and angelic Nativity scenes.

As a child, Rollins spent time with her grandmother, a former slave, who taught her about the game Christmas Gif'. "Two people, meeting for the first time that day, would compete to be the first to call out, 'Christmas Gif'!" Rollins writes in the foreword. "The loser happily paid a forfeit of a simple present—maybe a Christmas tea cake or a handful of nuts. . . . The practice spread from the slave cabins to the 'Big House,' and soon became a traditional part of the celebration of Christmas, a joyful time felt and shared even by an enslaved people."

All told, this literary work must have been a welcome balm during the stormy days of the civil rights movement. ❧

His Finest Party Recipes, Based on a Lifetime of Successful Catering

FRANK BELLAMY

....

1965
63 pages

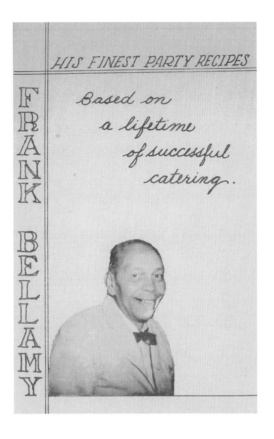

IT HAS BEEN SAID that most cooks create one or two memorable menus in a lifetime if they are lucky. The party dishes organized and served to moneyed households in Roswell, Georgia, were so elegantly done that the people whom Bellamy had helped entertain over the years created this handmade manuscript as a permanent tribute. His party dishes, typed and proportioned to serve twenty-four, were "compiled at the request of his friends" and "in appreciation of his many years of serving and befriending all of Roswell." There is no sales price listed anywhere on the collection, so I have to assume those fans gave the books away in order to spread his knowledge to anyone cooking for a crowd.

No printer, transcriber, editor, or coauthor signed his or her name to his collection. Bellamy's formulas for just over a hundred of the community's favorite dishes are clearly written, for the most part, and follow standard measurements, though an ingredient or a cooking step might be missing here and there. Organized into classic sections, the variety of dishes ranges from casual chafing dish meals easily served buffet style to more formal items best suited for plating. Some suggested menus are included as well.

A number of the dishes contain the signature of a woman from the community, but we don't know whether she submitted the recipe or it was a favorite at one of her parties. Others specify name brands for the constant stream of laborsaving and shelf-stable products then flooding the market, such as Eagle Brand condensed milk, Velveeta cheese, and 49¢ bags of king-size Fritos (corn chips).

The recipes also reflect an interest in international cuisines: Chicken Chow Mein, Chicken Curry, Spanish Pork Chops, Sweetbreads and Chicken Veloute, Tacos, and Mexican or Swedish Wedding Cakes. Time-saving, one-dish casseroles incorporate meats, pasta, potatoes, canned vegetables, cream, and cheese. Fancified brownies sport a topping of fudge frosting, and in Jelly Cake homemade lemon curd is smoothed between layers of basic yellow cake. ❧

Flossie Morris
Unusual Cookbook and
Household Hints

FLOSSIE MORRIS

....

Nashville: Rich, 1967
39 pages

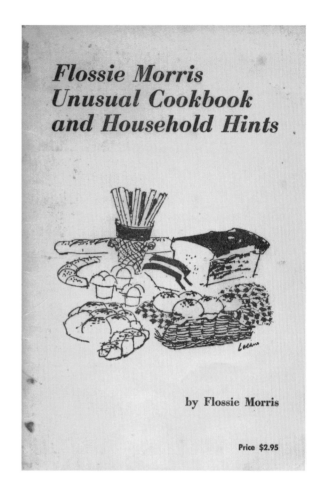

Flossie Morris
Unusual Cookbook
and Household Hints

by Flossie Morris

Price $2.95

T HIS "UNUSUAL" COOKBOOK is just plain unusual. The enterprising combinations and quirky recipe titles herald the continuing evolution of soul cookery. Its author relies on charisma to encourage other black cooks to settle into their own culinary identity—the kind of individualized artistry that rids the culture of the ignorant-cook stereotype and illuminates the concept of cooking with one's soul.

But first, we have to get past the bizarre mechanics.

Morris forgoes expected organizational devices such as a table of contents, chapter headings, and an index. Instead, the contents flow in a stream of consciousness from a woman we learn surprisingly little about. Other than providing some basic information on the title page, she is mysteriously silent about her background and the motivation behind this venture; no foreword or preface gives a peek into the author's character. And yet we do learn at least one thing about Morris: she had a thoughtful, albeit whimsical style.

She grouped more than 125 dishes according to standard categories, occasionally interrupted by an unrelated recipe. To start, a dozen standard southern bread recipes, including yeast breads, rolls, and biscuits, are complemented by several Old World slave dishes based on cornmeal—a spoon-bread-like dish called Southern Grit Bread, a treatment for leftover bread named Crown Cush Bread (a stewed cornbread casserole once popular with Confederate soldiers), Crackling Bread (cornbread spiked with crisply fried pork skin)—and a curious combination in which hot roll dough is stuffed with a mix of prunes, cream cheese, spices and walnuts. The recipe begins: "Wash 12 new clothes pins in hot water and dry."

In the next section, she parades her talent for adapting classic one-pot vegetable dishes. She douses bread cubes, vegetables, and eggs in canned soup and then bakes this imaginative side dish in a popular new brand of versatile bakeware. In Creole Eggs Corning Ware Casserole, aromatic vegetables and mushrooms are sautéed in chicken fat, stirred into mushroom and tomato soup, Worcestershire and A1 steak sauce, and then poured over sliced hard-cooked eggs. Other dishes in this section of the book include Cubed Bread Casserole, Cubed Potato Casserole, Quick as a Wink Okra and Tomato Casserole, and Supreme Carrot Logs.

Once you get past oddball mixtures like the ethnic hybrid Chicken Lasagne Curry, the next batch of dishes are American traditions and meat recipes that appear to be much more sensible. The author bounces quickly back to the unusual though, revealing a penchant for stuffed stuff, including miniature beets, cauliflower, and veal. She fills green peppers with a seasoned mix of rice and ground meat; piles creamed cheese, cream, and walnuts into canned pears; and packs cooked peaches, pineapple, apples, and grapes (spiked with sherry) into orange shells.

Finally, Flossie's series of "Unusual" dishes helped readers reimagine established black food: Flossie's Unusual Cream of Wheat Pan Cake Mix; Flossie's Unusual Just Around the Corner Egg Custard; Everybody Should Enjoy Making Pralines Candy; Very, Very Unusual Egg Nog; This Tea Just in Time for Summer; and Flossie's Unusual Why Cook if You Don't Have To Uncooked Fruit Cake. ❧

A Good Heart and a Light Hand

Ruth L. Gaskins' Collection of Traditional Negro Recipes

RUTH L. GASKINS

....

New York: Simon and Schuster, 1968
110 pages

*"Far and away the best cookbook to deal with soul food."
—Craig Claiborne, Food Editor of The New York Times*

A Good Heart and A Light Hand

Ruth L. Gaskins' Collection of Traditional Negro Recipes

THE AUTHOR doesn't set out to focus on herself. Instead, she draws readers into the world of African Americans by reclaiming the diversity of their cookery and her own expressions of charity. What we get here is a panoramic celebration that basks in the accomplishments of others in order to inspire tolerance. She credits the South as the source of her dishes: "Most of my friends who contributed recipes live in Alexandria, Virginia, although many were originally from other parts of the South. They are all Negroes, as am I; many are professional cooks—I am not; and they all have and use the two basic ingredients—'a Good Heart and a Light Hand.'"

The instructional book begins with a metaphor for southern hospitality, a practice Gaskins calls "A Negro Welcome." The "welcome" is symbolized by the pot on the stove, and it is omnipresent—at home, in the company of friends, at church, at club meetings, and at family reunions. The welcome pot in Negro kitchens relies on "six basic ingredients," Gaskins reports: corn, pork,

chicken, greens, seafood, sour or buttermilk, and molasses, foods that "have stayed with us for 300 years, and still form the heart of Negro cooking." She adds that soul cooking has kept its identity while evolving: "We've added sauces, spices, butter, relishes and wines—we've pretty much replaced molasses with sugar, and new houses have taken away most of our small game, but essentially we still start with the same foods . . . and, of course, a good heart and a light hand."

Illustrations of the "six basic ingredients" and delightful anecdotes give readers an appreciation for the habits and rituals behind the mysterious "soul" of African American cookery, something the author defines as "cooking everything anyway." Readers learn how soup is served on Negro tables. We are treated to the intricate instructions for killing and shelling a turtle, "a social event" that begins with getting the shy creature to stick its head out of the shell. Another dish that is somewhere between a thick soup and a stew is served once a week, along with cornbread, for dinner. Lima bean soup is seasoned as in Africa, with flaked corned (smoked) fish, not pork parts; bacon, one ham bone, or two ham hocks enliven bean soup. Wine Soup is a popular cold palate cleanser served at weddings and birthday party buffets.

Gaskins leads the meat section with a Negro cook's revelation: "Eating without vinegar is like eating without salt." She explains that every dinner table includes a condiment tray and that vinegar holds the place of honor, respected for everything from preserving food to improving appearance. Comprehensive meat, poultry, and fish selections reveal a cook's understanding of the process of "denaturing" and preparing protein in liquid and heat to ensure that it is cooked safely and yet tender, also known as braising or stewing.

She describes her way to cure, bake, and glaze ham, and gives general directions for today's nose-to-tail cookery: chitlins, hog maw, pigs' feet, tails, ears, hocks, neck bones, homemade sausage, and spareribs. Beef gets the same treatment—roasted, baked in a crust, braised with dumplings, sautéed with eggs. As a bonus, we learn about the oldest Negro settlement in the area and how small game became part of local menus.

Moreover, Gaskins creates an inventory of soul delicacies from a few, limited ingredients. Fried chicken is made special for Sunday dinner: smothered, fruit glazed and roasted, mixed with oysters and baked in a pie, or stuffed with cornbread dressing and served with giblet gravy. Fish is baked African style, in the ground between layers of grass and hot coals. There are fried eels (which were popular in seventeenth-century English cookbooks as well as African American ones), crab cakes, and five ways with oysters, including barbecued and baked in a pie.

Vegetables are front and center in Gaskins's menus because, she says, "Every backyard used to be a vegetable garden." Her vast repertoire features dried okra, spiced sweet potato balls, cooked greens with a dash of sugar, squash cakes, three variations on potato salad, and a dish that reminds her of chicken salad but is made with hog maws instead.

The section "Hot Breads" shares the history of cornmeal breads and teaches leavening methods as well as a way to make noodles (dumplings). The recipes include Cornbread for 25, which brings the welcome pot to "every large church or family function"; strip and drop dumplings; biscuits; and rolls so feather light that her father couldn't be satisfied until he had eaten a dozen.

Gaskins's desserts demonstrate the skilled use of things at hand: fruit from backyard trees goes into puddings, soufflés, and custards; nuts and berries gathered by the children every fall are used to accent cakes and doughnuts; and a dozen pies, "are our food": "We make them out of practically anything and eat them hot, if possible, usually with vanilla ice cream, at least 2 to 3 times a week."

The book concludes with the "Catch All" chapter, which provides a close look at fermentation processes and includes pickles, relishes, preserves; butters and wines made from elderberries, plums or peaches, potatoes, rice. The summer favorite that most black families think of as a prime example of making do is also here, made from crushed cornbread and cold buttermilk. She calls it Cornbread Cooler. ❧

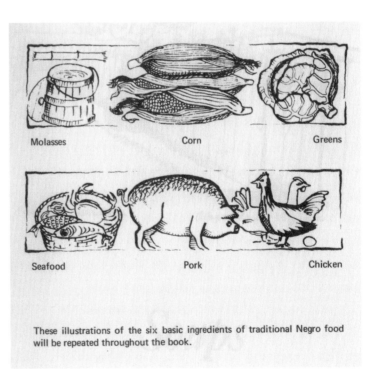

Molasses   Corn   Greens

Seafood   Pork   Chicken

These illustrations of the six basic ingredients of traditional Negro food will be repeated throughout the book.

Soul Food Cookery

INEZ YEARGAN KAISER

....

Revised edition
New York: Pitman, 1968
112 pages

Meticulous and delicious. Kaiser's enterprise begins with a dual-purpose definition of the term "soul" as it relates to food that strives to bring balance to a new image of black cookery. One side makes a declaration of science; the other is spiritual.

The author employs techniques that denote culinary discipline and reflect knowledge of scientific processes and culinary terms. Colored tab dividers are printed with typed chapter titles. Fundamental cookery hints, ingredient substitutions, storage tips, and procedural variations are sprinkled throughout. Lengthy and informative advice, such as uses for aluminum foil, tips for saving money at the food store, emergency substitutions, and time-saving strategies, conclude most chapters. A series of standard charts for common measurements and for herbs and spices, probably inserted by the printer, draw the book to a close.

Kaiser choreographs her recipes to establish a scientific pattern. She arranges dishes according to today's commonly used, modern recipe format, along with her own offbeat twist: the title and number of servings are listed first, followed by the ingredients in the order used. The cooking action required for each step is capitalized.

She notes that she wrote this straightforward book "with 'soul' people in mind . . . no delicacies—just basic 'stick to the ribs' staples . . . fresh vegetables, chicken, ground beef and other parts of the hog and cow that were either unused or cheaply bought." Even so, hers is not a stockpile of formulas for innards and vegetables boiled with side meat until mushy and greasy. She dresses up classic southern dishes with her own style: honey sweet potatoes join candied yams and baked yams, oven-fried chicken is soaked in evaporated milk before breading with cornflake crumbs. For salmon patties, she stirs cooled boiled potatoes into the classic mixture for salmon croquettes; tuna casserole takes a trip east, becoming spiced with fruit, pickle relish, and curry powder; sliced sweet potato pie is transformed into cobbler when topped by a second crust.

Knowing the value that her reputation would contribute to establishing credibility for soul cooking, Kaiser peddled her authoritative product with clarity and the compelling precision of a good merchant. From the account printed on the dust jacket flap, readers learn that she owned a public relations firm that specialized in what she called the "ethnic market," promoting food and beverages to "Negro consumers of all age levels."

She held a master's degree in home economics and put her expertise to good use: speaking to audiences about home freezing, convenience foods, and new cooking equipment; writing a syndicated column, "Fashionwise and Otherwise," which ran in African American newspapers; lecturing on college campuses; and appearing on radio and television. She was listed in the 1968 editions of *Who's Who in America* and *Who's Who in the Midwest*.

In these ways and more, Kaiser delivered on her plan to "develop an appreciation for food that has been prepared and enjoyed for years by minority people, especially Negroes"—even though many of the humble dishes were economical, such as Sardine Salad, Baked Cheese and Rice, Fried Pigs Feet, and Milkless, Eggless, Butterless Cake.

Here is Kaiser on soul: "The emotional part of man's nature; the seat of feelings or sentiments . . . well-seasoned, savory dishes that are difficult to eat without delight, enjoyment, and satisfaction. There is a spirit connected with the following recipes so that when one who is familiar with them and hears the name, he has a certain feeling of nostalgia, pleasure and anticipation."

CAKES

ONE-EGG CAKE

2 c. flour	1 c. sugar
pinch of salt	1 egg
2 1/4 tsp. baking powder	1 tsp. vanilla
1/3 c. margarine	2/3 c. milk

SIFT . . . . together flour, salt and baking powder.
CREAM . . . . . margarine until soft.
ADD . . . . sugar and egg gradually, beating until light and fluffy; add vanilla.
FOLD IN . . . . dry ingredients and milk alternately and mix well.
TURN . . . . into well-greased 7-inch cake tin.
BAKE . . . . in moderate oven approximately 50 minutes.

MILKLESS, EGGLESS, BUTTERLESS CAKE

2 c. flour	1/3 c. lard
1/2 tsp. baking powder	1 tsp. cinnamon
1/4 tsp. salt	1/4 tsp. ground cloves
1 1/2 c. seeded Sultanas	1/4 tsp. nutmeg
1 c. brown sugar	1 tsp. bicarbonate of soda
1 c. water	1 Tbsp. warm water

SIFT . . . . together flour, baking powder and salt.
BOIL . . . . raisins, sugar, water, lard, cinnamon, cloves and nutmeg for 3 minutes. Cool.
DISSOLVE . . . soda in warm water and stir into boiled mixture.
ADD. . . . . flour gradually, blending well.
BAKE . . . . in 8-inch square pan in moderate oven for 45-50 minutes.

SPICY DARK CHOCOLATE CAKE

2 c. brown sugar	3 c. plain flour
1 c. butter	1 tsp. vanilla
2 eggs, well beaten	1 1/2 Tbsp. cinnamon
1 c. buttermilk	1 tsp. allspice
4 sq. melted cooking	1 tsp. cloves
chocolate	1 tsp. baking soda
	1/2 c. boiling water

CREAM . . . . . sugar and butter.
ADD . . . . eggs, then milk and chocolate.
BEAT IN . . . . flour lightly, then vanilla and spices.
DISSOLVE . . . soda in the water and add to mixture.
BAKE . . . . in layer pans in moderate oven about 30 minutes.

280   -69-

Cooking with Soul

Favorite Recipes of Negro Homemakers

COMPILED AND EDITED BY
ETHEL BROWN HEARON

chairman, Home Economics Department,
Rufus King High School

....

Milwaukee, Wisconsin, 1968
193 pages

For this community cookbook project, a high school teacher rallied students in her family living classes to provide a snapshot of soul that would contradict the confused notion that black food was unhealthy food. Specifically, their goals were "to share with other cultures foods generally liked by Negroes, to indicate the nutrients in certain 'soul' foods, and to develop a sense of race pride by sharing with others the knowledge and experiences of the Negro in the art of food preparation." The kids hung signs and solicited nourishing recipes rich in taste and in nutrients.

A drawing of the front of the school served as the frontispiece. The editor's biography, the names of her student contributors, and a chart of the nutritional content of popular soul foods follows. Photographs of students making ice cream, stirring potato salad, and arranging bowls and platters of food on a picnic table, taken by the *Milwaukee Journal*, accompany chapters that cover a wide range of specialties, probably tested over and over again—including wild game (opossum, raccoon), mainstays (oxtail stew), and novelties such as Aunt Hattie's Muscadine Wine.

Each chapter starts with a brief history. Some explain the types of vegetables that would have been common in the home garden, the ways corn (fresh or dried) was cooked on the farm, and the benevolent art of Negro baking for bake sales, church suppers, and family dinners. There is also a definition of soul food: "Soul food is any food which allows itself to be prepared according to the dictates of an individual's taste buds . . . Anyone can cook with soul; the only requirement is to season while preparing and be absolutely sure it tastes just the way you intended it to."

To ensure that readers can find a wide spectrum of those varying flavors, and to perhaps avoid offending contributors by rejecting their submissions, the book presents some popular southern dishes multiple times: Chicken and Dumplings occurs in triplicate; Macaroni and Cheese appears five times or more (made with and without eggs, starting from a packaged mix); and Tuna Casserole, a mix of canned soup and tuna, is baked with or without peas, with potato chips, mixed with macaroni, or served over rice; Cornbread shows up in a dozen ways—and that number doesn't include the classic meal breads: spoon bread, hot-water cornbread, pone. 🌿

Barbara Fowler, Homeroom 304 prepares potato salad for mock picnic dinner.
Photo: Courtesy - The Milwaukee Journal: Jack Hamilton, photographer.

90

Michael Anderson, Homeroom 414, makes homemade ice cream using the hand-turning freezer.

163

POTATO SALAD

6 - 8 med. white potatoes	1/2 c. celery
6 eggs, hard boiled, diced	3 sweet pickles
	1/2 c. salad
1 t. salt	dressing
1/2 t. pepper	

Peel potatoes, cube and wash. Boil in saucepan. Hard boil eggs in separate container. Wash celery and chop finely; also finely chop pickles. After potatoes have cooked, drain off water, cool. Combine all ingredients, except 1 egg, and mix thoroughly. Slice remaining egg, cut slices in half, and arrange around bowl as garnish.

Barbara Fowler

COLE SLAW

1 med. size cabbage	3 T. vinegar
6 carrots	1 c. salad
3 T. sugar, or to taste	dressing

Grate cabbage and carrots in large mixing bowl. Add sugar, vinegar, and salad dressing. Mix thoroughly. Add more sugar if desired.

Dianne Stubblefield

91

Soul Food Cookbook

HATTIE RHINEHART GRIFFIN

....

New York: Carlton, 1969
32 pages

CONTENTS

THIS COMPACT LITTLE EFFORT is basic and understated. The author does not seem preoccupied with providing her full repertoire of specialties or the totality of southern cookery. Instead, the goal, as described on the dust jacket, is to attribute value to the fundamental foods "that the existing cook books have neglected, the style of cooking known as 'soul food.'"

The brief list of thirty-four dignified dishes includes cornbread, cornbread dressing, beef stew, meat loaf, chitterlings, short ribs, beef goulash, chicken and dumplings, baked beans, smothered cabbage, collard greens and smoked ham hocks, potato salad, navy beans, fried okra, candied yams, black-eyed peas, bread pudding, sweet potato pie, rice pudding, and three kinds of fried pies.

Fresh Pig Hocks Dinner, a boiled one-pot meal made with carrots, potatoes, onions, and cabbage, and Spinach and Beet Tops (simmered with salt pork and bacon fat) are two unique prescriptions created as proof of the ingenuity of this Michigan mother of four. ❦

Soul Food Cook Book

JIM HARWOOD AND ED CALLAHAN

....

San Francisco: Nitty Gritty Productions, 1969
210 pages

HOPPING JOHN

1 cup cooked rice
2 T butter
2 cups dried black-eyed peas
¼ lb. salt pork

Soak peas overnight. Add pork and cook peas until soft. (Take care to keep them whole while cooking.) Peas should be cooked enough when there is just a small amount of "likker" left on them. Mix cooked rice and peas together, season with salt, pepper, and butter. Serve with bread and butter.

117

*T*HIS HISTORIC RESOURCE could just as easily have been titled *Betty Crocker Cooks Soul*. The more than two hundred hybridized southern classics that appear in its pages, along with the in-depth introductory history of black people as the "caretakers of Soul Food," make it a comprehensive overview of African American cookery as it evolved from the Atlantic to the Gulf Coast: a modern oral-history project.

According to the authors, contemporary soul food originated during slavery in the staples of the "Dixie Diet," which derived from combined "Native American methodology, European class and food distinctions, and African farming and cooking practices." The authors' account demystifies soul food as innately devised and concludes that the pig "best symbolizes" soul food. It goes on to describe slaves' corn wizardry; explain why salt pork, vinegar, and hot pepper sauce are soul food seasonings; identifies the role of rice in dishes of the Carolinas and Louisiana; and details the "prodigious" job skills required to make wild game such as turtle and opossum a delight.

The book overflows with intricate illustrations of ingredients, completed dishes, cooking vessels, serving tools, and butchering charts. The list of soul ingredients is long, too: discarded pork parts, particularly ribs and chops; fried and baked breads made from corn meal, plus biscuits, pancakes, griddle cakes, and waffles; wild and domestic vegetables such as greens, okra, squash, tomatoes, turnips, potatoes, yams, sweet potatoes, and beans; sea and swamp foods like flounder, mackerel, shad, shrimp, oysters, and catfish;

chicken and rabbit; and sweets made with molasses, nuts, apples, peaches, and chocolate.

The authors emphasize that these "lowly" foods, though born in poverty, do not produce unpleasant dishes that make you "close your eyes and curl your nose and let a mouthful slide down untasted"; rather, "You can simply enjoy soul food for the taste." Barbecued spareribs, black-eyed peas and rice, Creole gumbo and jambalaya, hearty bean soups and stews such as burgoo, fresh chicken pies, and gingerbread cake certainly do speak of resourcefulness and a make-do spirit. They also point out that as ancestral black dishes disappeared into the existing southern cuisine, they became mainstream. ❧

Soul Food Cook Book

BOB JEFFRIES

....

Indianapolis: Bobbs-Merrill, 1969
116 pages

JEFFRIES'S UNPRETENTIOUS, soulized southern dishes will be familiar to anyone raised below the Mason-Dixon line. He mined much of his compendium from the food of his youth, making relatively few crucial differences. He defines soul food as both a series of ingredients and a talent for cooking without recipes. He never really succeeds at setting apart his soul food from established southern food. The book does, however, place the fundamentals for both in the hands of ingenious slaves and their traditions.

The book was composed after forty years of cooking and catering for an illustrious clientele, including luminaries such as Joan Crawford, Van Johnson, Ella Fitzgerald, Angela Lansbury, Salvador Dali, and David Merrick—a career that began on his father's farm and ended at Daly's Dandelion, a "cool saloon" in New York City run by Ruth and Skitch Henderson (the same duo who operated the Bird & Bottle Inn, in Garrison, New York, where the author Lena Richard earned fame).

"All soul food is southern food, [but] not all southern food is 'soul.'. . . Soul food, differs from southern food in its use of plain ingredients, its ways with inexpensive cuts of meat and its original uses for what was available—fresh-caught fish, rabbit, possum, truck garden vegetables, easy-growing yams, sweet potatoes and corn."

As for the ingredients, they were moderate in cost, originally chosen by slaves and poor people because they were available in the natural environment. Examples of the dishes were "collard greens cooked for long hours with salt pork or fatback, 'pot likker' (the juices from the bottom of the pot), hoe cakes (crisp cornbread taken to the field when the hoeing was done), hush puppies (like corn fritters), watermelon pickles, fried pies, dubie (a berry cobbler), buttermilk biscuits, soda biscuits, smothered steak, deep-fried liver, grits, rice, assorted beans (black-eye, purple, butter, hoe, and a dozen more), all cuts of pork whether high or low on the hog—from 'chit'lins' to trotters, hog's head, pig tails and feet to ribs and roasts."

So how does Jeffries distinguish the remaining hundred-plus soul recipes for meat loaf, croquettes, leafy greens, wild game, and sweet cakes from classic southern cooking? With pizzazz. His soul food soups are rich, hearty, and stick-to-the-ribs nourishing. Fish is treated like a throwback to a time when fishing cost nothing; the book includes rules for frying fish. Chicken, the soul bird, is most often roasted or fried; Jeffries suggests that chicken be cut into small pieces and singed to remove the pinfeathers and improve the flavor. Pork is soul itself: bacon fat for frying, salt pork in boiled beans, "cat bits" (minced ham) used to flavor vegetables, baked ham, barbecued ribs, fried chops, and roast baby pig for weddings. ❧

The Negro Chef Cookbook

LEONARD E. ROBERTS

....

Falmouth, Massachusetts: Kendall, 1969
196 pages

Y OU CAN TELL Leonard Roberts's recipes are enlightened by numerous culinary experiences and travels, although here they are "written with simplicity so they may be conveniently done by anyone whenever they get that urge to cook." Roberts was a classically trained chef who memorized Carême's *Le Patissier Royal Parisien* (1815), Dumas's *Dictionary of Cuisine* (1873), Dubois's *Classic Cuisine* (1864), and Escoffier, Gilbert, and Fetu's *Le Livre des Menus* (1912). He carried a pocket-size book of French terms and techniques as a reminder. He studied at Le Cordon Bleu in France and completed the chef's course at Edison Technical School in Seattle.

Roberts's repertoire ranges from humble to haute and relies upon his "chief tools: buttermilk, peanut oil, salt pork, paprika, sage, thyme, bay leaf, file powder, chili powder, oregano, garlic powder, rosemary, cumin seed, mint leaves, Tabasco, vinegar, Worcestershire, and liquid pepper seasoning (a combination of hot pepino peppers covered with cider vinegar and allowed to stand until the liquid is hot)."

He gives simple cakes and sauces royal titles, and provides a separate section to accommodate his full complement of sauces. There is a glossary of seasonings ("The Spell of Spice"), and a wine chart recommends food pairings and explains some viticulture. The desserts range from those made with French *choux* paste to Southern Shoo-Fly Pie and Jim Crows, a chocolate-peanut candy.

Savory meat dishes are accented with "South of the Border" style, including the flavors of mole and red chile. The section titled "Classics I" features noisettes, timbales, medallions, amandine, and *sabaione* (sabayon); "Classics II" is an A-to-Z list of simple salads such as Alexis, romaine with celery, chopped nuts and French dressing, Black-Eyed-Susan (shredded lettuce with orange sections, dates, mixed nuts, and French dressing), and Strawberries Romanoff.

Vegetables are treated the southern way: navy beans with pig ears and pig tails, collard greens with hog jowls or salt pork, pot likker with cornbread, and candied yams. Okra is steamed with butter and lemon juice and seasoned with a little salt and pepper, fried *à la Fitte*, simmered with chili sauce, baked au gratin, and stewed with tomatoes.

There are many, many more dishes that sound just plain delicious. ❧

Soul Food Cookbook

PRINCESS PAMELA

....

New York: New American Library, 1969
248 pages

❦ Milk-Baked Ham ❧

A 2"-thick slice of ham
1 tablespoon flour
2 heaping teaspoons dry
   mustard

2 tablespoons brown sugar
Sweet milk

Combine the flour, dry mustard, and brown sugar. Work the mixture into both sides of the ham. Place in baking dish and cover completely with milk. Bake at 350° for about 1 hour, or until the ham is tender. When ham is done, its surface should be browned and the milk almost entirely disappeared.

Princess Pamela's Soul Food Cookbook

From Chicken n' Ribs to Buttermilk Biscuits and Blackeyed Peas - A Mouth-Watering Treasury of Afro-American Recipes from Manhattan's Most Spirited Chef

$\mathcal{B}$EGINNING WITH the opening line of the preface and the publisher's advertisement, Pamela communicates the spirit of a cook, her view of what slaves ate, and the philosophy that soulful cooking and hospitality coupled with folk wisdom are important virtues that transcend race.

On the first page we learn that "what Julia Child did for beef *bourguignon*, Princess Pamela does for ham hocks and turnip greens" and other inventive recipes from the "fabulous cooking of Black America," such as Peanut Butter Biscuits, Chicken Fried Heart, Fried Collards, Southern Candied Pumpkin, Milk-Baked Ham, and Peach Skillet Pie.

The author reached deep into the plantation story for evidence of the nuanced black cookery that existed as a "loving art rather than a domestic science." Her clever retort to scientific cooking also grew out of the menus (meats, vegetables, salads, cornbreads, desserts, beverages) and wisdom that she dispensed at Princess Pamela's Little Kitchen, a tiny soul food restaurant on East 10th Street in Manhattan. Reportedly, Pamela's was one of the favorite soul spots of the *New York Times* food editor Craig Claiborne.

She believed that southern cuisine and soul food were so inextricably connected that "one may seek in vain the clear line of demarcation between where Southern cuisine ends and soul food begins . . . The aromas wafting from the grand plantation kitchen and the slave quarters could not help but co-mingle with the larger-than-life presence of the bandana-headed mammy stirring the pots in both places."

The book is laced with artsy flourishes—line drawings, curvy scripts, delicate typography—all arranged delicately around the author's life smarts, culinary prudence, and traditional soul food dishes calling for pork parts, grits, cornmeal cakes, oxtails, and possum.

"Soul food, black folk cooking is compassion food," Pamela proclaimed. ❧

Soul Food Cookbook

TUESDAY MAGAZINE

....

New York: Bantam, 1969
214 pages

I N THE PANTHEON of soul food cookbooks, this one is the most avant-garde. Composed of more than two hundred "delectable, imaginative, easy-to-make" recipes passed down through generations, the dishes were supplied by readers from across the United States and first printed in the magazine's popular Soul Food column before appearing here to "reawaken" interest in old favorites.

For readers unfamiliar with the style, the editors defined soul food this way:

Soul food was born in the slave quarters of Southern plantations. It is a form of cookery that developed from the need for economy, simplicity and creativity. Soul food has its emphasis on country-fresh vegetables with a variety of meats, golden fried chicken and fish, cornbread, flaky light biscuits, grits, dark, rich gravies, sugar-baked yams and sweet, irresistible desserts. It grew out of a need for economy, simplicity and a basic dish that could be set on the back of the stove in the morning to await Momma's return from work in the evening. It has emerged into a legitimate and quite delicious form of cookery. Soul food is the best of America's past brought up to date.

Each of the magazine's formulas includes a precise list of ingredients and carefully worded cooking instructions. Even usually short recipes are long, printed one per page, and include intricate details to ensure the reader's success.

Those who knew and loved soul food well must have appreciated the contemporary take on time-honored dishes. Roast Suckling Pig is marinated in brandy and herbs then stuffed with a sherry-spiked sausage-vegetable mix; barbecued spareribs are accented with lemon juice; Roast Duck with Apricot Stuffing and Plum Sauce is laced with soy sauce; and shredded collard greens Brazilian style are sautéed with onions and red pepper. Sweet potatoes are boiled, broiled, french fried, roasted, and candied; mashed into croquettes; sweetened with brown sugar, cinnamon, and apples and baked in a casserole; folded into soufflé; and stuffed into apples. Persimmon Bread and Garlic Bread join the usual lineup of cornmeal batter breads, dodgers, journeycakes, biscuits, and hot yeast breads. Powdered chicory is stirred into Dark Chocolate Cake. A full three pages are devoted to a wedding cake, and squash pie is spiked with rum.

Pork parts and other offal are covered in a chapter entitled "Variety Meats." Here, innovative recipes run the gamut: Chicken Heart Stew; Gizzard Appetizers; Basic Chitterlings I and II; Chitterlings sautéed, deep-fried, in butter, or Creole style (with tomatoes, onions, garlic, celery, and green peppers); two ways to prepare pig feet; pig tails, peas, and rice enlivened with coconut; and a dish of pig Zen, called Parts of the Pig, French Style, composed of pig feet, ears, and tails. ✸

West Oakland
Soul Food Cook Book

EDITED BY DOROTHY KUFFMAN

....

Oakland, California: Peter Maurin Neighborhood
  House, c. 1960s
47 pages

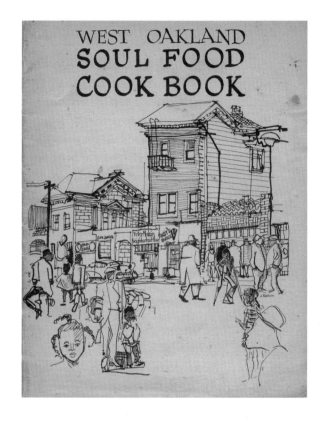

*T*HE NEIGHBORHOOD HOUSE opened in
the Bay Area in 1963, and by 1966 it had
expanded its outreach to offer daily activities that
included adult literacy classes and boy's carpentry instruction. It housed a community preschool
and provided home rehabilitation. This eclectic
fund-raising cookbook offers a snapshot of a
community struggling with dilapidated housing,
overcrowding, hunger, and homelessness and trying to make its way back to stability. Its mission
needed some cash.

A publishing team tapped the neighborhood,
volunteers, and staff members for more than one
hundred recipes for dishes that put the "soul" in
soul food. Dozens of illustrations depict West
Oakland street scenes and families at table and
in educational and work settings. The distinctive artwork is richly illustrated with decorative
lettering—a kind of handmade memento that
conveys a personalized outreach to supporters.
A donation of two dollars benefited the Peter
Maurin Neighborhood House on 7th Street.

We don't know exactly when it was published,
but the David Walker Lupton Collection esti-
mates that the year was 1969, which seems about
right, given the number of dishes made from
pieces, parts, and "secret" ingredients cooked in
idiosyncratic ways. Canned milk, fruits, and vegetables, for example, were everywhere. Beatrice
Hall added a tablespoon of butter to her potato
salad. Mrs. Ivy Tillman laced her fish fry batter
with vinegar. Mrs. Gertie Carey's Fresh Lemon
Cake was anything but, getting its tang from
lemon flavoring and canned lemon juice. And
Dorothy Fulcher stretched her dessert dollars
by substituting vanilla wafers for flour in Vanilla
Wafer Cake.

What we have here on display is the main
ingredient of soul cooking, improvisation, as the
adulteration of the multicolored pepper dish
confetti rice into "Confetteratte Rice" plainly
signifies.

'Nuff said. ❧

Gumbo. First get everything ready.
dried Shrimps & fresh shrimps.
1 cup each. dried & fresh shrimps
1 cup chop Selvery. finely chopped
1 cup Crab meat.
Garlic as many buttons as Desire.
1 large chicken or 1 guart crab meat
1 quart Okra.
2 ears of corn on cobb cut of cobb &
      scrape cob
Salt & Pepper to taste.
1 large onion cut fine.
First cook crust up chicken almost done
Then add ingredients to COOK untill done.
(Mrs Annie G Corner.
1015½ W Grand Ave. Oakland 7. Calif.)

P.S Brown your flour in ½ cup of
shorting Crisco. or oil any kind of fat.
Then put all ingredients in a
large pot cook tell done.
      Season to taste with
hot peppers.
add 1 cup of selvery chopped fine
      to mixture

CREDITS   DOROTHY KUFFMAN   EDITOR

           JOHN BALDWIN   ART

           AUDREY DEJOURNETTE

           BOBBIE THOMAS   TYPESETTING

WEST OAKLAND SOUL FOOD COOK BOOK

MRS. VIOLA TAYLOR'S
CHITTERLINGS

Take 3 lb. chitterlings. Wash well in several water. Put in deep pot with salted water. Put a potato in to keep down the smell. You may add one cut-up onion and 2 cloves garlic to the water if desired. Simmer 45 min., or until tender. Serve with hot sauce.

MRS. PERNELLA JOHNSON'S
FRIED CHITTERLINGS

Wash 3 lbs. of fresh chitterlings in several waters. Parboil in salted water, with 1 T vinegar, until barely tender. Drain and dry thoroughly. Dip in flour seasoned with salt and cayenne pepper. Fry in deep hot fat (375⁰) until crisp and brown. Drain on paper towels.

MRS. DOROTHY BRANNON'S
CHITTERLINGS

Clean 5 pounds chitterlings thoroughly in luke-warm water. Boil in fresh water until barely tender. Add:

2 T vinegar   4 stalks celery, chopped
1 large onion, chopped 1 bell pepper, chopped

Cook until tender. Season with salt, pepper, to taste; it will take quite a lot of salt.

MRS. RANDOLPH West End Nursery CHITTERLINGS

Take your parboiled Chitterlings, about 2 lbs. Drain. Dry.
Season with salt and Black Pepper , Accent, and Cayenne.
Dip in: Two Eggs, beaten well. Then in 4 T flour, until well coated.
Fry in hot deep fat, about 4 minutes, until browned. Drain.
Dip in seasoned Chile Sauce or use Hot Sauce to season.
Serve with Potato Salad. Serves 4.

MRS. LILLIAN JOHNSON'S
RABBIT SAUSAGE

1 Jack rabbit or tame 1/2 tsp cayenne pepper
  rabbit, ground   1/4 tsp sage
2 lb. salt pork, ground 1 10¢ pkg chopped red
1/2 tsp black pepper   chili pepper

Mix all together. Form into 12 large patties. Fry in pan until well done.

MRS. LILLIAN JOHNSON'S
STEWED RABBIT

1 rabbit, cut up   2 tsp salt
1 large onion, chopped 1/4 tsp black pepper
1 small can mushrooms 1 small bell pepper,
  or use fresh   chopped

Flour, season and brown the rabbit in hot fat. Pour over 1 C hot water and the vegetables. Cover and simmer until tender.

Soul Food Cook Book

JIMMY LEE

....

New York: Award Books, 1970
158 pages

YOU COULD CALL Lee's work a lifestyle book. The volume is packed with delightful anecdotes and so much culinary history that it sounds like the kind of cooking story an old cook would have told as he or she rocked in a worn and tattered chair on the front stoop, picking beans.

Lee is that old cook.

He was a native of Louisiana who cooked in Creole kitchens from Natchez to Mobile and from New Orleans and Charleston, and his recipes reflect that pedigree—Creole mustard, Louisiana Hot Sauce, and a prodigious use of rice. Curiously, he omits the usual discussion of beverages and preserves. And there are no desserts.

He explains his style like this: "Soul is everything that happens in the black experience.

Soul food is part of that experience. It's unique, succulent, stick-to-the-ribs style of cooking that was created by slaves in the Old South—culinary genius sparked by necessity."

The "Fish and Shellfish" section is packed, including requisite recipes for catfish fried and stewed. The "Gumbo and Jambalaya" chapter features four gumbos, one a murky mixture (attributed to Mahalia Jackson) made with beef stew meat, pork sausage, chicken gizzards and wings, salt pork, crab, shrimp, tomatoes, and okra; plus traditional jambalaya and Jambalaya au Congri, composed of black-eyed peas, salt pork, ham, and rice. Nods to Deep South and make-do dishes prepared in ramshackle cabins make no mention of the African practices and preferences that spawned it all.

The chapter "Barbecue and Brunswick Stew" tells the story of Brunswick stew, differentiates it from squirrel stew, and lists a recipe that yields 3,500 servings. All parts of the pig are found in "The Pleasures of Pig," and the art of frying country ham and making Red-Eye Gravy are in the section "Heavenly Ham."

"Colossal Chicken" boasts three fried chicken recipes, including Juicy's, which is laced with a hint of curry powder; battered southern style; and the author's own version of "the Colonel's 11 herbs and spices." "Great Game" provides ways to roast and stew southern muskrat, possum, woodcock, squirrel, and rabbit.

"Good Greens" sheds light on the comprehensive inventory of wild greens that black families foraged, figured out how to cook, and learned to relish. As was customary, his recipes all rely on bacon, salt pork, or streak-o-lean for flavor. Rice is Nice Red Beans and Rice by Lucille Armstrong, Louis Armstrong's wife; beans, tomatoes, and sweet potatoes round out the "Vegetables, Vegetables" department. "Of Breads and Biscuits" covers skillet as well as batter breads, including Green Corn Spoon Bread, made with young, tender green corn.

"Anyone can cook soul food with the right recipes," he concludes. "Here at last is the first fundamental soul food cookbook." ❧

A Pinch of Soul

*Fast and Fancy Soul Cookery
for Today's Hostess*

PEARL BOWSER AND
JOAN ECKSTEIN

....

New York: Avon, 1970
288 pages

DELECTABLE DINNERS
from
Bread Pudding with Brandy Sauce
to
Kentucky Burgoo

SUPER SUPPERS
from
African Bean Soup
to
Congo Chicken

All with
very little effort, a lot of style
and

A PINCH OF SOUL

$\mathcal{E}$VERY INCH OF THIS TOME, from cover to cover, seems to be written for the eat-drink-and-be-merry crowd, with standard soul and southern fare embellished with new ingredients and ethnic personality for a new generation. These dishes demonstrate reverence for the accomplished cooking of the past, without unnecessary nostalgia or a reliance on discarded or unpopular meats. The emphasis is on economy cooking, yes, but this is also a book about what soul food had become: "a very real and legitimate addition to the repertory of American cuisine."

The book was published in the year when health experts reminded consumers that America's foraging ancestors ate enough leaves, fruit, and organ meats to contribute preventive amounts of ascorbic acid to the diet, and the year before General Mills introduced Hamburger Helper to help homemakers stretch their food dollars. The authors promote the notion that stretching meat off the bone with "fifth quarter foods," consuming a bounty of fresh vegetables, and enjoying simple dumplings or macaroni are not new ideas.

These two friends spice bland foods with flavors having deep African bloodlines—garlic, pepper, bay leaf, hot pepper, vinegar—whether they declared those cultural roots or not. They pick up the classic one-pot meal as a way to get through tough times, and show modern audiences how other techniques in the black culinary tradition avoid waste and fill stomachs at the same time.

And like most of the other soul food cookbook authors discussed in this chapter, they offer a definition of the cuisine: "Soul food is a kind of music. The melody has been shaped by the land, mellowed by the many who have played its different tunes—from the chefs and cooks in the kitchens of the South, to the black cowboy cooks of the Old West, to the average momma keeping her own kitchen—and interwoven with the themes of many cultures." 🐦

Mammy Pleasant's Cookbook

A Treasury of Gourmet Recipes from Victorian America

HELEN HOLDREDGE AND
MARY ELLEN PLEASANT

....

San Francisco: 101 Productions, 1970
159 pages

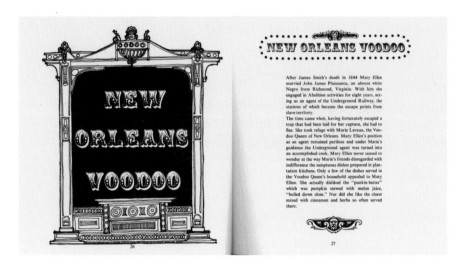

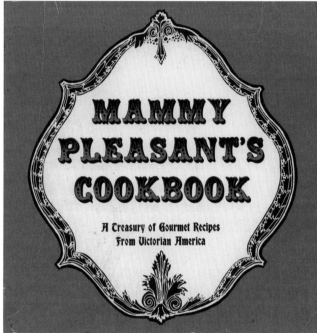

MUCH HAS BEEN WRITTEN about the woman portrayed in the nineteenth-century press as "Mammy Pleasant, angel and arch fiend and madam and murderess," not to mention voodoo priestess and "Mother of Civil Rights in California," but it took Holdredge, author of the biography *Mammy Pleasant*, to weave together yarns about Mary Ellen's accomplishments through recipes. The work forecasts a future approach to African American cookbook publishing: personal narrative.

This book is like a travelogue, recording the colorful dishes and flavors of high-society Nantucket, New Orleans, San Francisco, West Virginia, Missouri, and Mississippi, all of which Pleasant perfected in her travels. As brought to light by Holdredge, these accomplishments express the same cultural pride of ingenuity that marked the early days of the soul food movement and its connection to black migration out of the South. Yet Pleasant's life story strays quite a bit from the make-do aspect of the trend.

Words, vintage typefaces recalling the lettering on a majestic theater marquee, and line drawings of the townhouses, plantations, mansions, and homes where Pleasant lived and worked as a housekeeper and caterer artfully chronicle her dexterity with local ingredients and regional cookery styles. That skill helped her amass a fortune between 1824 and 1876. Pleasant purchased several magnificent boardinghouses, and, in 1876 she built a mansion of thirty rooms at a cost of $100,000. But by 1935, the property and other remnants of her culinary life had disappeared amid ghost stories and voodoo tales. ❧

Mahalia Jackson Cooks Soul

MAHALIA JACKSON

....

Nashville: Aurora, 1970
174 pages

J UST WHEN IT SEEMED as if everything had been said about soul food, the Queen of Gospel recorded her favorite recipes, plus some from friends, in this orderly ledger of no-frills preparations, published two years before Jackson's death at sixty. Her recipes share the kinds of festive meals that a celebrity enjoyed and served to guests who gathered in her home. Perhaps as a result, they seem less preoccupied than previous cookbooks with sustaining the soul food craze.

Cultural influences appear right up front. Four West Indian and African recipes on the opening pages—Peas and Rice from Nassau, Jamaican Fried Plantain, Nigerian Ground Nut Stew, and Ground Nut Soup from Zambia—tie ancestral cookery to Jackson's interpretation of modern black American food. Cajun and Creole adornments (New Orleans Chicken, Shrimp Creole, Creole Style Eggplant, New Orleans Red Beans

and Rice) pop up, too, though the number seems paltry considering that Jackson was born in New Orleans and was brought up by her Aunt Duke, "one of the great cooks of her time."

Time- and money-saving hints and suggestions help homemakers avoid cooking disasters, and many mainstays of soul cookery—barbecued bones, fried tripe, neck bones, wieners, ground meats, boiled garden vegetables, batter breads, griddle cakes, pound cake, and fruit desserts—convincingly fulfill the soul food mission of her title. But the number of economical treatments for pig parts and offal in the chapter "Meats and Main Dishes" represent just a fraction of the large inventory. Chitlings, Eggs and Brains, Hoghead Souse, Pigs Feet, salt pork marinated in milk and fried, and a concoction of chicken giblets and rice that she calls Soul Bowl exist in the shadows of dressier eats, such as Oven Beef Burgundy, Ham with Orange-Wine Sauce, and Tuna Burgers.

Page layout and the use of art and fonts connect readers not just to culinary and publishing trends of the time, but also to a worldly woman with a historic way of life. The book is easy to read and practical to use. Helpful features include the table of contents, index, lists of recipes to introduce each chapter, and chapter headings that float at the top of each page. Pages are adorned with black-and-white photographs of Jackson at the stove. And she has a comprehensive take on soul:

> Courage, fervor, and action convey the feelings (that's really what it is) of cooking soul. It takes courage to try to fill many mouths with little food. It takes fervor to find the ingenuity to combine the proper herbs, spices, etc., to make simple foods, say chitlings, edible—to say nothing of palatable and enjoyable. It takes action to gather and prepare all the ingredients necessary to make the stews, soups, and stuffed dishes, which provide sufficient quantity to many from small bits of costly items added to plenty of the bounty of the good earth. These are the essentials of cooking soul, the recipes of black folks the world over. 🐾

Vibration Cooking or The Travel Notes of a Geechee Girl

VERTAMAE SMART-GROSVENOR

....

Garden City, New York: Doubleday, 1970
Reprint, New York: Ballantine, 1986
220 pages

ORN IN FAIRFAX, South Carolina, the granddaughter of a slave, Vertamae Smart-Grosvenor was mother to Kali and Chandra. She performed on radio, television, and stage—in fact, loved the theater. She was not a writer. She got mad easily, did not like hospitals or taxis, and never held a serious nine-to-five job. She loved her beautiful friends, bon voyage parties, and cooking. She considered collard greens a delicacy. And she had great food memories and experiences.

Smart-Grosvenor could not help being creative, so she wrote this colorful diary with recipes. It serves as a broad pathway for reaching beyond the soul motif in order to find equity for black cookery within the culinary mainstream. Run through with bits of sarcasm, contempt for

dishonesty or prejudice, obvious empathy for the black power movement, and enough intimate dialogue and detailed imagery to fill a black-nationalism screenplay, Smart-Grosvenor's demystification of black cooking is comprehensive.

The introduction to the 1986 edition explains her thoughts on the "nonracial aspects of black-eyed peas, watermelon and other so-called soul foods." She believed in a universal and globally diverse kitchen: any dish, from any country, composed of any ingredients, could be soulful. She went on to admit, however, that she wrote about African American cookery, for several reasons: "Because I'm black and know the wonderful, fascinating culinary history there is. And because the Afro-American cook has been so under-appreciated."

She details just how underappreciated it is: "In reading lots and lots of cookbooks written by white folks, it occurred to me that people very casually say Spanish rice, French fries, Italian spaghetti, Chinese cabbage, Mexican beans, Swedish meatballs, Danish pastry, English muffins and Swiss cheese. And with the exception of black bottom pie and niggertoes, there is no reference to black people's contribution to the culinary arts." By capturing her life experiences through the lens of food, she intended to change that.

Her book is organized around seven episodes—"Home," "Away From Home," "Madness," "Love," "Mixed Bag," "Some Letters to and From Stella and one to Bob Thompson," and "Continued"—each with its own subset of folkways, reminiscences, tributes, and gossip about special people, places, and events. And some recipes.

In "Home," she describes her upbringing in the rural South. Recollections are gathered under the heading "Birth, Hunting and Gator Tails," and there are recipes for stewed small game, Kangaroo Tail Stew (canned and imported from Australia), and bear paw served like ham.

"Away From Home" covers her time spent in Paris, set in two periods: 1959 and 1968. There are recipes for pasta, ambrosia, pumpkin soup, *salade niçoise*, and Upright Ragout, a mix of chicken and leftover meat she prepared in a tiny apartment on the rue des Ursulines.

In "Madness," she tells stories about mean taxi drivers, unpleasant hospital stays, and her work ethic —or lack thereof.

"To tell the truth," she writes,

I ain't never really had no serious job working from nine to five. The ones I had I didn't keep 'cause my nerves would not take it. It's just not my rhythm . . . not my style. I have had some freakish jobs. I used to sew for a photographer. I made special effects such as aprons for elephants and six-sleeved shirts for a shirt ad. But my cooking jobs were the funniest . . . I had become the cook in Pee Wee's Slave Trade Kitchen. It didn't last long. But everyone dug my cooking.

Work

To tell the truth I ain't never really had no serious job working from nine to five. The ones I had I didn't keep cause my nerves would not take it. It's just not my rhythm . . . not my style. I have had some freakish jobs. I used to sew for a photographer. I made special effects such as aprons for elephants and six-sleeved shirts for a shirt ad. But my cooking jobs were the funniest. I remember "Obedella, Obedella, I want to be your fella!" That's what Jean used to say every time I came to work. Obedella was my new name since I had become the cook in Pee Wee's Slave Trade Kitchen. It didn't last long. But everyone dug my cooking. One of the things that everyone dug was chicken in peanut butter sauce. It is a West African dish sometimes called

GROUND NUT STEW

Cut up and season and sauté the chicken in peanut oil. When brown, add chopped bell pepper and chopped onions. When the onions are transparent, add red pepper and chicken broth and lots chunky-style peanut butter. Sauce should be on the stiff side. Serve with rice or plantain.

91

She then gives a representative example:

One of the things that everyone dug was chicken in peanut butter sauce. It is a West African dish sometimes called

GROUND NUT STEW

Cut up and season and sauté the chicken in peanut oil. When brown, add chopped bell pepper and chopped onions. When the onions are transparent, add red pepper and chicken broth and lots chunky-style peanut butter. Sauce should be on the stiff side. Serve with rice or plantain.

As anyone can tell, Smart-Grosvenor cooked by "vibration"—determining doneness by sight and smell, with approximated measurements and seasoning added according to taste. She preferred simple, plain, and ordinary food that was readily available, and in a smug act of reverse racism, she urges readers to check out their "kitchen vibrations." "*What kind of pots are you using?*" she asks. "Throw out all of them except the black ones.

The cast-iron ones like your mother used to use. Can't no Teflon fry no fried chicken. I only use black pots and brown earthenware in the kitchen. White enamel is not what's happening."

"Love" includes a hilarious account of a black cook named Honky, who knew lots of ways to fix cheap meals. One of his favorites: Stuffed Heart Honky Style. "Mixed Bag" covers assorted experiences with greens, a warning about aphrodisiacal foods, a rundown of cocktails and beverage recipes from family and friends, and an insightful study called "White People and Fried Chicken." Laugh-out-loud letters exchanged between Smart-Grosvenor and her cousin Stella, and a few random tales about the cultural aspects of her cooking, wrap up her travel notes.

She dedicates the book "to my mama and my grandmothers and my sisters in appreciation of the years that they worked in miss ann's kitchen and then came home to TCB [take care of business] in spite of slavery and oppression and the Moynihan report."

You dig? ❧

The Mother Waddles
Soul Food Cookbook

CHARLESZETTA WADDLES

....

Second edition

Detroit: Perpetual Soul Saving Mission for
  All Nations, 1970

39 pages

THE DEVOUT WEIGHT WATCHER

Here I am at another family party
This is another scheme for them to torture me
Just look, there's food as far as the eye can see
In three months I've lost three pounds
It's so hard to keep this weight down.
They always teased, and said I was the fattest thing in town
Why every one knows I have to eat
Look at uncle Bill eating all that meat
Boy, I wish I could have about 10 Bar-B-Que pigs feet
They said because of calories, I can't eat what I please
Therefore, I just have myself some cottage cheese
If I get uptight, I eat some ice cream in a squeeze.

WHEN GOVERNOR William G. Milliken proclaimed October 19–26, 1970, as Mother Waddles Week, he praised the altruistic spirit of the Reverend Charleszetta Waddles and recognized her for leading Detroit to "a fuller understanding of the mandate to 'Love Thy Neighbor as Thy Self,'" by, among other things, publishing a collection of just over a hundred recipes for soul food standards as a community-service project.

She founded the Perpetual Soul Saving Mission for All Nations, Inc., in 1957 and offered a twenty-four-hour emergency services program that provided food, shelter, clothing, medical and dental care, legal aid, transportation, job placement, training programs, and drug addiction services. Its kitchen served seventy thousand meals annually for thirty-five cents each (or free to the indigent).

The recipe booklet displays best wishes from prominent members of the community, including a pediatrician, a reporter for the *Detroit News*, and a director of juvenile court; testimonials from a few of her friends; a Proclamation from Governor Milliken; a list of her humanitarian and service awards and certificates of appreciation; and a legislative resolution.

"I was inspired to write this book, during the time I was confined to my hospital bed, after experiencing the misfortune of falling down a flight of stairs," Mother Waddles writes on the opening page. Two pages of recipes "for all us weight watchers," submitted with best wishes from the president of Weight Watchers of Eastern and Central Michigan, tell readers that Mother Waddles may have been refocusing her attention on healthier eating while in recuperation. ❧

Simple

PLEASURES

*A Soul Food
Revival*

In the intellectual realm a renewed and keen curiosity is replacing the recent apathy; the Negro is being carefully studied, not just talked about and discussed. In art and letters, instead of being wholly caricatured, he is being seriously portrayed and painted.

ALAIN LOCKE,
1925

I N 1969, three rebellious French restaurant critics founded a magazine devoted to food and wine. Henri Gault, Christian Milau, and Andre Gayot called their publication *Nouveau Guide*, and the monthly journal competed with the illustrious restaurant-rating guide *Michelin* by presenting a less conservative approach to cooking and dining.

By 1972, the style chronicled by the *Nouveau Guide* had become a well-established alternative to classic French cuisine. Chefs such as Paul Bocuse and Michel Guérard earned fame by serving vegetables slightly crisp or in pureed puddles, replacing flour-based sauces with meat essences, stocks, and pan reductions, and arranging tiny portions artistically on large plates. The light and quick cooking movement became known as nouvelle cuisine and it took America by storm.

Throughout much of the 1970s, black folks who had spent decades cooking in other people's kitchens or observing someone close to them who had confidently challenged established notions of food and cooking, too, were claiming new mantles as gourmet cooks, health experts, cultural archaeologists, and archivists. They flaunted stellar dishes not shrouded in the soul mystique, finding just as much inspiration for their menus in the heritage cuisines of Africa and the Caribbean and in the Creole cookery of the Carolina Lowcountry and Louisiana as they did in the rest of the South. Some got caught up in the ethnic aspects of Jewish kitchens; others were animated by China or Spain.

Buoyed by their new gastronomical black power, dashiki-clad cooks imbued their cooking with creative elements that matched those of nouvelle cuisine and cultural ethnic identity. The obsessions of flower children, hippies, and health fanatics energized feisty black cooks, too, who got excited about the healing properties of plants and about avoiding certain animals, unhealthy fats, and too much sugar. The shift gave a whole new meaning to cooking with soul.

Soul food, wrote the scholar Doris Witt in *African American Foodways: Explorations of History and Culture* (2007), a collection of provocative essays edited by Anne L. Bower, "reappeared as an emblem of ethnic and racial pride in developments such as the self-conscious creation of the African American celebration Kwanzaa."

Nostalgia for the South was manifested in a desire for a return to simple pleasures, advice collected from learned authority figures, and recipes culled from folklore and recollections. The authors Edna Lewis and the Darden sisters became grandes dames of southern food based in part on family reminiscences that associated African American heritage cuisine with country cooking.

These garden-to-table impulses naturally led to heart-healthy cooking and discussions about what it meant to be a chef. The comedian Dick Gregory and the Nation of Islam published strongly worded guides that remind me of today's locavore treatises. Both endorsed varied and balanced menus, avoiding known high-fat and high-sodium dishes, choosing fresh foods in season, and limiting intake of processed foods. And both were adamant—soul food is "unclean food unfit for human consumption." Mary Jackson and Lelia Wishart took a more positive tack, charting the nutritional values of soul food ingredients in *The Integrated Cookbook* (1971) to prove its worth.

Others focused on achievement rather than health. In New Orleans, Rudy Lombard gathered the recipes of two generations of elite chefs into his book, and in Georgia, *Four Great Southern Cooks* (1980) introduced three acclaimed women (and one man). And in Austin, Texas, Mitchell Mays was inspired to tell the story of how he helped transform a historic family home into one of the city's finest restaurants and party venues.

All this may sound as if new African American cooking lost its soul along the way, but I think it was the label—not the food—that lost its relevance. The essence of black cooking is a spirit of experimentation and originality, not just poverty ingredients and foods of the fifth quarter. In the new millennium, the term "soul" can affectionately describe a talented country-and-western singer, and "soul" is used by a theater company to convey that their hot new show is nurturing, satisfying, and comforting.

As I wrote in an article for volume 7 of *The New Encyclopedia of Southern Culture* (2007), the African American culinary frontier had by then expanded so that soul no longer adequately characterized the cultural and social choices made by people of color. We chide the make-do nature of soul food and along with it the aura and mystique that once cloaked our cooks as if they possessed innate powers of "black magic."

The pull of nouvelle cuisine, rising middle-class values, and improved social conditions made it perhaps inevitable that a new and improved soul cooking would emerge, one emphasizing health and nutrition by using finer cuts of meat, lighter styles of cooking and seasoning, and new ingredients (new to the region, at least) such as soy, uncooked greens and other vegetables, and pastas other than macaroni. African American authors were engaged in culinary reform—what the executive food editor for the *Atlanta Journal-Constitution*, Susan Puckett, called a "soul food revival"—just as esteemed white chefs were reimagining southern food as "new southern cuisine." Sentimentality ensured that the appetite for slowly cooked and highly seasoned vegetables, macaroni and cheese, sweet potatoes, pork in all its manifestations, chicken, hot breads, sweet tea, and cobbler would never disappear. Yet the times and the food changed. So did the cooks.

The more I read about the new identities emerging during the New Soul movement, the more my own passions seemed to overlap with the messages they instilled. These authors preserve cultural heritage, promote health, and use food to teach or entertain or both. Through my writings and the nonprofit foundation that I founded, the SANDE Youth Project, so do I. Here is how.

Several years ago, a morning news show invited me to appear on its black history month segment. My assignment: explain the health risks associated with eating soul food and discourage people of color from eating heritage cooking. I understood the rationale. Who better than the coauthor of a recipe book infused with chef-inspired dishes like chitlin pizza and sautéed collard greens tucked into crepes, and boldly titled, *A Taste of Heritage: The New African-American Cuisine* (2002), to declare, "Mama's down-home cooking is killing us."

I declined.

What I agreed to do instead was to talk about the valuable nutrients found in African American cooking, which had sustained our ancestors through generations of hardship. I associated our increased risk of developing chronic conditions such as diabetes, heart disease, obesity, and high blood pressure with a number of factors, including smoking, drinking alcohol, indifferent cooking practices, sedentary lifestyles, and eating too much fast food. I encouraged viewers to make a variety of colorful foods part of a balanced diet, to eat fast food and processed food less often, and to get up and move around a bit, for heaven's sake. My sermon, in other words, was "don't believe the hype."

Of course, the wellness community did and still does have a point. Making a regular diet of foods that are fried in oils and butter, drowned in rich sauces, or laced with sugar is not a good idea—for anyone. But we now know that all black people didn't live off fatback, fried chicken, and gooey cake. And that many of soul food's ingredients—beans, whole grains, vegetables, and small servings of meat—are ones recommended for optimum health. These staples, which offer a taste of healthy African heritage cooking, are the stuff of a soul food revival that began with the noteworthy comfort cooking of the black power movement and attracted a sophisticated, racially diverse audience. "Soul food" as a term has continued over the years, but without ever intending to represent the totality of the African American culinary experience.

For all of us figuring out what to say about the imaginative side of soul food today, the words of the great French chef Paul Bocuse are worth remembering: "One can only cook well with love—it is a matter above all, of promoting around the table friendship and fraternity among men. This seems to me essential: the home cook, as well as the grand chef, must prepare only dishes that he or she loves to prepare. . . . Cooking is easier and better when it is done for people that one loves . . . and it is always necessary to leave some part of cooking to improvisation."

Right on! ❧

The Art of African Cooking

The Original "Soul Food"; 307 Exotic Recipes from the First Ladies of the New African Nations

SANDY LESBERG

....

New York: Dell, 1971
214 pages

WHETHER A READER's interest in African cooking resulted from curiosity about one's roots or stemmed from a fascination with people from foreign lands, Lesberg intended for Westerners to "do more than just observe" African culture; she wanted us to taste and know that Africans had an exciting cuisine all their own.

She didn't take the next step and relate African cooking to soul food—directly or indirectly—even though the connection between the two is clearly visible in African dishes such as *jollof* rice (jambalaya), green mealie bread (cornbread), mealie meal pudding (spoon bread), okra sauce (okra and tomatoes), *injera* (hoecakes/griddle cakes), chicken okra soup (gumbo), and *akara*, or black-eyed pea fritters (hushpuppies). These foods suggest that African slaves had their own cooking methods before arriving in the New World, and it is one that, in Lesberg's words, "We can share, participate, identify—perhaps even understand."

The author explains that Africa is a hugely diverse continent: thirty-nine independent countries and eighteen independent territories at the time, with hundreds of tribes speaking myriad local tongues and dialects. Lesberg divides more than 300 recipes into sections representing four large regions (Northern, West, East and Central, and Southern), organized by foodways. Chapter introductions give some history and a few general facts about the countries in that region: political leaders, topography, population, religious practices, national mottoes, and government facts.

She generalizes about African cooking this way:

> Starch is more of a staple than protein. Meats are usually one- or two-course affairs and you won't find sweets as such on the menu. Rather, where fruit abounds that's it. A lot of papaya, pineapple, guava, and mango. The most common meals include meat of some sort—often mutton or goat. In West Africa, palm nuts, rice, plantains, or bananas are part of the everyday diet. Corn, millet, or sorghum are staples in other areas. In Southern Africa, cornmeal mush is one of the staples. Peanuts are a common food. Cassavas are pounded into flour and palm oil is frequently called for.

A list of some African foods in Lonkundo (a language of the Congo) is useful for researchers: peanuts (*nguba*), greens (*banganju*), fish (*nse*), oranges (*ilala*), sweet potatoes (*baenge*), beans (*babinsi*), onions (*batungulu*), rice (*loso*), and bananas (*mankondo*). 🐾

The Integrated Cookbook or The Soul of Good Cooking

MARY JACKSON AND
LELIA WISHART

....

Chicago: Johnson, 1971
135 pages

*T*HIS UNIQUELY SHAPED book takes its title from the authors' philosophy that food should not be segregated by ethnicity and race. "Integrated participation in soul food will lead to a deeper, better understanding for us all," they proclaim. "This book is a combination of old and new recipes 'blended well.'"

Recipes are printed two per page, side by side horizontally, with titles shaded in green ink to make them easy to read. The well-written formulas circulated in magazines and cookbooks for ten years, and were modified by a few additions from Jackson's eighty-one-year-old North Carolina–reared mother as well as research conducted in the Schomburg Collection in the Harlem branch of the New York Public Library.

The authors theorize America's transition from soul to southern this way: "Soul food originated through a kind of cooking lore, created and perpetuated by black people whose only means of communication was word-of-mouth. Like jazz, it had a solid base, but the rest was improvised." It was "prepared with the Black mother's love for her family, developed with great care, and served with dignity. Tenant farmers and blacks fortunate enough to have a plot of ground developed the 'in-between' Southern cooking—fried chicken, barbecued ribs, self-rising corn bread, etc. But somehow, everything retained something of the original flavor—the 'soul' of good cooking."

That "good cooking" included soda and baking powder biscuits, cornmeal batter cakes, croquettes, smothered steak, Brunswick stew, pigs' feet boiled or barbecued, tripe boiled or fried, ribs, chitterlings, ham, pork chops, whole barbecued pig, fried chicken battered or floured only, and small game stews.

A section entitled "Melting Pot/Foreign Adoptions" reminds me of Freda DeKnight's cookbook, which featured "a few popular 'foreign' recipes that are being adopted by Black Americans." Jackson and Wishart include recipes for Chinese chow mein, Hungarian Chicken Paprika, Italian Spaghetti and Meatballs, Jewish Potato Pancakes (Latkas), Polish Stuffed Cabbage (Pigs in a blanket), Mexican Chili Con Carne, and Puerto Rican rice dishes.

The book's useful kitchen tips and hints are still relevant today. A list of soul food restaurants on the East Coast and a group of sample menus conclude the book. A chart of the nutritional values in soul food, based on the U.S. Department of Agriculture's *Agriculture Handbook No. 8: Composition of Foods*, shows the ways that "soul food may combine the greatest concentration of food values known to man." ❧

The African Heritage Cookbook

A Chronicle of the Origins of Soul Food Cooking, with 200 Authentic—and Delicious—Recipes

HELEN MENDES

....

New York: Macmillan, 1971
247 pages

ONE-THIRD OF THIS scholarly work is devoted to establishing a link between soul food and sixteenth- and seventeenth-century West African heritage cookery. Five chapters cover the history and background of cooking in Africa, the ways that food and the agricultural past influenced the culinary practices of the New World, the adjustments that Africans made to the indigenous foods and established cultural culinary practices of their masters and the Native Americans, and finally the practices visible in the established soul food cookery.

A few headnotes introduce more than two hundred recipes for soul food traditions such as barbecue, chitterlings, gumbo, and sweet potato pie, all contributed by relatives and friends of the author. The recipes include the name of the cook who provided the dish, the author's own culinary memories, serving suggestions and accompaniments, and practical tips. There are menus for breakfast, lunch, everyday and company dinners, New Year's Eve, and "What to Take to a Soul Dance." Drawings depict African cooks preparing meals over an open fire, carrying produce from market, and American cooks over the stove and behind the table. A rich bibliography provides references to African tribal, horticultural, and cultural practices, slave culture, folklife, and social history. It also covers West Indian customs and cookery.

The following story of heritage cooking is quite compelling, and future books on the subject quote it. Often.

Slaves came to the New World with a distinct cooking style that they practiced in limited ways in the master's kitchen and more widely when they cooked for themselves. In every tribe, cooking was "one of the most important skills which the young girl had to master." As a toddler, she learned to recognize wild foods as her mother picked fruits, gathered herbs, and foraged for wild tubers, mushrooms, and bush greens. She learned to build and camouflage traps for small bush animals and to catch fish with small nets and baskets. At the age of around six, she went to live in the "House of the Women," where she learned her tribe's way of getting food.

In adulthood, she demonstrated proficiency in a wide assortment of culinary arts that show up as the backbone of soul cookery. She understood sauce making, seasoning with aromatic spices, and the ways that seeds, nuts, oils, vegetables, and fruits provide variety as well as flavoring and refreshment. Her economical practices included pickling, sun drying, and salting. Steamed and fried breads made from ground roots of manioc or cassava resemble soul's large, thick hoecakes, griddle cakes, dumplings, and pone.

Africans practiced the art of fermentation, too. Palm wines were important for religious and social occasions, as were those distilled wines from corn, sugar cane, and pineapple. Travelers observed Africans brewing corn beer. ❧

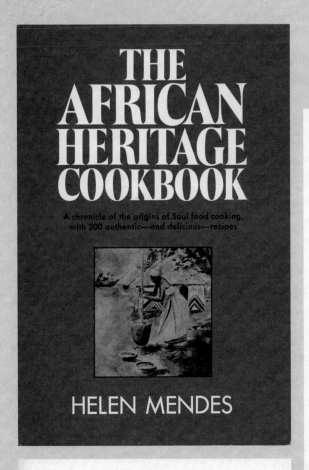

THE AFRICAN HERITAGE COOKBOOK

A chronicle of the origins of Soul food cooking, with 200 authentic—and delicious—recipes

HELEN MENDES

7

Meats and Sauces

ROAST PORK

5 pounds rib pork roast	1 cup water
1 teaspoon salt	2 stalks celery, chopped
¼ teaspoon black pepper	3 onions, minced
¼ teaspoon ginger	4–6 medium potatoes
1½ tablespoons flour	1 tablespoon brown sugar
2 tablespoons bacon fat	

1. Season pork with salt, pepper, and ginger. Refrigerate for 1 hour or more.
2. Preheat oven to 350 degrees F.
3. Dredge pork with flour. Quickly brown roast in the bacon fat. Place meat in a roasting pan. Add water, celery, and onions. Roast, uncovered, for 4 hours or until the meat thermometer temperature is 185° F. Baste frequently.
4. Peel and quarter potatoes. Place them around the roast. Sprinkle pork with brown sugar. Baste pork and potatoes frequently. Bake for 30 minutes or until the potatoes are tender.
5. To make the gravy, pour the stock into a skillet. Thicken it with a paste made of 1 or more tablespoons flour mixed with an equal amount of water. Correct seasoning. Simmer 2 minutes.

[Serves 4–6]

The Art of West African Cooking

DINAH AMELY AYENSU

Drawings by Diane Robertson

....

Garden City, New York: Doubleday, 1972

145 pages

AYENSU WROTE THIS BOOK to introduce some of the best recipes of indigenous West Africa to American tables. The recipes concentrate on fundamentals, including dishes with seafood, particularly herring; stewed meats with vegetables; and rice and vegetable dishes. Notes explain slaughtering rites, sacrifices, and ceremonial or religious occasions. We learn from the soup section, for instance, that hearty and nourishing soups are the mainstay of a main meal at lunch or supper, accompanied by *fufu* or a vegetable; lightly seasoned, clear fish soups are preferred for invalids; and soup is not served as a first course.

A "Shopper's Guide" directs readers to the "exotic and enticing assortment of sweet-smelling spices, tangy sauces, tropical fruits and vegetables of the African gourmet." ❧

Shopper's Guide

74 *The Art of West African Cooking*

BEEF HEARTS CASSEROLE

Bomunam Forowee (Fante, Ghana)

1 medium beef heart, sliced	1 large tomato, diced
Salt and cayenne pepper to taste	1 green pepper, sliced
3 tablespoons butter	3 sliced celery sticks
1 tablespoon flour	¼ cup Worcestershire sauce
1 medium onion, sliced lengthwise	¼ teaspoon cinnamon or nutmeg

Season sliced beef heart with salt and cayenne pepper, and brown in 1 tablespoon of the butter until tender. Cook slowly.

Brown flour in remaining butter, sauté onion until slightly browned, and add rest of ingredients. Cover and simmer slowly for 20 minutes, stirring occasionally.

Serve hot.

Serves 4
Cooking time: 30 minutes

ACCOMPANIMENTS:
Lima beans
Baked potatoes
Curried Rice with Raisins
Yams

Note: Kidneys or liver may also be prepared using this recipe.

Black Academy Cookbook

A Collection of Authentic African Recipes

(MONICA) ODINCHEZO OKA

....

Buffalo, New York: Black Academy Press, 1972
188 pages

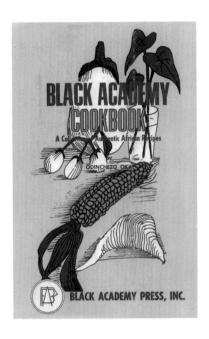

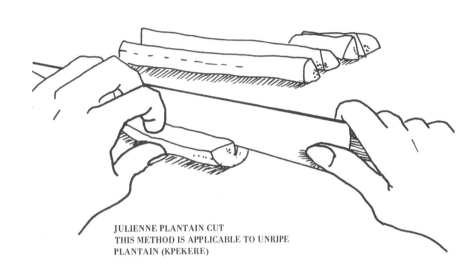

JULIENNE PLANTAIN CUT
THIS METHOD IS APPLICABLE TO UNRIPE
PLANTAIN (KPEKERE)

THE BOOK JACKET SAYS IT ALL. The author, who was a Nigerian-born graduate student studying social science education at Syracuse University, believed that knowledge of African food and cooking would help the world understand African ways of life and culture and would encourage black people to adopt their true culinary lineage.

According to the author: "Black Academy Cookbook presents to the housewife, bachelor, scholar or chef, authentic recipes from over twenty-three black African countries. Before he can get others to respect his past, the African in diaspora must first discover his authentic heritage. Black Academy Cookbook sets out to do this and hopes that before long, authentic African cuisine will take its rightful place at the table in and out of the home."

Her tribute to "our great ancestors" is not intended to be "an encyclopedia of African recipes." Instead, she collected simple recipes that were easily adapted to "Euro-American" tables; translated African terms and methods; provided substitutes for indigenous ingredients such as plantain, cocoyam, melon seeds (*egusi*); and explained the African cook's shopping, measuring, and seasoning habits. A helpful chart of African ingredients listed by their American, Igbo (Ibo), and English names makes shopping easier for Africans living in America. Line drawings illustrate cooking tools and ingredients and provide visual cues for techniques such as properly holding a knife, shaping plantains, and dicing okra.

Harmony McCoy's
Diet Cook Book

Secrets of a Renowned Health Spa Chef

HARMONY MCCOY

....

Murrieta, California:
Harmon-E-Enterprises, 1972
166 pages

MURRIETA HOT SPRINGS was a kind of "food clinic" where the chef and author tested and retested recipes and chemical reactions between foods for his four-week weight-loss program—an alternative to trendy starvation diets and boring regimens. The difference between McCoy's approach and other weight-loss plans, according to the introduction, is that "this one works!"

The program offers tips to increase diet discipline, menus with serving sizes and calorie counts (about seven hundred calories a day on average), perky sayings and encouraging thoughts to help the reader "color yourself healthy," plus essential cooking tips that would make anyone a better cook. Fresh vegetables are cooked in chicken broth. Ethnic ingredients such as rice vinegar and mirin make salad dressings low calorie. Fruit is spiked with liqueur for extra flavor. Fresh juice sweetens custard.

The oversized book opens flip-chart style and stands on the countertop without support, making each day's menu and recipes accessible and easy to read. It is lavishly illustrated with watercolor images of fresh fruits and vegetables, line drawings and sketches, several photographs, and a cute story in the preface about a girl, her spa chef, and his magic diet equation. A protective cardboard cover adds to the delightful presentation. ❧

The Jemima Code

Once upon a time there was a little girl who loved to eat yummy things, the fattening kinds of yummy things...so she grew and grew until she looked like this . She ate so much of everything that her breath came in short 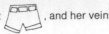, and her veins and arteries were gasping for air...so Miss Big went to a picturesque spa. She ate yummy things there, too, but not the fattening kind, for at the spa they gave her unfattening delights, in small portions. She cheated a little in the late afternoon or early evening or late evening...but not as much as the day before or the day before that; and soon her breath became deeper and her

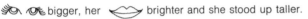 bigger, her brighter and she stood up taller.

Most of all, she loved feeling so good all the time that little things, and some of the big ones too, didn't bother her as much. Then one day she had to leave the beautiful spa because she missed her family. It made her sad to leave because she wanted to take the Spa Chef home with her, but couldn't. Chef Harmony had to stay at the Spa to give all the other people the happiness he had given her. She pleaded long to take him home ...so frightened was she to get along without him. Chef Harmony had a wonderful idea. "I promise to put all my

magic menus in a beautiful book so that you can smile and eat and breathe more easily. But you must make me the following promises or I won't be able to help you:

1. Never feel guilty about eating yummy things, because super yummy things aren't always fattening.

2. Always enjoy eating. It's one of the nicer things in your life — even as nice as shiny jewelry, pretty clothes or even beautiful new cars, or even lots of other yummy things like kissing and hugging.

3. Always read all the magic menus carefully, and do as Harmony says or the food won't taste yummy, and you'll want to eat more of the things that are bad for you; and you'll cry more often and start gasping for air again, and *always always* and *never never,* if you're still dieting, cheat by not watching your portions; because remember, *always* remember this simply magic equation:"

$$\bigcirc + \bigcirc = \bigcirc$$

$$\bigcirc + \bigcirc = \bigcirc$$

WEEK 1.

	Ounces	Grams	Calories
BREAKFAST			
1 — 2" slice melon or ½ grapefruit . (Honeydew, Crenshaw, Casaba or, Cantaloupe). For substitutes, see "Happy Hints" in back of book.	3½	100	47
1 cup black coffee or hot tea	8	236	0
LUNCH			
Fresh pineapple salad	4	114	50
Oil and Vinegar Dressing (1 Tbsp.)			70
Cheese-Mushroom Omelette	3½	100	200
DINNER			
Combination Salad (½ cup)	4	114	40
Baked Cornish Game Hen (½)	8	228	350
Baked Zucchini	3½	100	50
Orange Lady Finger	4	114	75
TOTAL CALORIES			882

The Edna Lewis Cookbook

EDNA LEWIS AND
EVANGELINE PETERSON

············

New York: Ecco, 1972
Reprint, 1983
198 pages

FOR A LESSON IN ELEGANT African American cooking, take Edna Lewis into the kitchen. In style, her book is eerily like those terrible, early twentieth-century cookbooks in which the wise white author translates for the black cook. Thankfully, Peterson stresses Lewis's culinary grace—sweet potatoes are cooked with lemon, corn is boiled in the husk, fresh herbs are used for seasoning, country ham is used to flavor vegetables, greens are stemmed—and the opinion that poverty food defines African Americans is soundly dismissed.

The book's untraditional organization reflects life on a Virginia farm. The recipes revolve around the seasons. The text is printed in a light typeface that conveys a delicate charm and spirit. Italics set off the headnotes as if to whisper cooking lessons in the cook's soft voice.

Informative recipe headnotes include serving suggestions, details about the dish itself, cautions to the cook, and tips for success, such as how to fit dough into a baking pan and the best time to ease a cake from its vessel. There are few extravagant ingredients. Where expensive meats are called for, detailed instructions explain how to avoid waste. Fresh herbs are everywhere. Blender mayonnaise becomes an exotic and savory sauce for seafood or cold chicken. A *poulet à la crème* is quite delicious with just a sprinkling of freshly cut parsley, but "a sprinkling of fresh tarragon so enhances its taste and aroma that it becomes a dish special enough for any occasion." As a lady of the farm, Lewis, of course, cooks with all sorts of offal (veal kidneys) and game (quail).

Elsewhere in the book, her methods tell not just how best to accomplish a task, but why. Look for suggestions on stocking the pantry; succeeding at baking; and ensuring success with the proper cooking equipment—heavy-bottomed and sturdily made saucepans and skillets made of aluminum, tin-lined copper, or stainless steel with cast-aluminum bottoms; enameled cast-iron casseroles; a Pyrex double boiler for sauces; and an electric mixer.

A list of some of the author's favorite cooking stores adds a personal touch. 🌿

Stories and Tales of
Green Pastures

MITCHELL MAYS

....

Austin, Texas, 1972
20 pages

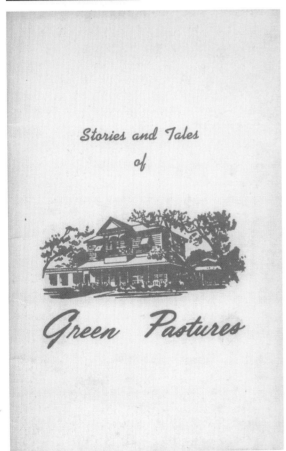

T HE STORY BEHIND the early days of the
majestic Victorian home of Judge Henry
Faulk in Austin, Texas, its transformation into a
restaurant, and the author's household management memories come to life in this teeny family
scrapbook with recipes by a former employee.

In 1945, Faulk's daughter, Mary Koock,
opened the home for luncheons and dinner,
eventually hiring several maids and waiters,
including Mays, who was later named maitre
d', and his wife, Marie, as one of the cooks. This
handmade, typewritten treasure features photographs of Mays at his college graduation, aboard
ship in Saipan, and entertaining guests in the
restaurant dining room. Two recipes hint at the
stately atmosphere—a ground-meat-and-bour-
bon dessert called Beef Cake, and Brandy-Bust-
er, a flamed fruit dish. ❧

How to Eat to Live, Book No. 2

ELIJAH MUHAMMAD

....

Chicago: Muhammad's Temple Of Islam No. 2, 1972
126 pages

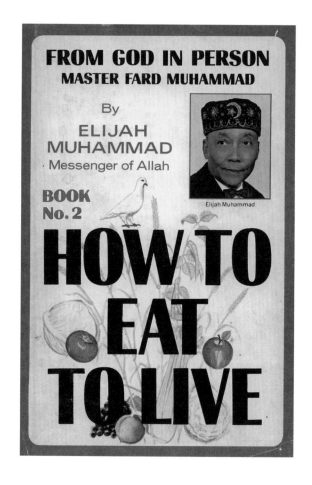

IN SEVERAL WAYS, this sometimes harshly worded missive aimed at the black Muslim community resembles a modern foodie's complaints against big agriculture and the processed-food industry. The author supported humane animal slaughter and eating clean, fresh food you raised and prepared yourself. He railed against overeating—especially processed carbohydrates and sugary foods. He begged consumers to make all their grains whole.

It was a case Muhammad had begun five years earlier, in *Book No. 1*: dietary ills, disease, physical weaknesses, and ailments can be attributed to the diet created by the "white race."

Book No. 1 is written in a narrative form that lists specific foods to avoid, many of them traced to the slave diet. *Book No. 2* refocuses the same information as food rules to be followed in order to preserve long life. The directive to limit mealtime to once every twenty-four hours is chief among them.

For example, *Book No. 1* provides the following directives regarding vegetables: All of them are good, except collard greens and turnip salad. Cabbages are good, but take away the green leaves. No kale. Eat some spinach, but do not be a "habitual spinach eater." Eat rutabaga occasionally. Unlimited intake of onions and garlic is okay, but no sweet or white potatoes. Sweet potatoes are good for hogs; white ones are only for people who live in frigid zones. "Potatoes and rice are too starchy for you and me," he says, adding that they are "friends to diabetes . . . full of gas."

Allah forbids eating peas, according to the book. No black-eyed peas, field peas, speckled peas, red or brown split, since these are "cheaply raised foods used by slave masters to feed slaves." Navy beans are permitted.

Book No. 2 is the rule book. Its cover claims that it comes from "God in Person Master Fard Muhammad," who founded the Nation of Islam. Among its strictures are the following:

"A sick mother's milk is better for her baby than a healthy cow's milk or any animal's milk."

"Lay off all those sugar and starchy foods and just eat common foods."

"Eat one meal every twenty-four (24) hours."

"Use no drugs to keep blood-sugar down. Just eat right . . . the sugar in your blood will clear up."

"Choose common foods: navy beans, cooked well done with a little salt and pepper."

"Never think to go near the hog and do not help prepare the hog for anyone else to eat. . . . in Arabic its name means, 'I see foul and very foul.'"

"Do not eat leaf vegetable, such as collard greens. . . . Eat the white heads of vegetables, such as cauliflower and white heads of cabbage . . . the roots of turnips, but do not eat the salad (leaves)."

"Eat rice, but do not eat the rice without washing it thoroughly until the water becomes clear . . . Parch in a little butter, vegetable oil, corn or olive oil." ❧

Pearl's Kitchen

An Extraordinary Cookbook

PEARL BAILEY

....

New York: Harcourt Brace Jovanovich, 1973
211 pages

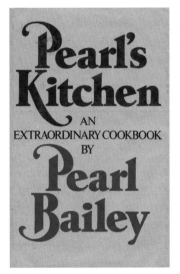

"The most down-to-earth, common-sensible, loving cookbook that's appeared in many a moon."
—The New York Times

78435•$1.50

*T*HERE ARE SO MANY wonderful, amusing, entertaining essays about food and life at the kitchen table here that you may forget this is a cookbook. The singer, actress, and Tony Award winner tells you her culinary ideology right up front, so there is no confusion: cooking is an expression of love and affection, not just "ingredients and technique"—soul with a dose of sass.

And then she sets off to prove her point through memories of favorite aromas, family, and cultural folkways and traditions; health practices (like her Papa's daily yeast regimen); the power of learning by watching Mama; cooking as a grand form of giving; life wisdom (pride in keeping house and, my favorite, the kitchen as sanctuary—a place of physical and emotional nourishment achieved through sharing and mediation and thanksgiving).

The kitchen, she believes, is not a place of pretense where gourmet cooking should be "so French" that you cannot pronounce the name of a dish or fully enjoy it. This is informal cooking, with techniques highlighted throughout, and enough personal insights to remove the soul mystique. In Bailey's words: "I believe in simplicity, cleanliness, nutrition and good flavor."

Next come the recipes—each designed to teach the sensory cues that good cooks have understood forever. She shares the best way to determine the proper amount of water for cooking rice and explains how to cook okra without the slime. When she says to add a little bit of vinegar to the pot, she doesn't just leave you hanging in the dark, but her soul style requires that you get over the need for precise measures: "What do I mean by a little bit? I don't know, do what looks right and if it doesn't come out the way you want it, do it differently the next time."

She likes recipes that bring simple satisfaction: hamburger casserole, plain vegetable soup, hard-shell crabs in beer, a hamburger "all the way." And she offers dishes to serve to guests—Veal Chops Ad Lib, a creation resembling parmigiana; Lamb Chops Sumpin Else, oven-braised and topped with cheese; Stewed Tomatoes Michelangelo, oven-roasted with toasted bread crumbs; White Potatoes How Did You Do This, a nutty dish that perches a whole potato on top of a foil basket so that it rests in Italian dressing and garlic. A few cultural specialties are present, too: Mexican Chocolate Cake, Antipasto *a la Pastor*, and a Chinese dish, Three-Part Noodles from the Dumpling Inn.

Dishes from performers and celebrities (Jane Churchill, Douglas Fairbanks Jr., Bing Crosby, Rose Tizol, Victor Borge, Tony Bennett, Carol Burnett) are assembled in the section "A Little Help from my Friends" to dispel the notion of performers "as boozers, dope peddlers, users, and everything of the sort." ❧

Dick Gregory's Natural Diet for Folks Who Eat

Cookin' with Mother Nature

DICK GREGORY

Edited by James R. McGraw with Alvenia M. Fulton

....

New York: Perennial Library, 1973

171 pages

*T*HE *NEW YORK TIMES* described Gregory's work as "an introduction to natural foods written with an eye to good health and an ear for the witty line." The popular comedian's book, largely instructional along with some recipes, was aimed at redirecting the eating habits of black folks.

The chapter "A Body Owner's Manual" describes proper organ function and the burdens that dietary habits place on essential filtering functions of the liver, kidneys, lungs, and colon. He explains the difference between food and "somethin' to eat" in chapter 5, which includes a shopping list of essential minerals and the foods that provide them. Next, he takes a critical view of the soul food movement, calling it "genocide," and lectures parents (and prospective parents) on the benefits of teaching kids to eat right from the start. The final chapters provide a prescription for living a wholesome and healthy life, with an emphasis on the "curative" powers of a natural food diet associated with regular fasting. There are also recipes for juicing, and menus and recipes for maintaining a balanced diet and healthy weight. ❧

The Way I Do Things

DELMA MILLSAP

....

Columbus, Ohio, 1974

124 pages

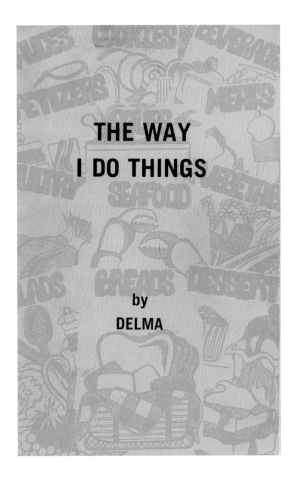

THE WAY
I DO THINGS

by

DELMA

MILLSAP SELF-PUBLISHED this book as "the best way to share my love of people, my love of food and the experience gained over many years." Her book is straightforward and uncomplicated, with a plain, almost impersonal quality: no photos, standard printing-company chapter dividers, two or three recipes per page. Recipes lean toward fresh ingredients (mostly), simple preparation, and a generous use of wine—marsala, sauternes, Madeira.

A few southern standards are present—Black-Eyed Peas with Ham and Okra (seasoned with sliced ham), Skillet Cornbread, Spoon Bread, Benne Wafers, Cafe Brulot—but gone are the vegetables long-simmered with pig parts and the cheap foods of the soul experience. The book is intended to appeal to a broad range of tastes and ethnicities. Cases in point: pizzalike canapés she calls Bambinos, a dish of chicken sauced with Madeira, the Italian custard zabaglione; *kefta* (Greek meatballs), Malayan Curry, Curry Broiled Chicken Wings, Bijon Buffet (a dish of pork, chicken, shrimp, and rice sticks simmered in soy sauce), an Asian-flavored salad of water chestnuts and bean sprouts, Huevos Picantes, and Mexican Pork Chops. Maida Heatter's Chocolate Mousse-Torte gives a nod to celebrity chef cooking. An index would be useful.

"Delma Millsap earned her reputation as a gourmet cook," writes Sally K. Roberts in the introduction. She "became familiar with almost every phase of food preparation" at the Maramor restaurant in Columbus, Ohio; headed the salad department at Columbus Coated Fabrics Company; cooked for the Beta Theta Pi Fraternity at Ohio State University; cooked at the Columbus Beach Club in northern Michigan; and operated her own catering company, which proved to Ohioans that "a Delma Dinner is not only a culinary experience, but it is truly a conversation piece." ❧

Vegetable Soup Activities

MARY AND RAY SHEPARD

....

New York: Citation, 1975
86 pages

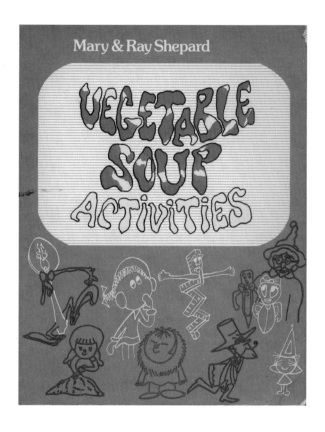

T HE PURPOSE OF THE *Vegetable Soup* children's television show (1975–1978) was to
"counter the negative and destructive effects of
racial isolation" on children who "almost never
see, play with, or go to school with children of
ethnic or racial groups other than their own."
The series encouraged young viewers to discover
by "doing" in different ethnic ways, including
crafts, games, recipes, language activities, and
reading. This companion workbook ensured that
kids could benefit even if they never watched the
program.

The authors were educators, so it was natural
for their projects to be suitable for classrooms,
home, church, and school. There are nine games

and eleven crafts, including making an early
American immigrant house, designing a Chinese
kite, creating a Haitian drum, and doing origami,
the Japanese art of paper folding. Two additional
sections, "Children's Questions" and "Recommended Children's Books," explain the difference
between Asian facial features, show the use and
function of black American slang in American
language, and provide resources for further study.

"Cooking with Woody the Spoon" presents
thirteen recipes for ethnic cooking. Recipes for
Afro-American cornmeal pancakes, Brazilian
fudge, Puerto Rican Rice Pudding, Southern
Sweet Potato Pudding, and Soul Spareribs show
kids the meaning of diversity. ❧

Soul to Soul

A Vegetarian Soul Food Cookbook

MARY KEYES BURGESS

....

Santa Barbara, California: Woodbridge, 1976
158 pages

cALTHOUGH THE AUTHOR grew up in
Texas with a taste for pork-rich dishes
of soul food, health concerns for herself and
her family motivated her to change her eating
habits and begin experimenting with the meat
substitutes available on grocery shelves and in
the freezers of health food stores. She published
a catalogue of more than 250 family favorites
adapted in her kitchen "laboratory" to demonstrate the "delicious taste that was possible to
create without using any meat."

So what gives this author's soul food its soul?
Textured vegetable protein in bacon-like chips,
ham-like chunks (used in pink beans), beef-style
chunks (pepper steak), chicken-style chunks
(gumbo), bacon-textured slices called Stripples
(cracklin' bread and hot lettuce salad), La Lerma
Terkettes (fried chicken), canned vegeburger
(lasagne), canned Nuteena, canned gluten steaks,
and bouillon. Black-and-white photographs and
a sixteen-page color insert help readers envision
finished dishes that don't often look anything
like the meat-based originals.

Burgess demonstrates a spirit of improvisation
in low-cost recipes such as cactus (nopalitos),
green tomato pie, and melon cake. Dream Whip
stands in for cream in sweet potato pie. Pears,
apples, peaches, cantaloupe, honeydew, cherries,
and nuts make "a good summer dessert" in If You
Have Fruit Pie. ❧

200 Years of Black Cookery, Volumes 1 and 2

BEA MOTEN

....

Indianapolis: Leonbea, 1976
97 pages (vol. 1)
143 pages (vol. 2)

IN THE INTRODUCTION TO Bea Moten's collection of 250 soul recipes (with 33 African originals), she writes, "Cooking was one of the first creative art forms of Black Americans." And she hopes the two-book series "will help you to rediscover an appreciation for Soul and African Food."

Moten was the narrator of a United Nations radio program called *African Profilers*. She connected African American heritage foods and culinary practices to the motherland, adding to the work of other authors of the time to establish culinary expertise that predated slavery. Among the points she makes:

- Most kitchens in many parts of Africa were completely separated from the main house.
- Food was often cooked on an open fire.
- A common cook's grinding tool resembles the mortar and pestle: a large flat stone and small round stone rubbed together to crush red pepper, okra, and peanuts.
- Greens were grown in abundance and eaten in most regions. Soul greens were cooked with ham, jowl bacon, or salt pork. In West Africa, *zom* (spinach with meat) included tomato sauce or fresh tomatoes, finished with a dollop of peanut butter. *Zom*, she said, could be prepared with beef and fish, such as canned mackerel or tuna. Africans preferred dried fish.

- Cabbage was plentiful in the southern regions of Africa. In Zambia, it is served with ground raw peanuts, tomatoes, and onions; travel further south to Lesotho for stuffed cabbage or spinach sautéed with onions and a sprinkle of curry powder.
- Black-eyed peas prepared the soul way get their flavor from pork parts. In Africa, they were first cooked and then mixed into a paste and fried into patties. In Liberia, a country colonized by freed slaves, the protein-rich beans were soaked overnight and rubbed between the palms to remove the skins and black eyes. The naked beans were blended with a small amount of water, seasoned lightly with salt and pepper, and deep-fried as a snack. Ethiopian *metin shuro* is ground cooked black-eyed peas, beans, and lentils together.

Volume 1 contains more than two hundred recipes for old-fashioned southern dishes organized into four sections: "Main Dishes," "Desserts," "Breads," and "African Recipes." Each section concludes with a series of miscellaneous facts and tips, including vegetables as medicine; household and culinary uses of buttermilk; natural pesticides for gardens; tips for setting up a successful buffet; and freezing dos and don'ts. Her desserts are still popular today as old-fashioned favorites, such as Oatmeal Cake with Baked Frosting, Sour Cream Indian Pudding, and Blackberry Pickle (preserves made without sealing).

She collected the African dishes during interviews with at least one hundred African ambassadors, foreign ministers, and presidents. Curiously, the meat tenderizer Accent is used throughout, while at the same time the recipes are laced with natural flavor enhancers: cayenne peppers, onions, garlic, bell peppers, cardamom, cinnamon, cumin, and curry powder.

Volume 2 contains recipes only—no introduction or anecdotes—and merely expands the offerings, upping the proteins to include one-dish casseroles and skillet meals, adding many more personal touches, and playing multiple variations on a single theme.

"Appetizers, Beverages & Snacks" offers adaptations of traditional favorites—French salad dressing and crabmeat added to stuffed eggs, cooked chili spooned into the center of biscuits, green onions mixed with cottage cheese then shaped into a mold for a fancy onion dip.

Her bread recipes add cultural embellishments: Raised Mexican Corn Bread, a yeast bread rich with cheese, jalapeno peppers, and cheese; Monkey Bread, not a recipe so much as a technique for baking standard yeast dough in a tube pan; Pita Bread; Yorkshire Puffs; and Gyros Sandwich.

Cakes and cake mixes are decorated and imbued with Jell-O, mayonnaise, sherry, raw apples, butterscotch, 7-Up, a Harvey Wallbanger cocktail (Galliano liqueur, orange juice, and vodka), fruit cocktail, yams, Milky Way candy bars, vanilla wafers, and pistachio pudding mix. She laces pound cakes with nuts, bourbon, lemon, brown sugar, and five flavorings.

Dill and sour cream give summer potato salad a twist. Kahlua spikes a dipping sauce for lamb skewers and chili. Chittlin' Gravy is served hot over rice or potatoes. ❧

SQUASH FANCHONETTS

1 round tablespoon of butter	2 eggs well beaten
1/2 pt. of sugar	1/2 teaspoon pulverized cinnamon
1/2 teaspoon pulverized ginger	1 generous pt. of warm, rich milk

Line patty pans with pie crust; then fill with a custard made of winter squash, stewed and pressed through a sieve, and while warm add the ingredients above: After the shells have been placed in a moderate oven add enough more of the custard to well fill the shells, as the mixture shrinks in baking. When the custard is firm in the center the pastry should be removed from the tins. Serve when cold, placing a bit of whipped cream onto each top.

The Taste of Country Cooking

EDNA LEWIS

....

New York: Knopf, 1976
Paperback edition, 1990
260 pages

I AM NOT CERTAIN which I relish more: the recipes for delicious country cooking or the storytelling, and that is probably just the way Lewis would have liked it. The author relives her experiences of growing up on the family farm in Freetown, Virginia, and we, her readers, are right there with her, gathering wild strawberries, canning, rendering lard, finding walnuts, picking persimmons, making fruitcake—doing "the things that made life so rewarding." Learning history never felt so good.

Lewis's family was the last of the freed slaves who settled Freetown. She herself had "no children to remember and carry on," so she wrote to pass along ideas about natural farming to future generations, sharing how things were done in the past so that readers might "learn firsthand from those who worked hard, loved the land, and relished the fruits of their labor."

Her recollections, menus, and recipes are grouped seasonally: sheep shearing and a spring lunch to be eaten after picking wild mushrooms; an early summer lunch of the season's delicacies and a prepared-ahead summer dinner; a breakfast after hog butchering and a dinner for fall hunting season; in winter, a Christmas Eve Supper, a dinner celebrating the last of the barnyard fowl, and a dinner of chicken and dumplings and warm gingerbread.

Most pages are decorated with delicate illustrations of ingredients, livestock, pots, pans, tools, and equipment, and with images of hardworking people in the field, barnyard, or kitchen house. Lengthy sidebars and headnotes elaborate on subjects like Christmastime in Freetown kitchens, wheat threshing, and hog killing. Elegant typefaces and bold lettering convey femininity, and the recipes shine with intimate details, cooking tips, shopping recommendations, and preparation tricks.

If I could ask Lewis what she was thinking of when she published her second book of farm-fresh cookery, I am certain that without hesitation she would say, "You, my dear." I was awed

Summer

by Lewis from the first moment I saw her, some years ago at a professional meeting of registered dietitians in Los Angeles. I noticed a small crowd in the hotel lobby buzzing around a statuesque African American woman with a magnetic smile, her graying hair swept neatly into a bun worn low at the neck. I shamelessly joined the groupie gaggle, which was clamoring for autographs in the way that paparazzi scratch and claw for snapshots of superstars. The regal lady leaned in close, whispered a few tender words of encouragement, and then signed the paperback edition of her first cookbook: "To Toni Tipton With Best Wishes Edna Lewis." As we got to know each other better, I told her about my desire to reclaim the reputation of black cooks. Her tales of achieving culinary mastery as an executive chef and champion of artistic African American cooking strengthened my resolve. She emboldened me with a precious handwritten letter and an exhortation: "Leave no stone unturned." ❧

WHEAT-HARVESTING MIDDAY DINNER

Platters of Sliced Boiled Pork Shoulder

Beef à la Mode

Pan-Fried Chicken with Cream Gravy

Casserole of Sage-Flavored Pork Tenderloin

First Cabbage of the Season with Scallions

Pork-Flavored Green Beans

Spicy Baked Tomatoes

Whipped White Potatoes

Hot Buttered Beets

Corn Pudding

Cucumber Pickles

Pearl Muffins—Biscuits

Butter

Fresh Blackberry Cobbler

Jelly Layer Cake

Iced Tea

Lemonade

Buttermilk

103

The Secret of Creole Cooking

B. F. TRAPPEY'S SONS

....

Fourteenth edition
New Iberia, Louisiana, 1976
50 pages

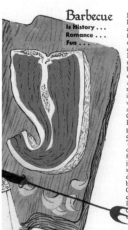

Barbecue

Is History . . .
Romance . . .
Fun . . .

Barbecue is a magic word.

Barbecue suggests the mingled aroma of wood smoke hovering lazily over pits and pans, and of brown-crusted meat oozing with spicy goodness . . . the cheer of bright, darting flames and the gay chatter of family and friends delicately hungry . . . appetites sharpened by fresh air and bright sunshine . . . good fellowship warmed outwardly by glowing coals and inwardly by pungent sauces exuding the fragrance of the Indies.

Everybody loves a barbecue! Small wonder—the taste for barbecuing is inherited. It is the second oldest form of cookery. Simple broiling was first. The first food ever cooked by the magic of fire was a chunk or joint of meat thrust on a reed or green stick and held over flames or coals. No barbecuing here: simply searing and heating.

Ages later, as cavemen's taste progressed from raw to broiled meat, they discovered the tantalizing savors of woodland herbs, roots, and berries. Long before they learned to boil in earthen vessels, they crushed leaves and berries over sizzling fowl, fish, or joint of venison. Perhaps they made a sauce of tallow melted in a clam shell, spiced it with herbs and drizzled it over cooking meat. Here, barbecue was born.

Our colonial forebears turned barbecues into day-long shindigs with political overtones. Freshly-dug pits underlaid with hickory coals and overlaid with succulent meat from pig, lamb, goat, and young chicken provided the main dish after long hours of slow cooking.

There are sauces of an infinite variety of flavors, colors, and consistencies. One that is cool to a Texan's tongue may scorch that of a Maine Down-Easter. Millions like a garlic flavor and others shun it. Millions more like onions, but some plead allergies and others just don't like them. But most Americans agree that barbecue sauce should have some sort of spice, sparkle, zing, zest, and kick, with more than a hint of wild, woodsy; outdoor flavor. It need not be fiery or fierce, but it should have a barbecue flavor. To any barbecue sauce that you make or originate don't overlook Trappey's Mexi-Pep Sauce. One or two ounces added to any sauce will produce the barbecue tang. Use according to quantity of sauce that is produced. This can be determined by taste.

For small barbecues, make the sauce at home and carry it in fruit jar or gallon bottle. Quantity amounts are often made at the site in hotel-sized kettles. Any leftover sauce will keep well in refrigerator.

— 38 —

Pot Barbecued Hamburgers

¾ pound beef, ground	¼ teaspoon Mexi-Pep
¼ pound pork, ground	fat, barbecue sauce
½ cup bread crumbs	3 tablespoons chopped onion
1½ teaspoons salt	
1½ teaspoons Chef-Magic Kitchen Seasoning	

Combine beef, pork, onion, crumbs, salt, Chef-Magic Kitchen Seasoning and Mexi-Pep. Form into patties and brown slowly in fat. Cover with barbecue sauce and cook 15 minutes longer, turning occasionally. Serves 6.

Pit Barbecue Chicken

4 fryers 2½ to 3 pounds	1 tablespoon paprika
2 tablespoons salt	1 teaspoon garlic powder
1 tablespoon black pepper	
2 tablespoons Spice-Up Table Seasoning	

Purchase chickens approximately 18 to 24 hours before barbecuing, clean thoroughly, split in half. Mix all seasoning ingredients thoroughly and apply to chicken using approximately 1 level teaspoon to each half of chicken, rub thoroughly on the inside and outside. Place all chickens after seasoning in large pan covered with aluminum foil and allow to marinate in refrigerator. You can't over-season because liquid from chicken will run during marinate period. To barbecue, place chicken on grill, bone side down, allow to remain for 20 to 30 minutes. Fire should be from 23 to 24 inches from the grill, and reduced to embers when charcoal and briquettes are used. With an oven type pit, more of the heat is re-tained. Turn chicken, flesh down and with barbecue sauce, southern style, paint the bone side. After 20 minutes or more, turn chicken again and paint flesh side. After two or three turnings, painting each time turned, the fire will have died down to a point where the heat will keep chicken warm until ready to serve. Total time for barbecuing between 2½ to 3 hours. Serve with garlic bread which has been heated in the oven. Serve 8.

Broiled Barbecued Chicken

2 chickens, about 2½ to 3 lbs. apiece
Season according to suggestion see Pit Barbecue Chicken

Salt and pepper chicken to suit taste, let stand overnight. Split down back, put into broiler pan and brush with southern style barbecue sauce. Brown well on both sides. Turn often, brushing with sauce each time. Broil slowly or if not ready to serve, when broiling is done, about 1½ hours, they may be set in a roaster and placed in oven, covered, until time to serve. Serve ½ chicken to a person.

Southern Style Barbecue Sauce

1 large onion, grated	1 tablespoon salt
1½ tablespoons brown sugar	¼ teaspoon black pepper
1 tablespoon dry mustard	3 cups tomato sauce
1 6-oz. bottle Trappey's Creole Barbecue Sauce	
1 cup vinegar	1¼ tablespoons Mexi-Pep
½ 5-oz. bottle Trappey's Worcestershire	
⅓ cup butter, margarine, or salad oil	

NOTE: For oven barbecuing, use same ingredients and add 1 cup water

— 39 —

Y OU CAN TELL by the bandana-headed mammy bent over an old black pot perched on an open fire that this promotional booklet for Mexi-Pep Louisiana Hot Sauce is yet another iteration of the Jemima code. Her full figure and words on the page together remind consumers that a black presence is the essence of all that is delicious and wonderful about Creole cuisine. The writers behind this collection of nearly 150 classic recipes made it their mission to translate value from black culinary mysteries to their product.

As expected, the objective is to convince consumers to buy more hot sauce. To do so, they spin a winsome history of the "petticoat rebellion which started Creole cooking," grumbling that no matter how closely one follows a recipe, the true gift of taste lies in the seasoning and spice—the realm of the Negro cook—unless you know their secret ingredient. To reinvent the tastes created by her knowledgeable hands, you simply stir or sprinkle a bottle of Trappey's into jambalaya, grillades, gumbo, okra and tomatoes, yams, and myriad Creolized meat, seafood, and vegetable dishes. Other revelations address her seasonings, the types of fat she uses, and the rule "season to taste," punctuated by an explanation of the role of Trappey's products in giving dishes that unique Creole *je ne sais quoi.* ✒

My Mother Cooked My Way through Harvard with These Creole Recipes

OSCAR A. ROGERS

RECIPES BY MRS. WALTER TILLMAN

············

Hattiesburg: University and College Press of
    Mississippi, 1972

Reprint, Orangeburg, South Carolina: Claflin
    College, 1977

102 pages

$\mathcal{T}$HE AFFECTIONATE tribute to a loving
mother is just as delicious as the 200-plus
recipes assembled here as an homage to her
life and work as a cook in the homes of leading
families in New Orleans. The author's mother
was known affectionately as Pinkie, and her
dedication to family, church, and community
were defined through food.

During the Depression, the family lived in
Natchez, Mississippi, and lived on grits, salt
meat, sweet potatoes, home-canned vegetables—
like little June peas—and fresh milk supple-
mented from grandmother's farm. The author's
memories reflect the seasonal eating that defined
poor folks back then. The recipes are well written, with clear instructions, precise amounts, and
cooking times. And a few Creole flourishes bring
life to otherwise standard southern fare. ❧

Penn School & Sea Islands Heritage Cookbook

PENN HERITAGE CELEBRATION
COMMITTEE

....

St. Helena Island, South Carolina, 1978
Reprint, 1987
120 pages

*T*HIS COMMUNITY cookbook is dedicated to the founding teachers of the freedmen's school, which offered industrial education in carpentry, blacksmithing, wheelwrighting, harness making, cobbling, mechanics, basket weaving, agriculture, and teacher training. The cookbook offers more than 250 southern staples and Lowcountry specialties, plus rich historical lore and photographs that fill out the sea islanders' culinary story.

A word of caution: the book's organization is a little hard to follow. Photographs introduce each chapter, and a brief summary of the image appears at the end of the chapter, following the recipes. The dishes don't necessarily match the image.

Still, I learned much about the food prepared and served at a gala Labor Day celebration held "on the green" in the 1900s, even though the accompanying recipes for gumbo, okra and tomato soup, and a variety of seafood dips, while interesting, didn't reflect the menu described in the historical sketch—although recipes for those dishes do appear in subsequent chapters.

Likewise, the photo that introduced the "Main Dish" section showed islanders harvesting white potatoes, which they raised for cash and food in the years preceding the Great Depression. The chapter recipes that follow are largely built around rice: Red Rice, Chicken-rice Purlo, Hoppin John, Shrimp Fried Rice, Wild Rice and Oysters, "A Good Jambalaya," Rice and Peas, Carnival Jambalaya, Stuffed Peppers, Indian Rice, and two wild-card dishes: Jamaica Pepper Pot and Butcherin' Time Scrapple.

The remaining chapters, photos, and recipes make a lot more sense. The image of an agricultural student feeding chickens, at the beginning of the "Meats and Poultry" section, paints a picture of the pride of island families, who displayed their harvest and livestock every year in late October at Penn School's Farmers' Fair. The photo accompanying the "Seafoods" chapter depicts a fisherman and his boat at the shoreline. An island native named Emory S. Campbell describes a sea island fisherman's handmade tools, the variety of fishes caught, and Saturday-night fish fries and oyster roasts.

A photograph of the school's Demonstration Farm stand introduces vegetable recipes. Home economics students working the dough bowl ("Breads"), displaying their sweet treats ("Desserts"), and serving beverages front the remaining divisions and recipes. Campbell's recollections of hunting without guns and ammunition highlight the dizzying effort required by uneducated bondsmen to secure meat for the family dinner table in the years before and after freedom, making wild game recipes such as Dove Supreme, Squirrel Fricassee, Boneless Deer Meat with Gravy, Deer Patties, and Barbecued Raccoon seem all the more dazzling. ❧

Recipes from
Our Best Cooks

Cooking with Soul

BLACK FAMILY ASSOCIATION,
CENTRAL CONTRA COSTA COUNTY
(CALIFORNIA)

....

Lenexa, Kansas: Cookbook Publishers, 1978
132 pages

Don't let the title fool you—this is more than another gathering of pig tails and greens. The Black Family Association believed that when it came to cooking with soul, the words "variety" and "cookbook" were "synonymically matched." The committee that compiled this nondescript fund-raising cookbook set out to prove that cooks of all cultures cook with soul. The book will be remembered more for the wide net it casts to catch the theme than for its design, composition, stock dividers, standard spice guides, and kitchen charts.

Recipes reflecting multiple ethnic and regional backgrounds were submitted primarily by Northern California friends and neighbors, but also from as far away as Mineola, New York; El Paso, Texas; and Pittsburgh, Pennsylvania. To illustrate the point that there is no cultural or regional limit to make-do cookery, the team included Italian, Asian, southern, Creole, Mexican, Hungarian, and Greek dishes, plus a whimsical dish called Mosquito Knees and Rice, a folk recipe of unknown origin that begins, "Catch mosquitoes, being extremely careful not to crush knees." ❧

Spoonbread and Strawberry Wine

Recipes and Reminiscences of a Family

NORMA JEAN AND CAROLE DARDEN

....

Garden City, New York: Anchor, 1978
Fawcett Crest edition, 1980
Harlem Moon trade paperback edition, 2003
288 pages

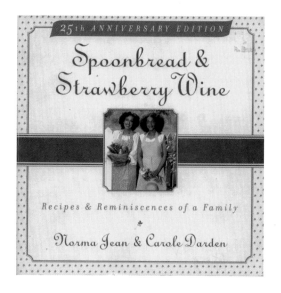

REMAKES OF Hollywood films are seldom as revered as the original. Not so with the twenty-fifth-anniversary edition of this charming family memoir with recipes, written by two sisters who loved to cook—especially together. After years watching the womenfolk do their eloquent dance around the family's kitchens, they decided it was time to "capture their elusive magic, strengthen family ties, and learn more about our ancestors' history and tradition." They wrote to long-lost relatives and friends and trekked across the United States in pursuit of heirloom recipes and memories. They describe the outcome thus: "This book is the reflection of our pilgrimage 'home,' which revealed to us not only good food but the origins, early struggles, and life-styles of our family."

In the introduction, the sisters recall fond childhood memories: catching June bugs and making mud pies under Aunt Lizzie's peach tree, watching Cousin Artelia making dandelion wine, listening to Uncle William's ham radio set, and walking along dirt roads to "old man Shade's" drugstore for pineapple ice. The duo also located photographs to illustrate the culinary skills they acquired along the way, such as wine making, canning and preserving, bread making, and preparing home cosmetics.

The book is organized around the Darden and Scarborough family tree. Photographs of beloved family members, tender anecdotes, and recipes capture each relative.

The 2003 edition is a delicate repackaging that has all the "culture and high drama" of the original and then some. The contents illuminate and are still affectionate—the adorable picture of the authors on the cover, their grandfather's mealtime prayer, the quaint illustrations, delicious interpretations of standard southern dishes, beauty tips, herbal cures, and all the heirloom family photographs. It is the layout that has changed.

The paperback edition, like so many of the black cookbooks published in the 1970s, squishes the recipes onto the page so tightly that no one could really be expected to cook from the tiny print, which often ran into the binding. That all changed in the 2003 version. Elegant script lettering sets off each recipe. The formulas are well spaced on the page, with plenty of white space, making the recipes simple and clear to use.

And please, do use them. They are lovely adaptations of southern standbys: North Carolina Turkey Butt Souse substitutes for the head cheese typically made from pork; pineapple embellishes cranberry sauce; barbecue sauce sweetens baked ham; and pimiento ornaments green beans. The Dardens bake deviled crab into a loaf, crumble cornflakes into the morning omelet, and create Aunt Lillian's cosmetics from ingredients grown in the garden. ❧

Face:

LEMON NOURISHING CREAM

1 egg yolk
½ cup olive oil

1 tablespoon fresh lemon juice
3 drops essence of lemon oil

Beat egg yolk with an electric beater at high speed until light and lemony. Add a few drops of olive oil at a time, beating vigorously until mixture becomes thick and creamy. Add lemon juice, then essence of lemon or a few drops of your favorite perfume. Blend well, jar, and keep this super-rich cream refrigerated. Massage into the skin as a night cream.

Two parting beauty secrets we received from Aunt Lil on our last visit:

"Peace of mind is radiated in one's countenance, and it's not so easy to come by in times of trouble unless you work at it every day. I begin and end my day by reading "The Daily Word" [a religious pamphlet with inspirational thoughts for each day]. And once a week I take a special, long, leisurely, floral-scented bath, preferably by candlelight.

"During my bath I sort out the weeds of the last week and sow the seeds for the coming one. In life you just have to keep moving—stepping higher all the time."

SOUL
FOOD

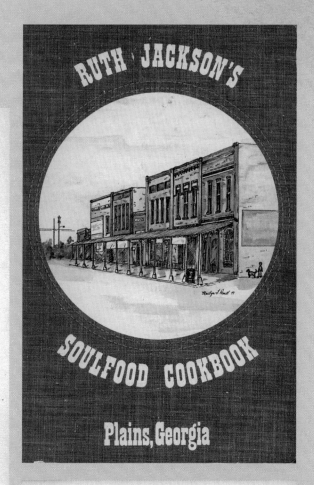

RUTH JACKSON'S

SOULFOOD COOKBOOK

Plains, Georgia

TURNIP GREENS

1 bunch turnips	1 tablespoon salt
1 pound side pork	1½ quarts water
1 tablespoon sugar	½ cup Crisco oil

Pick turnips and wash until there is no grit or dirt. Boil side pork about 20 minutes. Add turnips, salt, sugar, oil and water gradually. Cook 30 minutes or until done. Serves 8 to 10.
Carrie Evans

FRIED ONION WITH EGGS

1 stick oleo	6 eggs
1 cup water	2 large bunches fresh onion
1 tablespoon salt	1 teaspoon black pepper

Wash and cut onion. Melt oleo in large frying pan. Put onion in hot oleo and slowly add water. Cook until tender and then add egg. Cook 10 minutes longer.
Ruth Jackson

Ruth Jackson's Soul Food Cookbook

Plains, Georgia

RUTH JACKSON

....

Memphis, Tennessee: Wimmer Brothers, 1978
94 pages

Lebanon Baptist Church dinner in the annex.

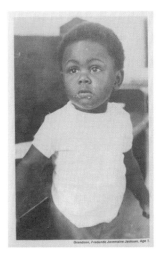
Grandson, Fredande Jeremaine Jackson, Age 1

To HEAR THE EDITORS of this book tell it, southern and soul cooking are creative arts "performed naturally" by rural cooks: "No one outside can capture its flavor on paper." But Jackson wrote down her secrets so that the rest of the country could be part of the "great tradition of Southern cooking."

Culinary theory handed down from family and perfected while cooking church meals developed Jackson's talents and her culinary spirit. With these recipes, you don't need to return to the "tiny farm cabins, with blue smoke curling up into the gentle Southern winter air," where southern and soul food was created. All you need is love.

The book capitalized on Jimmy Carter's presidency and the cooking traditions of their shared hometown of Plains, Georgia, to legitimize Jackson's spiritualized southern food. Some of the book's five sections start off with her words of wisdom. At other times, a history lesson and photos of family and friends enjoying food and fellowship complement the subject. Also included are a few recipes for favorite dishes by named contributors—probably fellow parishioners, given the amount of attention devoted to the spiritual aspects of soul cookery.

The first section, "Soul Food," is accompanied by an adorable full-page photo of Jackson's one-year-old grandson. It features a dozen dishes that Jackson claimed were "the very essence of the American rural spirit," such as head cheese, collards, fried vegetables (onions with eggs, okra, green tomatoes, cucumbers), chitterlings, liver pudding, and squash casserole.

Section 2, "Vegetables," promotes the "important spiritual qualities in soul food," a hearty fellowship created over steaming pots mingled with the spiritual fellowship of the church and the amount of love in the hands of the cook. Here, candied yams, peas, sweet potato casserole, macaroni and cheese, smothered cabbage, and a section on salads and dressings accompany photos of church members enjoying a buffet dinner while seated in the annex at long tables covered with tablecloths and flowers.

In section 3, "Dessert," Jackson looks back on her childhood and the women who gathered fresh fruits for rich, buttery pies and bubbling cobblers. Caramel cake and other sweet treats, such as a sugared piecrust snack called Butter Roll, which will remind some of Mexican crullers (churros), were central to the family's household.

Jackson tackles the "mystery" of southern cooking in section 4, but without all of the frou-frou observable in mainstream cookbooks. Her main dish offerings, in fact, are plain—meats, poultry, and fish seasoned with salt, pepper, garlic, and prepared condiments such as catsup and canned soup.

The closing chapter tells the black history of Plains, illustrated with a drawing of the Plains Community Center, where Jackson was employed, and photographs of distinctive residents and events. A glossary of cooking terms and a table of measurements finish off this intimate testament to country living, which is bound with front and back boards resembling a farmer's dungarees, the back cover like the butt of overalls or work jeans. ❧

Creole Feast

*15 Master Chefs of New Orleans
Reveal Their Secrets*

NATHANIEL BURTON AND
RUDY LOMBARD

....

New York: Random House, 1978
198 pages

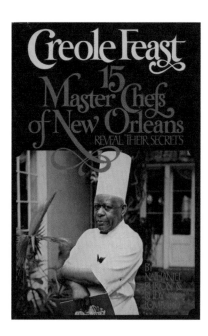

CATALOGUE OF revered Creole recipes gathered from friends who just happen to be professional chefs is a remarkable salute to the men and women who lived in the shadows of New Orleans's most acclaimed restaurants. These masters were self-taught as well as formally trained. They measured by touch, determined doneness by sound and smell. And as the introduction puts it, they "perfected the art of Creole cooking in almost complete anonymity and frequently in a hostile environment."

To understand the true accomplishment of these two authors is to understand the accomplishments of their subjects. The book is divided into two parts in order to help readers do just that. First, we are introduced to the chefs of a previous generation, including Louis Bluestein, Leona Victor, Lena Richard, and Christine Warren. Then in part one, elite chefs describe their work, methods, and expertise in a narrative style that is entertaining, engaging, and informative. The men and women who make up this prestigious circle must have talked for hours about their common experiences, training, methods, and favorite dishes.

Nathaniel Burton cooked and taught in many places, most notably Broussard's. He lists the characteristics that make a chef exceptional, including knowledge of fundamental techniques such as how to season with fresh herbs, make soups and sauces, and use quality ingredients.

Raymond Thomas Sr. of the French Market Seafood House loves to cook and it shows. He also is passionate about high-quality ingredients, fresh seasonings, and food that is "beautiful."

Leah Chase developed a family lunch counter into a landmark among New Orleans restaurants with her attention to detail, making sure that even a humble sandwich was made well on excellent French bread.

Annie Laura Squalls isn't afraid to experiment. When she encounters a new recipe, she works it out first in her mind, imagining new ingredients and the ways they can infuse excitement into trusted favorites.

Louis Evans says he is an old-fashioned cook. He doesn't take short cuts and believes that a culinary education is important, but adds that chefs must possess a confident work ethic and a "fierce pride about what they are doing in the kitchen" in order to be successful.

Austin Leslie reveals his secrets for the best fried chicken, the old-fashioned way to make potato salad, ways to keep vegetables tender and sweet, which seasonings bring out the best in seafood, and the process for pickling pork.

Charles Bailey is devoted to fruit and seafood, Coq au Vin and Roast Long Island Duckling. He tells readers how to handle delicate veal and confides the special ingredient in his potato pancakes: a splash of pineapple juice.

Henry Carr talks about the difference between sautéing and simmering, when to use water and when stock, and the best time to add herbs and seasonings to the pot.

"Corinne Dunbar's is a family affair," says the owner, James Plauche. "There are no chefs, no menu. Just one superb meal prepared by women who learned their art both from each other and from each generation of cooks that preceded them." As one of those women, Rosa Barganier progressed from dishwasher to head cook, and her unique ways with game hens, pecan sauce, and red bean soup are unfolded here. She assures readers that her technique for rolling biscuits won't "intimidate you."

Malcom Ross owes his skills to his training at Galatoire's, where he perfected trout amandine, eggplant, shrimp, oysters brochette, and even onion rings at the fry station. He devised a two-handed trick for making hollandaise sauce, applying a tactic involving vinegar that keeps the sauce smooth until serving time.

Expert advice from Larry Williamson, Sherman Crayton, Louise Joshua, Letitia Parker, Rochester Anderson, and Charles Kirkland instills a range of tips and techniques.

Part two, "The Recipes," is an elegant presentation of more than 300 revered Creole dishes, the most popular of them appearing more than once to allow for different interpretations of a classic dish (Red Beans and Hollandaise Sauce each appear four times, for instance). Of the chefs, the authors proclaim, "Their genius relies largely on experience, combined with the full use and development of all five senses."

Breads, Crêpes and New Orleans Specialties

French Bread

NATHANIEL BURTON

½ cup milk
1 cake yeast
5 cups sifted flour
1½ cups water

1 tablespoon sugar
1 teaspoon salt
1 tablespoon butter

Preheat oven to 375°. Scald milk and let stand until it gets lukewarm. Add yeast to milk. Mix flour, water, sugar, salt and butter together in large bowl. Add yeast and milk mixture to flour mixture. Cover dough with a cloth and let it rise in a warm place for 2 hours. Dough will double in size. Remove dough to table and knead for 5 minutes. Grease a baking sheet. Divide dough and shape into three loaves. Place on sheet pan and let it double in size a second time. Bake at least 25 minutes. *Makes 3 loaves*

Bless the Cook

BESSIE L. MUNSON

....

Arlington, Texas: Arlington Century, 1978
194 pages plus index

Bless the Cook

by
BESSIE L. MUNSON

COOKBOOK AUTHOR. Caterer. Community servant. Remarkable woman. Munson begins her story, with the pronouncement that this volume is "more than a cookbook." And so it is.

There is no table of contents to guide recipe foragers. The book jumps right into the meat and potatoes of her life and flows like a river from one fantastic food memory to another. It is an eloquent collection of essays with recipes, enacting the author's passion for teaching and empowering others through food. A handful of illustrations guide readers in the proper folding of egg rolls, fluting piecrust edges, and achieving the finished look of Raggedy Ann Salad.

The book begins with a loving tribute to life on her grandparents' farm near Bartlett, Texas, a table where the food was always plentiful and sumptuous. The storyline cascades as more fond food recollections emanate from grandmother's house—fried-fish suppers in the country, old-fashioned country picnics and after-church dinners on the ground, hot yeast breads for box suppers to auction as fund-raisers for the church and for the school lunch box.

As a caterer, Munson shared the "privilege of food service" everywhere—parties for governors, national leaders, statesmen, Hollywood celebrities, and singing groups. She dedicated "beautiful times" to cooking and eating with her children too, and helped plan and cook with emotionally troubled girls in Los Angeles. She taught cooking classes in Arlington, Texas, and wrote fondly of festive and wonderful gatherings around the family table.

A half-dozen photographs serve as the chapter dividers. They show off the Mexican- and Chinese-themed casseroles on her buffet, the fluffy pie display at the Fort Worth Air Traffic Control Center, and her "spectacular Christmas menu," the Holiday Cocktail Party. The Real Man's Patio Party features a tower of cheeses with fruit, assorted crackers with party breads, marinated lobster or crab claws, a relish tray of raw fresh vegetables, grilled burgers with "secret sauce," hot buttered herb bread and hot buns, and a mix of spinach, hard-boiled eggs, and bacon she called Men's Easy Salad. She built menus around vegetables and showed her cosmopolitan flair with dishes like Paella Concoction.

There are enough creative cakes here to fill a bakery—decorated with fresh or dried fruits; spiked with instant coffee and wine; laced with mayonnaise and corn syrup; and made dense from grated carrots, flake coconut, and nuts. She takes shortcuts, too, substituting pistachio or vanilla pudding mix for custard and saving time with cake mix, prepared sponge layer cake, and vanilla wafers. ❧

Method
In large saucepan, sprinkle unflavored gelatin over apple juice; stir over low heat until gelatin dissolves, about 3 minutes. Add cranberry juice cocktail and chill, stirring occasionally, until mixture is slightly thicker consistency than unbeaten egg whites. Fold in apples, celery and nuts: divide mixture into two 11x7x1½ inch pans and chill until firm. To serve, cut each pan into squares and serve on lettuce-lined plates. Makes about 30 servings.

ORANGE AND OLIVE SALAD

2 large oranges, peeled
4 tablespoons dry white wine
¼ cup olive oil
1 small green onion, minced
  salt and pepper to taste
  dash of oregano
1 cup pitted black olives

Method
Slice oranges in ¼-inch slices and place in large bowl. Mix wine, oil, onion, salt, pepper and oregano. Pour over oranges, add olives and mix gently. Chill about 20 minutes and serve. Serves 2 to 4.

RAGGEDY ANN SALAD

  peach halves
  celery sticks
1 hard-boiled egg
1 box raisins
  sliced pimento or cherries or red candy
  grated yellow cheese
  ruffled lettuce leaves

Method
Drain peach halves, then start to make the doll.

BODY-peach half, cut side down
ARMS AND LEGS-celery sticks
HEAD-half of hard boiled egg, cut crosswise; use with cut side down
EYES, NOSE, SHOES, BUTTONS-raisins
MOUTH-slice of pimiento, or cherry pieces or red candy
HAIR-grated yellow cheese
SKIRT-ruffled lettuce leaves

HORSESHOE EGGS
(discovered by Flora)

1 dozen eggs
6 tablespoons mayonnaise
4 tablespoons A-1 Sauce
2½ tablespoons prepared mustard
3 tablespoons Worchestershire Sauce
1 tablespoon butter
Dash of cayenne pepper
Salt
Black Pepper
2/3 cup grated American Cheese

Cook eggs well done, boil about 15 or 20 minutes.
Mash eggs through a potato ricer. Save one-third of
the whites of cooked eggs. Cut in 4 quarters. Place
in the bottom of a buttered baking dish. Add all
ingredients with the mashed eggs. Mix well. Put
the mixture on the top of whites, sprinkle grated
cheese over the eggs. Bake in a 350 degree oven on
the middle rack of oven until top is browned.
Serve hot!

HAM OMELET

1½ cup chopped ham
8 whole eggs
2/3 cup milk and cream
½ teaspoon salt
few dashes of pepper
quarter stick of butter

Beat eggs slightly. Add salt, pepper, milk. Beat
eggs a bit more. Heat frying pan. Melt butter and
spread over the frying pan. Pour the entire egg
mixture into frying pan. Cook until about done.
Let the eggs spread over the pan. Place the ham
in the center of pan, fold the eggs over the ham.
Dump on platter and serve hot.

Born in the Kitchen

Plain and Fancy Plantation Fixin's

FLORA MAE HUNTER

....

Tallahassee, Florida: Pine Cone, 1979
159 pages

*T*HIS IS SOUTHERN COOKING with a cherry on top.

In her introductory narrative, the author regales readers with tales of passion for pastoral living and time-honored dishes that will woo experienced and novice cooks alike. (She spent thirty-six years with the Baker family on Horseshoe Plantation, an 11,000-acre farm established around 1840 in Leon County, Florida, where cotton, corn, and bobwhite quail were raised and where she honed her creative culinary skill.)

Next comes a charming, contemporized recipe collection that reveals imaginative experimentation: cane syrup sweetens corn meal bread, pumpkin bread gets citrusy notes from lemon juice and orange rind, fried bananas (a nod to the ancestral use of plantains) garnish steak, and chicken fat tenderizes waffles. She adds catsup to macaroni salad and sherry to black bean soup. Curry flavors creamed oysters and crab, and oyster pie. Baking soda enhances boiled spinach. Quail is

served roasted, smothered, and pan-broiled; doves are baked into a pie with vegetables or roasted. Roasted coots (duck-like fowl) and snipes (a wading bird similar to woodcock or sandpiper), along with vegetables fried, smothered, stewed, creamed, boiled, baked, stuffed, and served in sauce testify to the plentitude of the farm.

She names some dishes curiously—a salmon-croquette-like dish is Salmon Fondue. Aunt Jemima's Jubilee Ham is basted with molasses and pineapple, orange, and lemon juices; thinly sliced ginger preserves pear slices in Pear Chips.

I was surprised that she specifies Brer Rabbit Yellow Label Molasses for her gingerbread and details the proper way to extract the milk-like substance from corn on the cob for her Fried Fresh Corn, yet she assumes that her readers would know the procedure for thickening with "flour paste," which I think is the classic French mix of butter and flour, *beurre manié.* ❧

Cooking for the Champ

Muhammad Ali's Favorite Recipes

LANA SHABAZZ

....

New York: Jones-McMillon, 1979
126 pages

MUHAMMAD ALI'S FAVORITE RECIPES
By Lana Shabazz

LANA'S BEAN PIE

3 cups sugar
½ pound unsalted butter
2 tablespoons cinnamon
2 tablespoons corn starch
5 well-beaten eggs
3 cups cooked navy beans, mashed through
   food strainer (may substitute carrots or
   butternut squash)
2 cups evaporated milk
5 drops yellow food coloring
1 teaspoon lemon extract

Heat oven to 450°. In medium-size bowl cream together sugar and butter. Add cinnamon and corn starch and blend well. Add eggs, one at a time; beat to blend. Add beans; beat. Add milk, food coloring and extract. Blend well; set aside.

WHOLE WHEAT CRUST FOR BEAN PIE

1½ cups whole wheat flour
¼ cup corn oil
½ teaspoon salt
3 tablespoons ice water
1 egg

Sift together whole wheat flour and salt. Blend in oil. Add water, egg; blend a little at a time. Mix until it can be formed into a ball of dough. Divide into 3 parts, roll each out ⅛ of an inch thick on a floured board. Place in greased pie pan, pour in bean mixture. Bake for 5 minutes at a high temperature, lower flame and bake at 325° for 45 minutes.

Yield: 3 pies

95

$\mathcal{E}$ ASY-TO-MAKE gourmet recipes that emphasize healthy eating, nutritious ingredients, and fresh herbs and spices: these are the foods that kept the heavyweight boxing champion nourished. They were published for "people who want to remain in top physical condition." Full-color photographs divide sections composed of recipes for lean proteins, the wise use of leftovers, a rainbow of colorful vegetable casseroles and side dishes, whole grain breads, a few sensible desserts, and some refreshing beverages. The author's menus also share her special way of tenderizing meats, quick meal solutions for working wives, baking tips for the champ's favorite butternut squash, and the killer bean pie with a whole wheat crust that Ali bragged "to everyone within earshot of the [training] camp" that she had left under his pillow. ◗

A Christmas Cookbook
from Williamsburg

FRED D. CRAWFORD

....

Williamsburg, Virginia: Williamsburg Publishing, 1980
32 pages

AFTER A BRIEF HISTORY tracing Williamsburg's Yuletide holiday tradition to December 1608, three menus, forty-five treasured "receipts," and more than thirty full-color photographs evoke the opulence of antebellum southern hospitality—elegant tables set with fine china, formal place settings, and sideboards decorated with sliver trays, candelabras, holly, and pine boughs.

Crawford was the executive chef at the Williamsburg Inn for thirty-four years, where, "as a culinary artist with a superior knowledge of wines, herbs and spices," he prepared banquets for royalty and dignitaries, received awards for his creativity, and was named master chef of the Commonwealth of Virginia and chef of the year.

For a memorable Christmas gathering, the classic country feast of Roast Tom Turkey with Chestnut Dressing features recipes for the wassail bowl and such delectable canapés as the Shrimp Tree, Deviled Eggs and Oysters Wrapped in Bacon, Carrot Soufflé, Scalloped Oysters, Broccoli in Cheese Sauce, and a tempting assortment of traditional desserts—Pecan Tarts, Black Forest Cake, and English Fruit Trifle.

A whole Chesapeake Bay rockfish is at the center of the menu called A Formal Setting. It is accompanied by asparagus wrapped with pimiento, Duchess Potatoes, Stuffed Baked Tomato with Green Peas Au Gratin, and Hot Spiced Cider. Chocolate Cream Pie, Coconut Layer Cake, Jellied Fruit Mold, and Grand Marnier Soufflé bestow a touch of class on the menu.

Finally, the menu An Elegant Presentation of the Traditional Williamsburg Ham sparkles with a baked country ham glazed with chaudfroid, Brandied Sweet Potatoes, Southern Corn Pudding, Brussels Sprouts with Browned Buttered Toasted Chestnuts, Wine Jelly Mold with Custard Sauce, Fudge Cake, and Fresh Fruit Ambrosia. ❧

The Buster Holmes Restaurant Cookbook

New Orleans Handmade Cookin'

BUSTER HOLMES

············

Gretna, Louisiana: Pelican, 1980
122 pages

YOU EAT AND YOU LEAVE. That's the way it is at Buster Holmes and it is delicious." Those are the words of the *New York Times* reviewer quoted on the back cover of the 2010 reprint edition of this book. This amazing historic record is a depository for more than 170 revered dishes and obscured but revealing views of the New Orleans restaurant's interior, menu board, customers, and employees.

We see the "second line" of a jazz funeral procession as it passes down the street in front of Buster's place, which was housed in a private home built in the 1830s with slave quarters at the rear. We are introduced to Hustler, the proprietor of the French Market vegetable stand where Buster bought his vegetables. Woody Allen is photographed while jamming with a few of the musicians hanging out at Buster's.

Many of Buster's dishes reflect his family's tradition of hunting. Creole classics abound, and an imaginative mix of southern and Creole victuals delivers the best of both culinary styles: pork rib jambalaya; creamed hen with a dumpling mixture poured over the top; Red Chick, a stewed dish resembling chicken Creole; Tomato, Okra, and Corn spiced with curry; and Cornbread and Biscuit Dressing.

Buster's inventive spirit hovers in out-of-the-ordinary concoctions—Pour Crust Chicken Pie, green beans spiked with Creole mustard, Bourbon Yams, Sweet Potato Salad, Okra Pancakes, Sweet Potato Rolls (fritter-like balls crusted with bran flakes), Louisiana and Mississippi Mud distinguished by a sprinkle of flake coconut. A few hard-times dishes are made with less expensive substitutes: molasses in pound cake, lard in place of butter for yellow cake, sorghum-sweetened gingerbread, and Ritz Cracker Pie. 🌶

Feast to Your Soul's Delight

U.S. DEPARTMENT OF HEALTH
AND HUMAN SERVICES, FOOD
AND DRUG ADMINISTRATION,
IN COOPERATION WITH THE
SODIUM REDUCTION CONSUMER
EDUCATION PROGRAM OF THE
NATIONAL URBAN LEAGUE

....

HHS Pub. No. (FDA) 84-1107, 1980

71 pages

I CAN'T EXPLAIN IT, but I came away from reading this book feeling that change may not be easy, but it is possible. This is a cookbook of favorites "passed from person-to-person over the years," aimed at average consumers who want to reduce their sodium intake in order to reduce the risk of high blood pressure, heart and kidney disease, and stroke. It is plain, with rudimentary artwork, but somehow its modified recipes nudge readers toward better health.

The strategy of prevention rather than intervention combines the standard health and nutrition recommendations of experts to eat less sugar, red meat, and butter, and more grains, cereals, vegetables, fish, poultry, and fruits. The bounty of sodium education inspires one to try,

try, try. There is a list of foods that are hidden sources of sodium (baking soda, baking powder, monosodium glutamate, self-rising flour), a glossary of common cooking terms, FDA definitions for the sodium content on food labels, shopping tips, suggestions for modifying recipes for a low-salt palate, two salt substitutes, and nearly one hundred recipes for appetizers, beef and pork, breads, desserts, grains and pasta, poultry and fish, salads, soups and stews, and vegetables. Dishes such as Stuffed Pork Chops, Macaroni and Cheese Supreme, Fricasseed Chicken 'N Dumplings, and Creole of the Sea (shrimp Creole) are shockingly simple, having been rehabilitated with wine, fruit, juice, and herbs as substitutes for salt. ❧

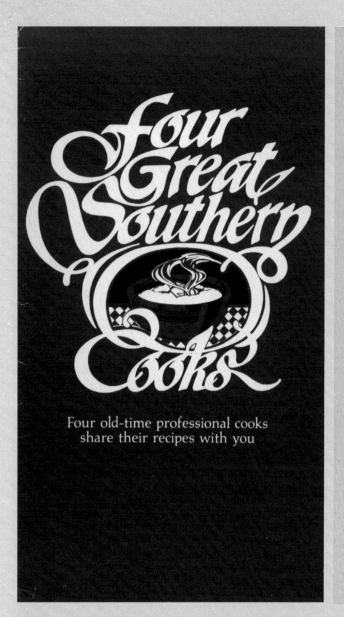

four Great Southern Cooks

Four old-time professional cooks
share their recipes with you

Rose Petal Wine

Bea collects the petals from fading roses and uses them to make a sweet white wine. Fermentation takes about five months. White or red petals can be used.

Ingredients
1 gallon white or red rose petals
1 gallon boiling water
6 cups sugar

Method
Crush the rose petals in a heavy Pyrex bowl and pour the boiling water over them. Cover with a clean cloth and set aside in a warm place to ferment for three days.

On the fourth day, add the sugar and stir until the sugar dissolves. Cover with a clean cloth and let stand in a warm place for three weeks.

Strain the liquid through cheesecloth into four quart jars. Tie a cloth over the mouths of the jars and let stand for four months, or until the wine is no longer effervescent.

Strain the wine into clean wine bottles, cork with a clean cork and store in a dark place until ready to serve. Makes about 1 gallon.

Four Great Southern Cooks

EDITED BY DUBOSE PUBLISHING

....

Atlanta: DuBose, 1980
198 pages

A UNIQUE FORMAT isn't the only thing that sets this book apart from the soul and southern tomes that weighed down shelves during the soul food revival. Four culinary biographies were crafted as a record of the South's "proud legacy" of hospitality, commitment to high-quality ingredients, and an approach to cooking that reflects the diversity of the region. An invisible narrator, presumably white, retells the story through "mouth-watering dishes made lovingly from scratch" by a "fab four" born and reared in Georgia. These domestic workers perfected their craft in the grand houses of southern legend with specialties ranging in style and substance from old to new, homely to fancy, casual to formal, and collard greens to caviar.

Daisy Redman grew up in Savannah, surrounded by good food and good cooks. She watched her grandmother practice the culinary arts, stirring hot pilaus, okra gumbo, and beef stew, and serving tea cakes in her restaurant in the Old Tybee Depot. Her celebrated catering menu included rich seafood dishes such as a creamy Crab Soup spiked with sherry; Shrimp Toast, a deep-fried appetizer; Lobster Thermidor; Stuffed Baked Shad with Shrimp Sauce; the Savannah specialty Low Country Shrimp; and a Coffee Liqueur Sauce for Ice Cream that is essentially homemade Kahlua.

Ruth Jenkins had a knack for pie perfection long before she became known for her fork-tender country ham, crisp french-fried cauliflower (served as an appetizer with a rich mustard dip), and her coconut cake. She "meticulously pinpointed" the measure of each ingredient to ensure that the book-buying public could achieve her results. Chilled Caviar Pie, Quail in a Bag, Barbecued Chuck Roast with a splash of bourbon, and fresh Coconut Cake are specialties that stand alongside southern staples.

Beatrice Mize was an innovative and resourceful cook who made her living by turning leftover ham into ham mousse and yesterday's chicken into today's chicken à la king. She began her career by cooking traditional southern specialties and earned fame for dishes with international origins as well. She ran the Dew Drop Inn in 1919, her father's small café in Cornelia, Georgia. She earned honors for the meals that she and her father cooked and served to three hundred workers on the Tugalo Dam project in Tallulah Falls. And she was remembered for her brown sugar pound cake topped with a pecan glaze and Rose Petal Wine.

William Mann Jr. contributed recipes taken from the handwritten cookbook he kept during the 1920s, formulas he attributed to the southern cooking teacher Mrs. S. R. Dull. Others he acquired from visitors to his employers' home. The remainder, such as Junior's Dove Pie, Roast Leg of Lamb basted with white wine, and the light gingerbread he adapted from an old English recipe, are his "own inspired creations." ❧

The Presley Family Cookbook

VESTER PRESLEY AND
NANCY ROOKS

....

Memphis, Tennessee: Wimmer Brothers, 1980
188 pages

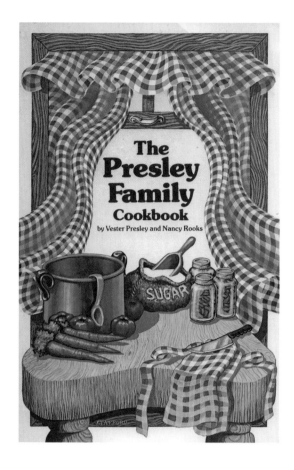

OVER THE YEARS, several cookbooks have claimed to house the King's favorite recipes, including the peanut butter and banana sandwich purported to be his favorite, but this project goes a step further. In more than five hundred recipes, Vester Presley, Elvis's uncle and the guard at Graceland for more than twenty-three years, along with Nancy Rooks, who had been a maid and cook for the family since 1967, paint a broad picture of the traditional southern table. The Presley name may have been employed purely as a marketing tool.

Curiously, their book is plain, with standard print-shop chapter dividers, stock food illustrations, a half-dozen underexposed black-and-white photographs of Rooks in the kitchen, and mostly generic southern covers—from watermelon rind pickles, pickled peaches, and chowchow to blackberry cobbler, with the customary savory meats and side dishes in between.

Rooks cooks fewer than ten make-do main dishes, including a curiosity called Ham Bone Dumplings. She shines when it comes to sugary things, though, sweetening tea cakes with molasses, spiking chess pie with cocoa, giving sweet potatoes a taste of the tropics with crushed pineapple.

But where are the headnotes describing Elvis's favorites? No charming anecdotes tell the origins of the dishes other than Twelve Flavor Ice Cream Dessert. The authors contend, "Some days this is all Elvis would have during the day." In fact, the only bragging that connects Rooks and the Presley family is the recipe for Elvis's favorite Peanut Butter and Banana Sandwich, a list of Elvis's favorite drinks on the final page, and this testimony by Rooks in the introduction: "His home was like my own home because I spent more time there than at my house."

VANILLA ICE CREAM

1 gallon milk
6 eggs
3½ cups sugar
Pinch salt

2 teaspoons vanilla
   flavoring
1 junket tablet

Cook milk over medium heat in top of a double boiler. Beat eggs; pour into milk. Mix sugar, salt and vanilla. Dissolve junket tablet in ¼ cup warm milk and add to custard. Pour into ice cream freezer and freeze.

NO COOK PINEAPPLE ICE CREAM

2 cans Eagle Brand milk
3 quarts sweet milk
6 eggs, separated

2 teaspoons vanilla
1 large can crushed
   pineapple

Combine Eagle Brand milk and sweet milk. Beat egg yolks well; add vanilla and crushed pineapple. Beat egg whites to soft peak stage. Fold into custard and freeze. *Makes 1 gallon.*

TWELVE FLAVOR ICE CREAM DESSERT

1 scoop each:
Vanilla ice cream
Pineapple sherbet
Black walnut ice cream
Banana split ice cream
Lime sherbet
Orange sherbet
Butter pecan ice cream

Strawberry ice cream
Chocolate chip ice cream
Black cherry ice cream
Lemon ice cream
Peach ice cream
1 pint fresh strawberries

This is a combination of different kinds of ice cream. Mix together in a large bowl. Center on the table for dessert with fresh strawberries on top. Serve with chocolate chip cookies. *Some days this is all Elvis would have during the day.*

SOFT GINGERBREAD

3 cups sifted flour
1 tsp. baking soda
2 tsps. ground cinnamon
2 tsps. ground ginger
1 tsp. ground cloves
1/4 tsp. ground nutmeg
1/2 cup butter
1 cup sugar
2 eggs, well beaten
1 cup light molasses
1/4 cup boiling water
1 cup soured milk*

Blend the first 6 ingredients; set aside.
Cream the butter and sugar together until fluffy. Add the eggs in thirds, beating vigorously after each addition. Add a mixture of the molasses and water gradually, mixing well. Alternately add the dry ingredients in fourths and soured milk in thirds to creamed mixture, mixing until blended after each addition. Pour batter into a well-greased (bottom only) 13x9x2 in. pan. Bake at 350° about 35 min. or until gingerbread tests done. About 12 servings.

*To sour milk, put 1 Tbsp. cider vinegar or lemon juice into a measuring cup; fill cup with milk to the 1 cup line. Stir and set aside.

Louise Knowles

A LOVE CAKE FOR MOTHER

1 can of "Obedience"
Several pounds of "Affection"
1 pint "Neatness"
Some Holiday, Birthday and everday
    "Surprises"
1 can of "Running Errands" (Willing
    Brand)
1 box of powdered "Get up when I
    should"
1 can of pure "Thoughtfulness"
1 bottle of "Keep sunny all day long"

Method: Mix well, bake in a hearty, warm oven and serve to "Mother" everyday. She ought to have it in big slices.

29

Bread And Rolls

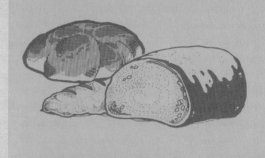

"This is that bread which came down from heaven: not as your fathers did eat manna, and are dead: he that eateth of this bread shall live for ever."
John 6:58

THE HOUSEWIFE

My days are days of small affairs
Of trifling worries, little cares —
A lunch to pack, a bed to make,
A room to sweep, a pie to make,
A hurt to kiss, a tear to dry,
A head to brush, a bow to tie,
A face to wash, a rent to mend
A meal to plan a fuss to end,
A hungry husband to be fed —
A sleepy child to put to bed.
I, who had hoped some day to gain
Success — perhaps a bit of fame,
Must give my life to small affairs,
Of trifling worries, little cares.
But, should tomorrow bring a change,
My little house grow still and strange —
Should all the cares I know today
Be swept, quite suddenly away,
Where now a hundred duties press
Be but an ache of loneliness,
No child's gay ribbon to be tied,
No wayward little feet to guide;
To Heaven then would rise my prayers,
"O God, give me back my little cares!"

Author unknown

8

Soul Food for Body and Soul #2

MRS. H. H. PETERS

....

St Louis: Open Door Ministries, 1980
96 pages

THIS UPLIFTING YEARBOOK is a keepsake of fellowship between Bible-believing women who came together to study God's word. It is packed with scripture, prayers, wisdom, dozens of household hints, 150 recipes, and more than 100 photographs of the cooks who submitted their favorite southern dishes. Brief biographies and photographs identify the class officers. One-dish casseroles made of tuna and ground beef, five different takes on gumbo, barbecue spareribs, chicken meatloaf, three recipes for chili and southern fried chicken (dusted with seasoned flour and browned in a small amount of oil, then covered with a tight-fitting lid and cooked until golden) are the kind of delicious recipes the ladies brought to special gatherings at Christmas and at the end of the program year. Imaginative mixtures that eventually became timeless classics such as 7-Up Cake, Dump Cake, and Bean Pie share center stage with charming combinations such as Recipes for Friendship, A Happy Home, and A Love Cake for Mother.

In 1948, the Reverend H. H. Peters founded Open Door Ministries to produce and distribute "black evangelical literature," claiming Revelation 3:5 as its motto: "Behold, I have set before thee an Open Door and no man can shut it." Twenty years later, his wife opened the chapel doors to a ladies' Bible class. One woman came. After much prayer and persistence, the attendance eventually grew to about 190 women, many of them contributors to this cookbook series, which began with *Soul Food for Body and Soul #1* in 1970. ❧

Mammy's

MAKEOVER

The Ever-Useful Life

We are blessed since we can find our ovens
and stoves and make up for some of what
we long for.

NTOZAKE SHANGE,
1998

THE 1970s were the decade when
African American cookbooks
celebrated culinary freedom and
turned the spotlight on the diverse
foodways of African American
culture. In the 1980s, it was the cooks' time to
shine. After years of existing in the shadows of
the food and hospitality industry, "me generation" authors deliberately emphasized personal
narrative and reflection. The book *If I Can Cook /
You Know God Can* (1998), a poetic tribute to the
culinary arts by the black feminist writer Ntozake Shange, transports me to their kitchens.

Small and humble, these are still sacred places
in my mind's eye, where miracles are performed
with a few simple raw ingredients, and the sil-
houettes of creative characters are obscured and
barely visible through the steam of bubbling pots.

In the 1980s, publications aimed primarily
at white audiences reshaped their messages to
appeal to the needs of as many gastronomes as
possible. Women's magazines repackaged their
approach to food and cooking, attaching themselves to the divided interests of feminists with
titles such as *Working Woman*, *Country Living*, *Victoria*, *Country Home*, *Country Craft*, and
Traditional Home. Advice columns "evolved to
accommodate the developing domestic/profes-
sional split" between professional women and
those working inside the home, wrote the feminist scholar Patricia Turner in *Ceramic Uncles and
Celluloid Mammies: Black Images and Their Influence on Culture* (1994). Cookbooks appealed to
new niche markets with a wide range of themes
and titles.

While white women pursued gender equality
and moved further away from the kitchen, African American authors humanized black cooking. Food memoirs written by and for everyone,
including football players and mixed-race cooks,
upheld the flair of individuality and authenticity
formerly attributed to cooking with soul. Catering experts proudly revealed secrets that would
help hostesses deliver quick weekend dinner
parties. Cooks who had served governors and the

wealthy translated their professional brand into tips for managing hectic households. Regional, Creole, and African cuisines were still all the rage.

Manufacturers couldn't help noticing.

I was food editor for a small weekly newspaper in Los Angeles when I received from Kraft Foods a series of feature stories and recipes about black cooking. The series had grown out of a research project that explored the culinary traditions of black communities in the United States. In 1982, Kraft published *The Heritage of Black Cooking* in a sturdy, twenty-five-page trifold pamphlet featuring the recipes and pizzazz of black cooks throughout the country. Everyone recognized the dishes: red rice, molded shrimp spread, jambalaya, caramel praline soufflé, ham hocks and black-eyed peas, Texican salad, and spinach dip, all laced with Kraft salad dressings, condiments, and sauces. But I am not so sure that anyone expected the report to substantiate what African Americans knew all along—that black cooks brought an "unmistakable African influence" to the culture and cuisines of the South and had demonstrated skill at "surviving off the land." Kraft asserted: "Black cooking has major differences from mainstream traditions, but it also has many things in common. It has tremendous regional variety, but some dishes appear again and again with only minor regional variations."

It wasn't long after these revelations that the company making sure that "a black woman was always in America's kitchens" gave Aunt Jemima a makeover. Quaker Oats had been gradually altering the controversial but profitable trademark for years. In 1969, the mammy image disappeared from the cover of one of Quaker's cookbooks, *The Morning to Midnight Cook Book: 340 Unexpected Treats from Aunt Jemima.* Two decades later, and a hundred years after the image was introduced, Quaker transformed Aunt Jemima in order "to make the symbol more acceptable to the black market," according to the award-winning journalism Professor Marilyn Kern-Foxworth, in *Aunt Jemima, Uncle Ben, and*

Rastus: Blacks in Advertising, Yesterday, Today, and Tomorrow (1994). "All that remained of the stereotypical Jemima was her effervescent, alluring smile," Kern-Foxworth said. "The headband was traded in for soft, gray-streaked hair, and to give her a more contemporary look she now wears pearl earrings and a dainty lace collar."

Both developments made it seem as if completely new horizons had opened up for African American cookery and that black cooks might finally get their due. Instead, mainstream media screamed the same old thing.

Proponents of new southern cuisine were particularly dismissive. For them, regional home-style southern cooking was more desirable than ghettoized soul food, and new southern cuisine was more sophisticated than both, something entirely different.

National food magazines published opulent feature stories about the modernized fare. *Bon Appétit* declared new southern cuisine "at once down-home but not old-fashioned, sophisticated but never pretentious." The food editor Anne Byrn Phillips of the *Atlanta Journal-Constitution* outlined the updated and streamlined changes taking place in southern kitchens, writing the following in *Cook's Magazine* in 1985:

The cookery of the South has become lighter, fresher, and more colorful while holding fast to many of its traditional roots. Frying remains the only acceptable way for Southerners to cook crab cakes or chicken, but other dishes are often broiled, grilled, or even stir fried. We're blanching quickly, not boiling forever, and shifting from fatback to fresh herbs. We are relying as always on native ingredients—oysters of Apalachicola and Bon Secour bays, shad roe from the Ogeechee River, quail of South Carolina, and Vidalia onions from southeast Georgia—to accompany those new creations. But we're using less lard, butter, and oil, less of the salty, smoky ham for which Virginia and Kentucky are famous, more lemon juice and herbs.

How new Southern cooking came about is easy to see. It is an amalgam of French cooking, of Italian cooking, and of the myriad other ethnic cooking methods, gleaned from a hundred sources and blended with our current affection for American regional food. It's rooted in our English ancestry, but it's come a long way. What is happening in the South and has always been going on is a perpetual exchange of culinary ideas among cooks. And the circle of influence is ever expanding.

The cover of *Food and Wine*'s November 1988 issue was just as harsh. If it didn't overtly put black cooks back in their place as the "other," it nonetheless narrowly shaped their contributions according to Old South habits. The headline "Southern Food Rises Again" jumped from the cover page. Inside, a recipe for Vertamae Grosvenor's Fabulous Fried Chicken predictably tied the black cook to a stereotype. The editor of *Southern Magazine*, Linton Weeks, pushed the New Southern agenda even further. A feature entitled "The Soul of Southern Cooking" capitalized on the added value brought by the word "soul." Simultaneously, the piece confined black edibles to "sweet potatoes, watermelon, black-eyed peas, eggplant, okra and other wondrous dishes."

Some of the most revered southern cookbook authors also experienced myopia when it came to the creators of the region's "glamorous dishes." Take Craig Claiborne, from Sunflower, Mississippi, for instance. In 1987, the former *New York Times* food editor organized three hundred recipes from "many of the South's best cooks," including Paul Prudhomme and Bill Neal. Only one of them, Edna Lewis, was black. Claiborne devoted little attention to the African foodways imbedded in his beloved southern cuisine. He explains that benne (sesame) wafers are a cocktail wafer and a vital part of the culture of Charleston, though his lesson on the etymology of "benne" does involve a rare, and brief,

association with Africa. But he blushes at never having heard of catfish in white sauce "until we experimented with it in my own kitchen, calling it 'an excellent Southern dish with French overtones.'" The free woman of color Malinda Russell called the dish Catfish Fricassee in her groundbreaking cookbook way back in 1866.

Marie Rudisill, on the other hand, didn't marginalize or ignore black cooks in *Sook's Cookbook: Memories and Traditional Receipts from the Deep South* (1989); she capitalized on them. In her lovingly written homage to Sook Faulk, Rudisill, who was Sook's niece and Truman Capote's aunt, assembled recipes from the files of the Faulk family of Monroeville, Alabama, many of them attributed to the clan's respected black cooks. The artist Barry Moser contributed stunning watercolor composites of real people, some based on old Faulk family photographs. The whole thing was "enriched by anecdotes and tales of family and Alabama history."

Rudisill retold the story of the faithful family mammy (Aunt Pallie); applauded the family's main cook (Little Bit), "a huge woman" whose cooking knew "no equal"; and gave kudos to Corrie: "Her strong love and her good cooking were integral to the Faulk way of life." The book commemorates the cooks "for whom this food was both sustenance and ritual" and "for whom the kitchen was a covenant."

In response, African American cookbooks of this era proclaim life lessons to set apart their great cooking.

Recipes for making friends accompany the message that cultural foods promote good health. One book recommends joy and laughter as the remedy when tragedy strikes, and another says we should stop being afraid to have a party. Other cookbooks admonish us to eat fresh and shop local; tell stories to keep traditions alive; and believe that home-cooked meals matter, spice is nice, authentic African American cooking is for everyone, and kitchen work builds character, courage, and faith.

What a gift! ❧

Cotton Patch Cooking

ESTHER NELSON

....

Sacramento, California: Folks Publications, 1981
78 pages

56

BEANS AND HAMBONE

1 pound soup beans

1 ham bone

1 pod red pepper or black pepper

salt to taste

1 small clove garlic

Wash beans and place in fresh water. Cook slowly with a ham bone for 2 hours. Add minced garlic if desired, and a small pod of red pepper. Remove the ham bone and trim off the meat; cut it up and add it to the beans. Season with salt. Serve piping hot with a dish of cabbage slaw.

ELEPHANT STEW

1 elephant	2 rabbits
50 pounds salt	25 pounds pepper

Cut elephant into small bits. Cook all on a kerosene stove at 400° for about 2 months. After cooking, cover with brown gravy.

This should be enough to serve 3,850 people. If you have more people, add two more rabbits.

THE CALIFORNIA Folk Arts Association "endorsed" it; I can't get enough of it.

The author, a college counselor, returned to the rural community of Hickman, Kentucky, where she was born, and recorded industrious recipes and folktales of former tenant farmers—men and women ages 84–93—who recalled the long, hard hours of plowing, harrowing, planting, hoeing, and picking up to 350 pounds of cotton a day for a pittance.

Amusing stories and delicate line drawings of flowers, herbs, preserves, and cotton-planting equipment entertain. Traditional southern and soul favorites such as dandelion wine, sweet potato biscuits, cornmeal breads, beans, greens, baked and fried fish, chicken and dumplings, oxtail soup, and watermelon rind pickles carry the survival cooking banner. But don't think *Cotton Patch* is a melancholy catalogue of uninteresting make-do recipes.

This tongue-in-cheek "blending of simple recipes prepared in the tenant farmer's kitchen" and black folktales told to "add laughter to an otherwise dreary day" recounts subsistence dishes inspired by what must have been bitter poverty and captivates the imagination. Amazingly.

Apple peelings bake in the sun into beer. Rice ferments into wine. Pumpkin Whiskey displays compelling resourcefulness. At the same time, a numbered, thirty-eight-step recipe for Corn Liquor with a diagram of an old-fashioned still stands out riotously. The first recommendation for novice moonshiners: "Find a hideout in the woods near a pond."

Yes, there are hardscrabble dishes, but they sound like something from a modern chef's trendy menu: Nasturtium Ice, Fried Elderberry Blossoms, Homemade Yeast, Carrot Preserves, Corncob Jelly, Moonshine Cake, and Home Made Soap. As an interlude to these recipes of scarcity, a ridiculous concoction of plentitude springs from page fifty-six without warning.

I am still smiling. ❧

Onje Fun Orisa
(Food for the Gods)

GARY EDWARDS AND JOHN MASON

....

New York: Yoruba Theological Archministry, 1981
143 pages

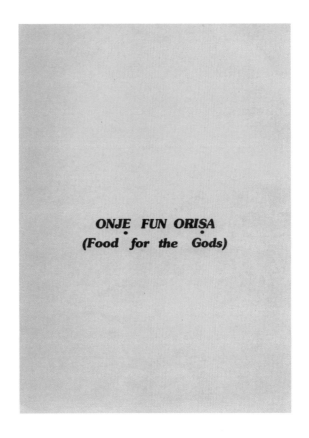

THIS FASCINATING typewritten report aims to provide some much-needed perspective on the culinary contributions that African slaves made to New World cuisines at a time when most writing was singularly focused on African or black American cookery, but few attempted to connect the two. The entire project is handmade, like a college thesis, including the title page. A sixteen-page photographic centerfold shows favorite African recipes. A glossary of African terms, an index, and a bibliography, all dealing with West African, American, and Caribbean foods, try to answer a simple question: How were black people able to hold onto African culture, despite the "intense cruelty, the brutality, and the cultural oppression of slavery?"

The authors use African ritual cooking to explain how foods eaten as part of religious ceremonies, offerings, and initiations were re-created across the Atlantic. The book describes African agricultural practices; lists the foods that composed the colonial West African diet and the techniques used to prepare them in recipes; shows how the recipes were eaten; describes rituals; names deities; relates Italian, Irish, and other European immigrants' acculturation to the adjustments fashioned by Africans in their new environments; and includes about ninety recipes.

Overall, the book is a generalized overview that draws some fundamental conclusions and brings forth research that will be used in years to come by future food scholars, including these five African cooking techniques (published in 1951 in an *Africa Magazine* article on Yoruba cooking by William Bascom):

- *se bo*: to boil in water, or steam in leaves
- *din*: to fry in deep oil
- *yan, ta*: to toast beside the fire, or in live embers or in a potsherd or dry pot over the fire
- *sun*: to roast in the fire
- *bu*: to bake in hot ashes 🌿

The Party Book

MILTON WILLIAMS AND
ROBERT WINDELER

....

Garden City, New York: Doubleday, 1981
224 pages

*T*HE BOOK JACKET lets you know right up front that this is a "complete handbook" of home entertaining, designed to help you "stop being afraid to have a party." The photos, recommendations, and recipes carry the assurance of a Hollywood caterer to the likes of Henry Mancini and Aaron Spelling.

It is a large book. Thirty photos, in full-color and black-and-white, help bring the reader along and add structure to the home-entertaining conversation. Because so few recipes are offered in such a large book, the first chapter's overleaf of an inviting table set for breakfast, with freshly cut flowers and a *Wall Street Journal* placemat to embellish the place setting with a touch of whimsy, is particularly valuable. Why? The layout helps spark the imagination of the home cook.

Among its other striking visuals are a table setting with hors d'oeuvres for Helen Reddy and Jeff Wald's tenth anniversary; an all-chocolate party from *Maida Heatter's Book of Great Chocolate Desserts*, in which even the wine coolers and the centerpiece tree branches are covered in chocolate; Easter flowerpots with *pashka* and other desserts surrounded by jellybeans, for a table that both kids and adults can enjoy; edible centerpieces of fowl or roast meat situated between sprays of greenery, fresh pears, citrus fruits, or votive candles tucked in hollowed-out baby apples.

And Williams's wise counsel just goes on from there in chapters that range from basic and essential knowledge (he doesn't approve of so-called "potluck" meals in home entertaining—if you are giving a party, you provide the food, always) to grand finishing touches that make guests feel special. Between suggestions for throwing different types of parties, creating invitations no one can refuse, and mastering the basics of table setting, the author reveals intimate knowledge known to professionals. There is a party-organizing schedule, decor and planned diversions in the room that get conversation started, and two sections that help hosts relax and enjoy the event along with the guests: "Help! When to Hire It" and "Disasters."

Within each section are menu recommendations that inspire all kinds of possibilities for creating nontraditional and original party ideas, but relatively few recipes. For Valentine's Day, a seeded papaya half filled with crabmeat and a dollop of curry sauce is served on red, pink, and white heart-shaped doilies, but no recipe is given. A late-morning or midday Sunday brunch menu features instructions for making a festive cocktail and Scrambled Eggs à la Milton, but the remainder of the menu omits measurements, depending instead on suggestions or "you-should-dos," as if to distinguish between the cook and the event planner.

According to Williams, you could cook smoked salmon in vermouth and orange juice; do a whole smoked salmon and a carrot, nut, raisin, and apple salad instead of sandwiches for high tea; and make parties colorful and economical with cultural themes. There are dinners planned around those with special dietary needs, like dieters, vegetarians, and kosher guests. Some dinners are devoted entirely to desserts, and to be complete, one party represents the foods of the American South, despite his angst about his roots: "I'm not at all crazy about the idea of putting a chitterling in my mouth," Williams concedes. ❧

West African Cooking for Black American Families

DR. ADELE B. MCQUEEN AND
ALAN L. MCQUEEN

....

New York: Vantage, 1982
91 pages

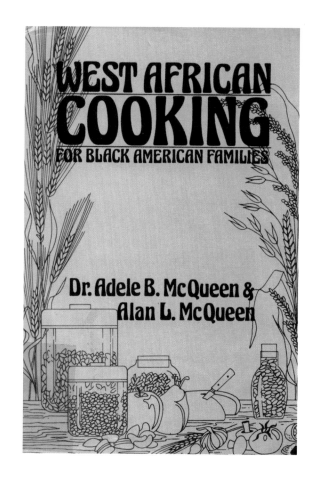

Guacamole, mashed potatoes, and luscious sweet potato pie might not be the first dishes you think of when you think of African cooking, but these scholars aim to change that.

Their compact book features more than two hundred recipes, ten menus, a glossary of African foods, and a table of substitutes, packaged as a laboratory tool for high school and college students in culinary courses. A doctor of human ecology at Howard University, Adele McQueen ran a test kitchen that specialized in African food preparation, and she collaborated with members of the International Women's Club of Liberia while living in that country with her husband. She lived and dined with African women in their homes, in restaurants, and on school campuses in an effort to blend their techniques with American methods and ingredients. Familiar recipes from previously published African American cookbooks, such as guacamole, are visible in the recipe for Butter Pear Dip. Palm Butter may have spawned Peanut Butter.

The glossary, a particularly useful research instrument, makes cross-referencing McQueen's recipes with those found in African and early African American cookery books a breeze. A few of those translations: leopard tongue (a reddish leaf used for tea), lights (cow lungs), meld (cow spleen), palm cabbage (palm hearts), pawpaw (papaya), potato greens (collards), and butter pear (avocado). ❧

Soul Food

Die Ernährung von Schwarzen in den USA
[Soul food: The nutrition of blacks in the USA]

MARIANNE GUCKELSBERGER

....

Hohenschäftlarn bei Munich: Klaus Renner
Verlag, 1982

142 pages

Marianne Guckelsberger

SOUL FOOD

Die Ernährung von Schwarzen in den USA

KLAUS RENNER VERLAG

<u>Rezepte</u>

<u>"Candied Yams"</u> (Süßer Yamsauflauf)

Yamswurzeln waschen, mit kaltem Wasser aufsetzen und
garkochen. Das Wasser abgießen, den Yams schälen und
in Stücke oder Scheiben schneiden. Ein Backblech mit
hohem Rand oder eine feuerfeste Auflaufform buttern.
Den Yams abwechselnd mit Zucker, Margarine, Vanille-
extrakt, Melasse oder Sirup und Zimt einfüllen. Ca.
1/2 Stunde backen.

*T*HIS FASCINATING study traces African American foodways, eating habits, and nutrition from slavery to the advent of soul food. The typewritten book looks like a bound thesis on black food ethnology, which the author says piqued her interest after an encounter with Rastafarians in Jamaica, if my translation is correct; it is written almost entirely in German, except for English footnotes, references, and interviews.

The scholarly work is a useful reference tool for several reasons. Recipes are included that establish a core black diet comprising candied yams, pigs' feet, cornbread, ham hocks, chitlins, pigs' ears and tails, navy beans and pigs' feet, mustard and collard greens, bread pudding, and rice pudding. A comprehensive bibliography cites established sources in culture and food, including several of the soul food cookbooks of the 1960s, plus black literature, such as Grace Halsell's *Soul Sister*. A comparison of grocery prices on Long Island and in Harlem seems intended to substantiate the claims about limited food access and barriers to healthier choices made by interviewees. Rich discussions about plantation society, domestic service, economic conditions in the black community, exploitation, survival skills, oral traditions, the use of cookbooks, restaurant food, black health practices, celebrations and social occasions, and the meaning of soul come together to form a complex picture of the African American experience behind the cuisine known as soul food. ❧

Uncle Herman's Soul Food Cookbook

HERMAN S. CLARK

....

Fresno, California: Mid-Cal, 1983
82 pages

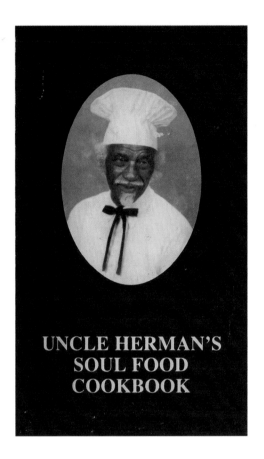

UNCLE HERMAN'S SOUL FOOD COOKBOOK

UNCLE HERMAN makes me want to cook. And cook.

His delicious-sounding dishes seem like they will go together in a cinch—making them good for everyday family feeds and informal gatherings alike. It is the kind of no-frills cooking that helps company feel right at home. This is unsurprising, since Clark cooked for several fraternities at Stanford University and provided lunch for the Mother's Club once a month.

In the foreword he explains that he prepares meals according to the "Basic Four Food Groups" and that he is always mindful of the health community's recommendation that cooks promote proper nutrition through fresh, flavorful combinations. Not bad for a man who began his career by cooking his experiments in his mother's wash pot on a wood-burning stove in Monroe, North Carolina—dinner fit for pigs, he said. But he improved: "After being qualified enough to satisfy the hogs so wonderfully, I decided that maybe I would try cooking for people, to see if I would satisfy them as well."

Satisfy he does, with roughly 150 quintessentially southern specialties such as gumbo, chitterlings (boiled and fried), fried chicken two ways, barbecued spareribs, pulled pork North Carolina style, and pig ear sandwiches. His small variations on classic themes belie a farm pedigree: celery leaves perk up beef stew, potato salad is made velvety rich with mashed potatoes, peach cobbler is sharpened with buttermilk, bacon is crumbled into cornbread, steak sauce is made from scratch, okra is combined with green tomatoes, cream cheese is baked into pound cake, and he offers up a few unconventional concoctions, too. The collection is grouped by food categories, without chapter dividers, and it ends unexpectedly. A section of eleven desserts follows the index, and they are attributed to Lossie S. Clark and Fannie Graves, but it is unclear who these women were or what they meant to the author. ❧

Mark May's Hog Cookbook

MARK MAY

....

Silver Spring, Maryland: Rosedale, 1983
65 pages

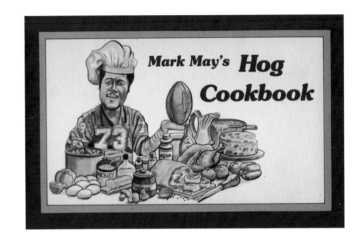

MARK MAY, the Washington Redskins' first-round pick in the 1981 NFL draft, became a member of the famous offensive line known as the "Hogs." He gathered thirty-two manly man recipes, each accompanied by a cli-chéd caption and a silly cartoon rendering of May in assorted positions and headgear as he prepares his favorite dishes. The winning recipes include helpful hints and tell you the type of equipment needed to prepare the dish. Serving sizes are given both for ordinary folks and for Hogs. ☙

First String Casserole

This would be a tough one to knock out of the line up. There is just no substitute for this first stringer.

36

300 Years of Black Cooking in St. Mary's County, Maryland

COMPILED BY THE ST. MARY'S COUNTY
COMMUNITY AFFAIRS COMMITTEE

....

Originally published 1975
Reprint editions, 1983 and 2005
118 pages

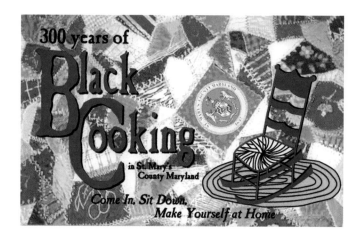

THE ORIGINAL EDITION of this cookbook was compiled in 1975 by Citizens for Progress, a community organization that worked to address social equity for poor people of color in St. Mary's County. The proceeds were used to fund a community survey covering politics, education, and employment issues. The survey was published in the *Focus*, a local African American–owned newspaper.

The book begins with a poem, "Come In. Sit Down. Make Yourself At Home," followed by more than two hundred familiar dishes separated into chapters by black-and-white illustrations of iconic African American buildings within the community.

I found it difficult to connect with many of the typewritten recipes for mostly southern staples, which appear in fonts of varying size. The dishes include beverages (Beef Tea and Dandelion Wine) as well as four versions of fried chicken, including wings dipped in plain pancake batter before frying and chicken seasoned with garlic salt or paprika and dusted with a secret ingredient—a sprinkle of sugar. The history of stuffed hams is followed by two ways to make the old-timey dish. To the stock selection of soul meats (sowbelly, pigs' feet, neck bones, other offal, and small game), the contributors add liver pudding, muskrat, and fried eels, a Victorian specialty.

A few imaginative choices did rouse my taste buds. Among them: five ways to make potato salad with a taste of the unexpected, a dish of fried leftover biscuit dough, a layered fruit pie, a recipe for blondies (white brownies) called Congo Bars, and a grapevine concoction combed through the hair and used to make curls set. 🍂

Forty Years in the Kitchen

A Collection of Recipes by
Dorothy Shanklin Russey

COMPILED BY
MRS. WILLIAM B. SCHMIDT

....

Dallas, Texas: Taylor, 1983
103 pages

WHEN IT COMES TO cookbooks written by white women about the black cooks who served their families, we have two choices. One viewpoint sees exploitation of the cook's life work. The other accepts the homage as a testament to the cook's expertise. I choose to be proud.

Russey, a caterer and mother of two, pleased palates in Elizabethtown, Kentucky. Her introductory words tell us that this book was "written with love" for the people she "worked for, dealt with, and loved." For years, she gathered notes, studied journals, and accumulated recipes for fine cooking, "trying to improve what I did in catering." The result is an easy-to-follow collection of party foods, organized and published by her employer, that sparkles with creativity.

Main course dishes, for example, are fancy—the recipe for each one comes with such detailed instructions as specific pan sizes, cooking times, the number of inches below the broiling element, or make-ahead options. And there are surprise

elements designed to entice guests to eat their vegetables. Bacon flavors broccoli; sour cream and horseradish sauce beets; carrots get souffléed; artichokes, eggplant, zucchini, and tomatoes are stuffed with herbs, mushrooms, and white beans; dill sauce smothers cucumbers. Russey's desserts make the mouth water.

There are no headnotes, so we have no way of knowing why $100 Devil's Food Cake is so expensive. We must find out for ourselves whether Pecan Pie I is denser or richer than Pecan Pie II. Or whether we should expect the additional sugar and corn syrup in Pecan Pie III to make it "Southern-style," as the title suggests.

"Dorothy was a wonderful cook!" Schmidt exclaims on the opening page of the book. "Many a Hardin County party hung its success on whether or not Dorothy was in the kitchen! And we all loved her. This is her book. These are her recipes. It is also her memorial."

And with that, we must be satisfied. ❧

Chachie Dupuy's New Orleans Home Cooking

CHACHIE DUPUY

....

New York: Macmillan, 1984
182 pages

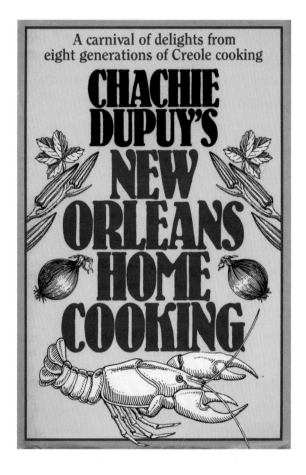

A carnival of delights from eight generations of Creole cooking

CHACHIE DUPUY'S NEW ORLEANS HOME COOKING

*I*N A MODERN TWIST on an old theme, the author believes it was the synergistic mix of her classical training and the black cook's "magical culinary touch" that produced this book's Creole classics—jambalaya, court bouillon, grillades and grits, eggs Sardou, and bread pudding—making it impossible to determine where the author and her muse begin and end.

The book is an outgrowth of a thirty-year relationship. Williana Pinkins traveled from Donaldsonville, Louisiana, to cook in the Dupuy family home. In the introduction to her collection of home-style Louisiana fare, the author remembers Pinkins as one of the finest cooks in New Orleans and her culinary mentor. Dupuy often sat in the kitchen with Pinkins, observing and listening while she worked. When Dupuy grew up and left New Orleans, she studied cooking in France with a French family and at Le Cordon Bleu.

But curiously, the collection contains few of the rich, complex sauces one might expect from a trained chef. In fact, recommendations are homespun and make-do, for example, creating an ice cream mold from cornflakes. In addition, the photographs tend toward the predictable—shopping scenes in the French Quarter, fishermen on the dock.

Then, the book ends where it begins, with Pinkins pictured smiling before a backdrop of kitchen shelves lined with canisters of seasonings and spices—a hackneyed perspective from slave days that perpetuates the conventional wisdom of the black cook as an unlearned prop, despite the love shared between the women. ❧

Reflections of an African American Kitchen

EDITED BY FRANCES M. HASSELL

....

Memphis, Tennessee: Hassell House, 1984
190 pages

T HE STAFF OF THE Universal Life Insurance Company in Memphis spent three years compiling recipes and cooking tips for this meticulous and informative tome. And it shows. With its emphasis on good health and weight management, the nutritive value of foods, and the importance of a well-balanced diet comprising a variety of foods rich in vitamins and minerals, the jam-packed book could just as easily have been published for today's health-conscious set.

The book is printed on buff-colored paper with recipes and dozens of illustrations sketched in brown ink. It opens with "The Meal Planner's Creed," a devotion focused on the role of the cook in maintaining a family's health, security, and pleasure. The standard chapter divisions include a section of special dishes, African dishes, helpful cooking hints, and homemade beauty aids and household cleaners. Tables of substitutions and equivalents are provided, as are measuring techniques and approximate boiling temperatures for altitude cooking, illustrations of ingredients and kitchen tools, and a couple of kneading how-tos.

The "Country Store" section is an homage to the old-time general store, where African American customers shopped, in the years following emancipation, for coal oil, calico for wedding clothes, home remedies, baby's croup medicine, snake root, and much else. This lovely narrative regales readers with the ways the general store served its community and how merchandise was "weighed up" on crude scales by members of the storekeeper's family. The recipes and chapter introductions tell you exactly what to do with the dry goods purchased there.

A cinnamon-nut crumb topping refreshes gingerbread. Soul Bread stirs cooked mashed hot sweet potato into cornbread batter. Salads are brightened with the addition of a few tender celery leaves, a sprig or two of parsley, young cabbage leaves, watercress, or tender raw spinach leaves added to lettuce, endive, and romaine. Salad mixtures are topped with any one of a half-dozen variations on French dressing—with cheese, a chiffonade of parsley, hard-cooked eggs, onions and beets, curry, pickles, or tomatoes.

General rules are offered to help cooks retain the color and nutritive value of vegetables, including when to boil or steam, whether to cover, serving suggestions, and what to do with the water in which vegetables have been cooked (pot likker). The recipes for stewed tomatoes, boiled greens, beans, peas, sweet potatoes, and cabbage are familiar. But a few unusual creations present a whole new taste for southern standbys, such as carrots dipped in milk and seasoned flour and then fried, to delight the palate and satisfy the soul.

The authors provide tips for purchasing, cooking, and handling fish, which is lauded as a complete protein, rich in vitamins and minerals and lower in fat than meat. Saltwater varieties are particularly prized for their iodine content. And common terms used by fishmongers are defined. Yet only seven recipes for fish are provided— boiled, fried, baked, and made into croquettes.

The same can be said about soups. Close attention is paid to stock making, followed by ten variations, including Grandma's Potato, Turtle Chicken Gumbo, Turkey Bone, Split Pea, Ham, Ox-Tail, and Mid-Summer (vegetable).

To build confidence and promote the intelligent cooking of meats and meat dishes, the reader is introduced to common cooking methods and a wide variety of cheap cuts and offal. Gravies are treated with as much respect as soups; celery tops, parsley stems, and leftover vegetables of every kind are tossed into the stockpot. The usual suspects are in the chicken section: chicken feet stew, chicken croquettes, rum-baked wings, barbecued chicken, and three ways of frying—with a coating of crushed Cheese Nips crackers; sprinkled with salt, pepper, and garlic powder and then fried in lard and pork grease; and browned then steamed until fork tender. Rabbit, squirrel, muskrat, quail, partridge, and squabs are fried, fricasseed, broiled, or roasted.

The rules for successful cakes and the recipes for classic southern cakes fill out a huge section that also includes a bizarre-sounding take on cinnamon rolls, in which they are doused in vinegar. Farina Balls, Jollof Rice, and an ambrosia-style fruit salad conclude the African-inspired comestibles.

The book ends with a section of lists: "Helpful Hints for Cooking," "Sugar Substitutes from *Vegetarian Times* magazine," "Food Substitutions," "Spice and Herb Chart," "How to Save Money at the Supermarket," "What to Do with Leftover Food." A section on homemade household cleaners and beauty aids, such as Egg Hair Conditioner, Toning Oatmeal Mask, Dry Skin Milk Bath, Cough Syrup, and Almond-Mayonnaise Scrub, provides a grand finale that is as interesting as it is useful. ❧

Chez Helene

"House of Good Food" Cookbook

AUSTIN LESLIE

....

New Orleans, Louisiana: De Simonin, 1984
64 pages

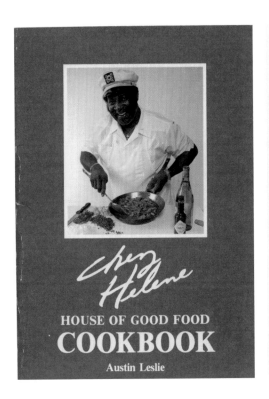

AUSTIN'S FRIED CHICKEN

1½ cups peanut oil for frying
1 3 to 3½ lb. fryer, cut up
Salt and pepper
1 egg, lightly beaten
1 cup light cream or half & half
1 cup water
½ cup A.P. flour

Preheat oil in frying pan to about 350°. Wash chicken pieces under cold water and pat dry. Sprinkle with salt and pepper. Make egg batter by combining egg, cream, water, salt and pepper. Dip pieces of chicken first in egg batter to coat and then in flour. Add chicken pieces to skillet, meatiest parts first. Do not crowd. Turn to brown on all sides. If oil pops, reduce flame. Cook until meat is tender and skin crisp, about 10 to 12 minutes. Serves 4.

32 ● CHEZ HELENE

EVEN FOLKS who had never traveled to New Orleans knew about this author's culinary swag, and his pocket-size compilation of eighty "haute cuisine" recipes enabled them to partake without ever leaving the kitchen.

His restaurant, Chez Helene, was located on the outskirts of the French Quarter. Was featured in the Time-Life cookbook series Foods of the World. And in 1987 he inspired a sitcom on CBS, *Frank's Place*. The chef blurred the lines between Creole cuisine and African American–southern–soul cooking so that every one of his recipes had broad appeal: a splash of wine in fine sauces; sautéed mushrooms caressed by a silky Madeira demi-glace; Grand Marnier Soufflé crowned with a polished English Custard Cream; Oysters Rockefeller; Bread Pudding with Rum Sauce.

It was the chef's special way with fried chicken that kept everyone talking. And eating.

Says Alton E. Harrell in the introduction: "His recipe for New Orleans' fried chicken has been the benchmark for which all other restaurants and fast food chain restaurants must set their taste buds. He reveals the secret ingredient here: a small measure of cream in the batter that coated the chicken so it fried up crisp, juicy and tender." ❧

The Black Gourmet

*Favorite Afro-American Recipes
from Coast to Coast*

JOSEPH STAFFORD

············

Detroit: Harlo, 1984
190 pages

*T*HERE IS MORE THAN A HINT of Louisiana Creole, regional adaptations, and a flair for the extravagant in this whopping treasury of "unusual, hard to get recipes not found in regular cookbooks," which may explain why the second edition added "Creole" to the title. Stafford tells us nothing about himself or what makes him a "black gourmet," devoting his preface instead to honoring the cooks who came before him.

We do learn that he thinks highly of naming certain dishes with regal status: "royal," "gourmet," "special," "deluxe," "supreme," and, when the creation is really beyond compare, "royal supreme." Otherwise, the emphasis is on meats, main dishes, and hearty appetizers: Creole Goulash, Daube, South American Beef Stew, Kentucky Meat Loaf with Bourbon Sauce, Delmonico Steak with Mushrooms, Brandy Blazed Porterhouse Steak, Gourmet Chitterlings, Pork and Veal Patties with Creole Sauce, Chop Suey Dixieland Style, and Creole Fried Chicken. 🐾

Thirty Years at the Mansion

LIZA ASHLEY

....

Little Rock, Arkansas: August House, 1985
Clinton White House edition, 1993
175 pages

BILL, HILLARY, AND CHELSEA CLINTON write in the introduction to their special edition of this gift-shop souvenir journal that Liza Ashley was a historic figure who listened to and counseled Arkansas governors and their families and staffs for thirty years, and lived her life with strength of character, common sense, and devotion to hard work and to her religious faith. They insist that besides being a very good cook, she represented the best Arkansas had to offer: "For three decades she has caused governors and their families to fight and lose battles of the bulge . . . a remarkable woman, an Arkansas treasure, and our good friend."

Clinton's assistant Carolyn Huber helped Ashley round up more than 150 recipes and dozens of photographs in which Ashley's enduring grin beams. She poses with staff members, the governors, their wives and children, and with important visitors to the mansion such as the actor Gregory Peck and former first ladies Barbara

Bush and Rosalynn Carter. The scrapbook-like collection concludes with recipes for dips, appetizers, sweets, and beverages scaled up to serve large crowds for holidays, luncheons, and teas.

Her repertoire evolved as each new family came to favor particular dishes. The family of Winthrop Rockefeller (governor 1967–1971) liked artichokes, Lobster Newburg, Vichyssoise, Clam Chowder, French Onion Soup, and Lemon Soufflé. Dale Bumpers (1971–1975) and his crew preferred simple family-style dishes like Hash Brown Potato Casserole, Stuffed Pork Chops, and southern icons such as Ham Loaf, Pickled Shrimp, and Charlotte Russe. Nearly all the dishes prepared for the family of Governor Frank White (1981–1983) were adapted from the recipe files of the first lady, Gay White, including her lasagna and several types of layered salads. The Clintons (1979–1981, 1983–1992) preferred lamb, veal, fish, quiche, and Mexican foods like enchiladas and King Ranch Chicken. Governor Clinton "loved pound cake and chess pie," she recalled. 🐦

GOVERNOR FRANK WHITE 131

Homemade Granola

2½	cups old-fashioned rolled oats
1	cup shredded coconut
½	cup coarsely-chopped almonds
½	cup sesame seeds
½	cup shelled sunflower seeds
½	cup wheat germ
½	cup honey
¼	cup cooking oil
½	cup chopped dried apricots
½	cup raisins

In large bowl, combine oats, coconut, almonds, sesame seeds, sunflower seeds and wheat germ. Combine honey and oil; stir into dry ingredients. Spread evenly in 13" x 9" x 2" pan. Bake at 300° until light golden brown for 45 to 50 minutes, stirring every 15 minutes.

Remove from oven; stir in apricots and raisins. Remove to another pan to cool. Stir occasionally during cooling to prevent lumping. When cold, store in tightly covered jars or plastic bags.

Yields 6½ cups.

Cleora's Kitchens

*The Memoir of a Cook and Eight
Decades of Great American Food*

CLEORA BUTLER

....

Tulsa, Oklahoma: Council Oaks, 1985
Second edition, 2003
213 pages

AT THE TIME THE second edition of
this noted Tulsa caterer's recipes and
recollections was published, her extraordinary
accomplishments were still virtually unknown to
the broader book-buying public, but those of us
in the food world knew all along it was a master-
piece, full of "great food, great reading."

The publisher achieved its stated goal: to
create a book that would be "as exciting as this
remarkable woman's life in food." The *Washington Post*, the *Chicago Tribune*, and *Bon Appétit*
all praised the work as "classic," "timeless," and
"inspirational." *Gourmet* magazine named the
memoir Best Cookbook of the Year. *Publishers
Weekly* praised it as a "valid lesson on the American black experience."

Traditions of fine cooking and entertaining
ran generations deep in Butler's family, but it
was the delightfully written tales of a young girl
coming of age in the kitchen—and eventually

owning a successful pastry shop and catering
business—that inspired such high praise for her
art of African American cooking.

The book begins with "The Memoir of a
Cook," an autobiographical account that highlights some of the staples of a survival kitchen:
fried chicken, greens, baking powder biscuits.
The recipes that follow (more than three hundred of them) reflect a woman defined by a lim-
itless repertoire developed in the kitchens of the
oil wealthy.

The dishes are organized by era—from "The
Early Days" to "The Twenties" and on through
"The Eighties." There are illustrations of vintage
cooking equipment and tools, such as a tin pudding mold from 1900, a cast-iron muffin pan
(1890), and a tinned-steel tube pan (1923), and
pictures of pickled condiments and dried herbs
in contemporary Spanish jars. Text boxes tell the
origins and history of commonplace foodstuffs:

the story of margarine; the difference between griddle cakes, pancakes, and crepes; a brief history of graham flour and of All-Bran cereal; the origins of wax paper.

The pages bring to life specialties from her bakeshop as well as her catering sensibility. Her anecdotes are wise, and her recipes wonderful, most of which cross the border from soul and southern to mainstream. Her takes on southern basics are fancified with imaginative additions: beef tongue with raisin sauce; okra and tomatoes with crab, shrimp, and mushrooms; roast squab stuffed with wild rice; polenta (cornmeal mush) with meat sauce; bran cereal fiber in cornbread; eggs poached in beer; olive oil pickles. There are only a few recipes for cabin staples such as offal and long-simmered vegetables with pork.

What is an aitchbone? Want to make mashed potatoes or pumpkin pie today to serve tomorrow (or any day in the future)? Butler answers questions such as these. And more.

The southern food writer James Villas once wrote that M. F. K. Fisher was the "guiding light, the source of infinite gastronomic and philosophic wisdom, the model of what a truly refined food writer should strive for." Cleora Butler was the M. F. K. Fisher of her day.

To hear her tell it, growing up the granddaughter of former slaves on a farm in Oklahoma energized her career. Her mother baked popovers, cream puffs, and all kinds of cakes on a wood-burning stove, and Cleora and her brothers often worked all weekend to deliver freshly baked bread to customers who paid twenty-five cents for each loaf. The family enjoyed cook-ins during winter months when they were housebound, baking two or three kinds of cookies or one of their favorite desserts. And she made fresh sausage at hog-killing time with her grandfather just before Thanksgiving. By the time she was fifteen years old, wild strawberries, blackberries, plums, and possum grapes converted into succulent jams, preserves, and fine wines were the beacon that spurred her interest in home economics classes, leading to a successful professional culinary career.

She summarized her "attitude about the art of cooking" with a verse that she adapted from John Ruskin. ❧

*To be a good cook means
    employing the economy of
    great-grandmother and the
    science of modern chemists.*

*It means much tasting
    and no wasting.*

*It means English thoroughness,
    French art and Arabian hospitality.*

*It means, in fine,
    that you are to see that
    everyone has something nice to eat.*

—Ruskin

Stirrin' the Pots on Daufuskie

BILLIE BURN

....

Hilton Head, South Carolina: Impressions, 1985
197 pages

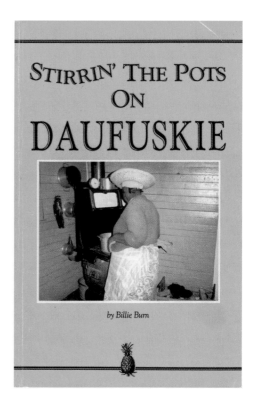

You know by the author's printed signature and inscription on the opening page—"With Love, Billie Burn"—that this is going to be a book redolent with a spirit that exudes community and love. The collection of more than two hundred "original and favorite recipes of those who live or once lived on Daufuskie Island" was gathered by a white woman who canvassed family and friends, men and women, black and white, current and former Daufuskie residents, for heritage cooking recipes. A few of Burn's own recipes, including her mother's handwritten formula for white fruitcake, capture the spirit of love and reverence for authenticity.

A winsome introduction paints a transactional picture of island women practicing their improvisational craft in mixed settings, each one adding different foods to the cooking pot until it tasted just right. No onions? No problem. These cooks simply ladled in whatever was fresh and available, whether that meant beans, potatoes, corn, or discarded animal parts, and in the case of Thomas Stafford's Roll Bread, "buttermilk, if you can get it." Crabs, oysters, and rice seasoned the pot, too. When times were particularly tough, some islanders roasted otter or "went so far as to eat pinebark bread and fiddler claw stew."

Next, like a reverential grace of thanksgiving offered just before a meal, the tribute gets underway with a litany of food-related Bible verses, the Pledge of Allegiance, and "Island Hints," a couple of dozen recipes from 1868 for simple preserves, puddings, beauty treatments, medicinal cures, baking powder, and several puddings—instructions that read like the kind of wise counsel neighbors exchange over hot tea and gingerbread in the late afternoon.

The book concludes with a feast of down-home life stories of nearly 125 cooks and a few of their favorite recipes. It is a style that can be traced to Africa, too: Fresh Fig Cake; Old Fashioned Biscuit Pudding made with leftover baked biscuits; Red Grits, tinted with mashed cooked pumpkin; Red Peas and Chitterlings. For cultural balance, there is a section of Swedish recipes from a 1907 cookbook.

Grainy photographs are scattered throughout, documenting important places, including the home where best-selling and award-winning author Pat Conroy lived. ❧

25 pond rice
10 pond grits
10 flour
5 pond sugar
1 half gallon cooking oil
2 Box salt
4 pond smoke Bacon
3 can cream small
3 large can
1 Bottle dish washing
1 Jar coffee
1 sweet roll
1 Box donuts
1 Box mush crackers

x

1 Bag Beans
1 Bag Black i peas
3 Bar octogan soap
1 scrub Brush
1 Jar sweet pickles
3 Can park an Beans
1 Bottle tomatoes Cautchup
2 tray Turkey wings
2 tray harm hook
2 tray Stew Beef
2 tray nick Bone
2 tray park Choops
1 Sack Corn

Tow loaf Bread

xi

Mrs. Susie Washington Smith's recipe
BLACKBERRY DUMPLIN'*

1 quart blackberries, washed and drained
Pot — half filled with water (a saucer in the bottom of the pot will prevent the dumplin' from sticking).

Make favorite pie dough recipe using flour, lard or oil, water and a little sugar. Roll out on floured board until rectangular in size. Spread berries over dough. Roll up dough over berries, folding over ends to seal them in. Put in a clean cloth and tie well with string. Lower in boiling water that completely covers dumplin'. Cook about 2 hours until dough is done. Take out of water immediately. Roll dumplin' out on a platter or in a pan. Serve with sauce.

Sauce:
1 can condensed milk
¼ cup sugar (optional)
1 stick margarine
½ tsp. nutmeg or vanilla/lemon flavoring
Mix and serve generously over dumplin'.

Susie is giving a recipe in memory of her mother.

Mrs. Agnes Washington's Recipe
OYSTER STEW OR GRAVY*

1 pint oysters   3 slices bacon
1 small onion, chopped   1 Tbs. self-rising flour

Fry bacon, remove from pan. Add onion and cook until done. Add flour and let brown. Add oysters and crumbled bacon. Add a little water if needed. Cook until oysters curl around edges. Serve over grits or rice.

(Everyone on the Island uses this basic recipe except some use white meat rather than bacon.)

140

Making a Blackberry Dumplin'

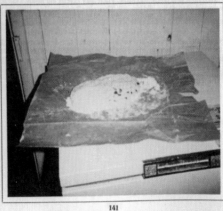

141

Ma Chance's French Caribbean Creole Cooking

JEANNE LOUISE DUZANT CHANCE

....

New York: Putnam, 1985
159 pages

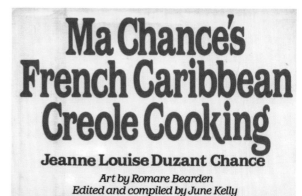

THIS COLLECTION OF OVER two hundred dishes representing the exotic flavors of the Caribbean island of St. Martin would be a treasure, even without the accompanying sketches by Romare Bearden. Its menus translate a cooking style that Ma Chance, short for Madame Chance, learned by watching her mother and experimenting. Her dishes trace back to a time when French Creole cooking meant food so fresh that "many times people did not even wash or peel the vegetables." They ate boiled potatoes with milk for breakfast; fish, cornmeal, and stewed peas for lunch. Dinner was fried fish, soup, and dessert. Cassava bread was the usual snack.

Her printed collection is dominated by island seafood—Conch Soup, Whelk (sea snail) Salad, Poached Kingfish braised with aromatic vegetables and herbs, Lobster Stew with Hot

Corn Balls, Crab Burgers, and assorted seafood omelets. As a nod to her African heritage, there also are fritters of every kind—savory codfish, oyster-cornmeal, crab, and sweet nuggets of pumpkin, banana, breadfruit, and tannia (a type of yam) seed. Other dishes include deviled eggs stuffed with crab; callaloo soup (made from dark leafy greens) crowned with dumplings; Stuffed Christophene (chayote squash); Cassava Bread; Gooseberries-on-Stick; Stewed Guavas; Coconut Pie; and a airy frozen mango treat, Mango Magique.

The book finishes with a selection of island punches juiced from papaya, passion fruit, soursop, and prickly pear; brunch, lunch, and dinner menus; and a shopper's guide for hard-to-find ingredients. ❧

Hot Stuff

A Cookbook in Praise of the Piquant

JESSICA B. HARRIS

············

New York: Atheneum, 1985
278 pages

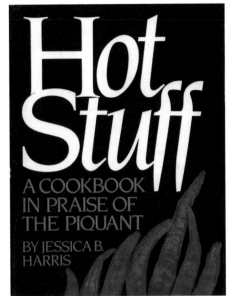

As a food and travel writer for leading magazines, Jessica Harris observed that the American taste for hot and spicy food was on the rise, so she traveled the globe in order to tell the history of peppers, dating back to early man. Her book provides medical claims for pepper consumption, an A-to-Z glossary of pepper vocabulary that describes piquancy, how-tos for purchasing and preserving peppers, menus, mail-order sources, plus 250 recipes for hot stuff from four regions: Africa, Latin America and the Caribbean, Asia, and the West.

Recipes are identified by their place of origin. Informative headnotes tell how dishes are traditionally served and suggest ways to improvise when preparing recipes without the usual kitchen tools. Personal anecdotes explain her first encounters with a dish.

Not every recipe proposed by the author, an assistant professor of English and French at Queens College in New York, will set the mouth a-blazin'—refried beans, guacamole, vegetables in yogurt, even alcoholic beverages with just a mild dust of chile.

Then there are those incendiary dishes taken from regions around the world:

"Hot Stuff in Africa"—In this section, chiles are cooked whole or ground and simmered into traditional stews, *wat*s (an Ethiopian stew or curry), and sauces for fish cakes and fritters.

Finely chopped chile pepper finds its way into Banana Snacks. And peppers turn salads of avocado, carrots, eggplant, and cucumber fiery.

"Hot Stuff in Latin America and the Caribbean"—"Peppers poke their red noses up through Martinique's Sauce Chien . . . Haitian chefs perform voodoo in creating Sauce Ti-Malice." Other peppery dishes abound: Puerto Rican deep-fried codfish fritters liberally doused with spicy hot sauce; Mexican breakfast eggs; even the classic margarita gets a dose of spice in the Sangrita, a tomato, orange, and lime juice mixture seasoned with onion salt and chile.

"Hot Stuff in Asia"—This is the land of Mongolian barbecue, Indian curries, sambals, chutneys, and hot condiments, but the love of chile extends to desserts such as Spiced Summer Fruit Salad and to spiced tea from India, *satay* sauce served with grilled meat and marinated meat appetizers such as kebabs and tikka.

"The Western Tradition"—The recipes here feature some expected formulas like Philadelphia Pepper Pot. But there are also some interesting surprises among traditional southern dishes, such as Ham Spread spiced with cayenne; macaroni and cheese, okra and tomatoes, crab cakes, and cornbread sticks all get a kick from chile pepper. Pickled jalapeño peppers give chicken livers pep. ❧

The Africa News Cookbook

African Cooking for Western Kitchens

EDITED BY TAMI HULTMAN

....

New York: Viking Penguin, 1985
175 pages

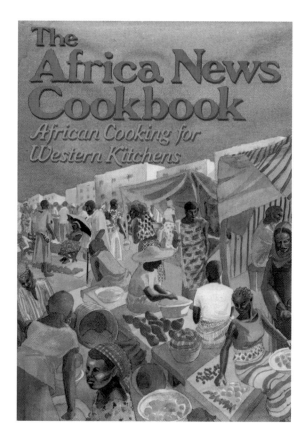

THE AFRICA NEWS SERVICE, based in
Durham, North Carolina, was a nonprofit
educational news organization that provided
content about Africa to the American media
and the public. The agency's stated objective for
writing this book was to introduce recipes that
contained "few of the high-fat, excessive protein
foods so prevalent in Western diets" and instead
were "rich in fruits, vegetables, and healthful
carbohydrates"—"perfect for today's new style
of cooking and eating."

In the introduction, the editor makes clear the
connection between southern and African foodways: "It is appropriate than an African recipe
book be produced in the Southern United States,
a region that long ago assimilated African ingredients and culinary techniques. Every 'southern cookbook' silently exhibits its debt to those
heartsick slaves who re-created a bit of home in
their stews and cornbreads and greens and fritters. African influences are pervasive, from the
jambalayas and gumbos of Louisiana bayous to
Charleston's characteristic bene snacks—peppery,
sesame crackers and sesame candies and cakes."

The book goes on to recount the continent's
topography, its precolonial eating habits, the
nutritive value of the typical diet, the role of
women's work on cuisine, and then to talk briefly
about corruption, discrimination, poverty, hunger,
and educational injustices. To further correct
perceptions about African cookery, celebrations,
and hospitality, and their connection to African
American foodways, the editor allows the wholesome simplicity of 165 adapted recipes to speak
for itself.

The story begins with some fragrant spices
that are integral to African cookery—cardamom, cinnamon, cloves, coriander, cumin, fennel,
fenugreek, garlic, ginger, mint, pepper, sesame,
and turmeric. She offers a word about the proper
handling and cooking of fiery chiles. She explains
how to clean shrimp, peel tomatoes, and deep-fry.

A wide range of regional dishes follows, adapted to American kitchens, schedules, and ingredients, each accompanied by fascinating anecdotes of its origins, its creators, and the traditions associated with serving it. Recipes for condiments, soups, snacks, meats, seafoods, vegetarian dishes, and a few desserts are presented (in many cases) with their African titles and places of origin. Each formula demonstrates how these aromatic roots and herbs, local ingredients, and culinary techniques give character to the savory *tagines*, *wat*s, chutneys, sauces, salads, and drinks of Africa, and how these national dishes found new life in the New World.

Illustrations by Patricia Ford pop up throughout. The map of Africa's colonial past shows how cultural boundaries influenced cooking and eating habits. There are depictions of a host and guests enjoying Senegalese *yassa*, a long-marinated dish of grilled chicken and rice; variations for folding savory filled pastries (samosas), pigeon or chicken pie (*bstila*) or stuffed vine leaves (similar to Greek dolmas); and a Western Saharan tea ceremony, *le thé*. ❧

The Griots' Cookbook

Rare and Well-Done

ALICE MCGILL, MARY CARTER SMITH,
AND ELMIRA M. WASHINGTON

....

Columbia, Maryland: Fairfax, 1985
201 pages

A STORYTELLER AND FOLKLORIST, an actress and yarn spinner, and a writer: these three women came together in a "circle of love," combined their passion for the creative art of storytelling with their desire to pass on black culinary and griot customs, and produced a book that raised money for Morgan State University's WEAA-FM radio station even as it celebrated African oral traditions.

It is a book on the art of cooking that is "as entertaining as it is useful," with tales that celebrate the "human spirit," Smith said.

The book begins brightly. Lengthy biographical sketches and photographs of each author mingle basic vital details, such as birthplace, education, marital status, and accomplishments with a few words imparting her philosophy for living.

Chapters labeled "Breads," "Eggs," "Meats," "Fish and Poultry," "Sweets," and "Vegetables"

come next. Breezy "commentary" relates how a recipe was created (as in, in a pinch), how recipes migrated from one part of the world into the hands of the authors, which dishes travel or store well, and how best to serve particular ones. There is also a miscellany the authors call "notes of interest." Smith's amusing poetry, African proverbs, and more than 125 familiar mixtures appear with a few unusual items, such as Potato Chip Omelette and Heart Chop Suey (made with beef or veal hearts). The names of the contributors are included.

The book draws to a delightful close with three stories, Smith's blueprint for how to be a storyteller, and a biblical reference, John 13:35: "By this shall all men know that ye are my disciples: if ye have love one for another." ❧

Tidbits For Telling Stories

Choosing a Story

Does the story appeal to you? In a quick reading or listening does it capture your attention and involve you in what is happening? (Does it "grab" you?) You **MUST** like it to expect others to like it.

Are the characters interesting, believable, and fun to work with? Are there enough contrasts among them for you to portray them or at least give suggestions of differing characteristics? It is wise to keep the major characters to a few in number.

Select a story filled with action - with one suspenseful event building on another to the climax.

Have an arresting introduction.

Be aware of sensory images as, "Her skin was like black velvet."

Be aware of the length of a story. Beginning storytellers may try to keep stories within five to seven minute range. Some may be shorter. Ten minutes may be long enough to tell a short story; the folktales may be shorter. As you gain in experience you will get a "feel" for length, by the reaction of your listeners. **Telling time** and **reading time** are not the same.

Be aware of telling the appropriate story for your audience.

Decide whether to use first or third person in the telling.

You may decide to change setting and nationality of characters.

You may adapt a story by deleting plot incidents, minor characters and description.

Using Dialogue, rather than constant "and the man said," "the queen answered," etc.

Focus your attention on **TWO THINGS:**

1. The story (see it and feel it happen **NOW**)
2. Your listeners (let them know you care about them)

Facing Stage Fright

1. There is no "pat" cure.
2. Gain experience
3. Be prepared
4. "Sense" the audience and react to it
5. I repeat Philippians 4:13:
   "I can do all things through Christ, which strengtheneth me."

Costuming

Use to highlight and personalize your sessions if you are comfortable doing so.

Pitfalls

AVOID:

Standing perfectly immobile

Having too many gestures

Ignoring disruptive behaviour

Using some ethnic language with some groups that find it objectionable

Looking **DRAB**

Seeming insecure/scared

Having a monotonous voice

Having your story **too long.**
When you see you're losing interest, cut/change/stop.

Pacing back and forth

Mary Carter Smith
© 1981

Alice McGill

Mary Carter Smith

Elmira M. Washington

The Second Best of Granny

Family Recipes

GEORGIA H. CARTER

....

New York: Vantage, 1986
67 pages

IN JUST 110 SHORT, simple recipes, Granny concocts imaginative entrees and pies that will make you want to go into the kitchen and cook. Right now. Educated in home economics and nutrition, the author adapted the favorite recipes of her friends and family for healthier eating.

She displays some of the same taste for game stews, gumbos, chicken and dumplings, cornbreads, and buttermilk biscuits as authors who were her contemporaries. Elsewhere, her swanky recipe inventory jumps off assertively with unique additions that boost the flavor and trim fat by, for example, stirring sweet potatoes into tea cake batter. But the most compelling part of the book is at the end—seventeen fabulous quantity-cooking recipes that take the guesswork out of entertaining and cooking for buffets or church suppers.

Granny's Season-All is a fifteen-ingredient aromatic mix of salt, garlic, curry, chili peppers, onion and celery, mustard, nutmeg, ginger, peppers, and paprika stirred together, stored in a covered container, and sprinkled on everything. She makes a seafood seasoning by adding allspice, mace, and turmeric to the rub.

Chicken and dumplings goes Creole with crawfish in the brew. She keeps an eye on fat and calories with Parmesan Chicken, a take on oven-fried chicken. Turkey stands in everywhere—for seafood in étouffée and for smoked pork in lima beans. Her amazing pies really do put it down: Chitterling Pie, Sweet Potato Pie in Raisin Crust, Pumpkin Pie in Pecan Crust, and Apple Pie in Cheese Crust. Go, Granny! ❧

GRANNY'S SEASON-ALL

2 C	salt
2 T	sugar
1 T	garlic powder
1 T	curry powder
1 T	chili powder
1 t	cayenne pepper
1 t	onion powder
1 t	allspice
6 T	paprika
1 T	Accent
1 T	celery salt
1 T	dry mustard
1 t	nutmeg
2 T	black pepper
1 t	ginger

Mix thoroughly. Store in covered container.

Makes 3 cups

1

"I Just Quit Stirrin' When the Tastin's Good"

CISSY FINELY GRANT

....

Cape May, New Jersey: Chalfonte Hotel, 1986
90 pages

In a 1954 photo taken at The Chalfonte, Helen (second from right) is pictured with her family -- (from left) Lucille, Dot and Helen's mother, Clementine Young. Dot's daughter, Tina, is in front.

SINCE 1876, family-style dinners composed in the traditional southern manner have graced the table at New Jersey's Chalfonte Hotel in historic Cape May. For thirty-two of those years, Helen Dickerson put the food on the plates. To finally get the "chief chef's" formulas down on paper, the author states that recipes were measured, "tested, re-tested, and tested again." At last, this little homemade souvenir book of eighty-five recipes was completed—a testament to the woman who welcomed summertime guests year after year with promises of seashore breezes and the alluring taste of her warm yeast rolls.

The book is airy, with recipes appearing in typewritten fonts, and the pages are dusted with a few illustrations of kitchen tools and ingredients. A dozen black-and-white images capture the Victorian structure's charming facade, with its quaint louvered doors and expansive porches, its spacious and elegant dining room, its owners, and Dickerson. She poses with her daughters, their husbands, and the tools of her trade. She also is immortalized in photographs showing her shaping her beloved rolls and flouring her world-class fried chicken. ✹

Big Mama's Old Black Pot

ETHEL DIXON

....

Alexandria, Louisiana: Stroke Gabriel, 1987
207 pages

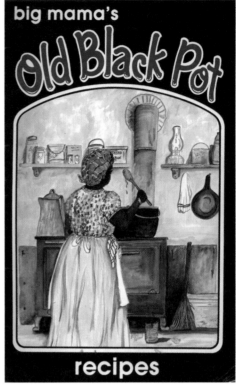

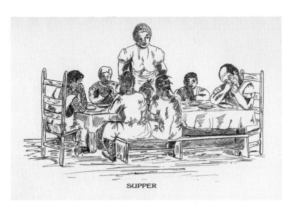

SUPPER

vegetables

YOU MIGHT THINK from the book's cover or from the clichéd illustrations of a busty mammy in a head rag slumped over and kneading a mound of dough or carrying a heavy dressed turkey on a silver tray, à la *Harper's Weekly* circa 1900, that this trip back in time is just another awful plantation cookbook written by a white woman to caricature her black cook. Thankfully, it is not.

In a peculiar twist, an African American author sourced the book's contents from old letters, photographs, journals, diaries, chats across fences, and stories shared on porches between generations. The register is useful and entertaining, with splendid illustrations, short stories, and folklore that depict a way of life scarcely recorded in history books, according to the author. It is the work of a woman who is proud of her culinary heritage. And it shows.

Dixon revels in the legacy left by Mama and a half-dozen other family cooks from whom she inherited a strong work ethic, a love of farm and family, and over 150 recipes for sturdy country

cooking. She dedicated these sentimental recipes for "good old-fashioned, calorie-laden, country-style cooking . . . to every wife, mother and daughter who toiled over a hot wood stove 'making-do' with whatever sparse staples that were available to provide for their family a tasty, nourishing meal."

Taffy pulls, stumpin' for catfish, forecasting weather by animal and insect behavior, and clever formulas for home remedies educate and captivate. There are recipes for Potato Biscuits, Syrup Bread, Huckleberry Muffins, Honey Beets, Ros-a-Nears (roasting ears of corn), Fried Pea Fritters, Pig's Feet Soup (with ginger, squash, tomatoes, and lima beans), Buttermilk Salad Dressing, Meatballs and Rice, Venison Sausage, Smoked Goose, Fried Turkey Breast, Garfish Balls, Crab Loaf, Butter Roll Pie, and the proper way to make the five country gravies (brown flour, cream, giblet, redeye, and tomato). In all, the book seems to administer a no-nonsense, Big Mama command: "Get your ass in the kitchen and cook." ❧

Down Home
Southern Cooking

LAMONT BURNS

············

Garden City, New York: Doubleday, 1987
Paperback edition, LaMont's Food Products, Inc.
176 pages

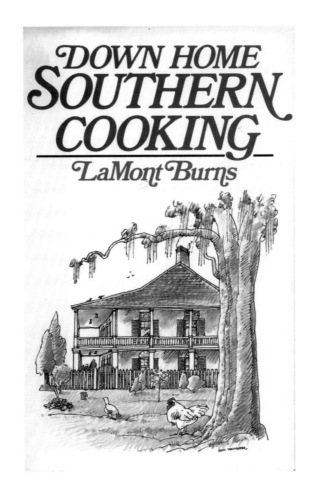

BURNS EXPLORES the roots of southern cuisine through the culinary legacy of four generations of black cooks and over one hundred recipes that proclaim southern hospitality. Inspirited by the culinary values of his ancestors, he transformed the classics of the Old South into a heritage cuisine so ageless that it spawned a reprint edition and a specialty foods company specializing in barbecue sauces, baking sauces, and marinades.

His knack for cooking with spices was a passion inspired by his grandmother. Here he adds a dash of coriander to a classic crab appetizer to enliven without overpowering the delicate flavor. Elsewhere, he takes his cues from Africans who thickened soups and stews with groundnuts or used them as a coating for fried meats and vegetables, as in his Almond Chicken

Soup. Old-school creamed chicken becomes new school when tender sweetbreads and sherry are added to the mix. Burns unwrites the rules of delicate, flaky piecrust too, substituting bread flour and hot water for all-purpose flour and ice water. And his Molasses Pudding with Foaming Sauce shows he understood food safety; he cautions readers to stir the sauce mixture over boiling water to ensure the eggs are cooked through but not curdled.

The book is illustrated generously with drawings of the kitchen hearth; farm, plantation, and coastal scenes; table settings; and the ingredients for his dishes. Miss Lucinda (his great-grandmother), Miss Aussiebelle (his grandmother), and Miss Thelma (his "Momma") appear in vintage photographs in the reprint edition. 🌸

Gene Hovis's Uptown Down Home Cookbook

GENE HOVIS WITH
SYLVIA ROSENTHAL

....

Boston: Little, Brown, 1987
235 pages

"Gene Hovis, to my mind, is one of the finest hosts of New York. To dine at his table is an absolute joy. He is a superb southern cook and the recipes in his new book are admirable testament to his taste and talent."

Craig Claiborne

W HEN IT COMES TO GIVING Granny a voice, Hovis does about as good a job as anyone can.

Hovis writes lovingly and with reverence about the woman he remembered as a superb cook and fabulous seamstress who always set her dining room with a lovely hand-crocheted cloth and pretty hand-embroidered napkins. This charming tribute recalls a bygone era through wistful re-membrances of feasts at funerals, laundry baskets that doubled as picnic hampers at prayer meet-ings, special birthday fare, and meals made in an electric skillet. A 1987 *Publishers Weekly* reviewer observed that the anecdotes about Granny are simply "delightful," and the recipes for more than 190 timeless southern emblems, "enticing."

Mary Cooper Dameron was born in the mid-1800s in North Carolina, the daughter of slaves. She was the cook in the home of a British-born family named Cooper, where she also learned to read but not to write. She had seven children, was widowed early, and raised her family alone. A bowl of fresh flowers on her dining table "looked opulent and lavish." But it was the exquisite food on her table that impressed Hovis most.

As evidence, he preserved Granny Dameron's culinary legacy and used it as the backdrop for his adapted southern style. The vegetable trays and tea sandwiches that were popular buffet luncheon hors d'oeuvres in Granny's day were redesigned around curried quail eggs rather than standard deviled chicken eggs.

He gussies up tea sandwiches as a way to channel the bounteous meals that Granny expertly packed, carried, and served in a shoebox to meet the challenge of satisfying adult and child appetites while traveling in the segregated South. There are tips for making seasoned butters. Suggestions for preventing sogginess, storing food properly, and serving sandwiches remain important considerations for modern cooks, whether they are packing brown-bag lunches or gathering friends over a cup of tea or coffee.

A few chef-like touches, such as wine in sauces, homemade stock, and kneaded butter (*beurre manié*), help the whole thing along. Particular specialties suggest that Granny's legacy will be safe, and sometimes updated, in Hovis's creative and competent hands: Skillet Meat Loaves (braised versions of the usual potted meat entree); Chicken Breasts glazed with an orange-cognac sauce; chicken crowned with a mélange of fresh summer vegetables; roast capon bathed in rosemary butter; roast turkey marinated in soy sauce, white wine, juniper berries, rosemary, and honey; Shad Roe Soufflé with Lemon-Dill Butter (Granny's Shad Roe Pudding); Beets Filled with Peas; cornbread exploding with corn kernels and sour cream; Bacon Bread; and an upside-down lemon pie baked in a meringue crust. ❧

The Black Gourmet Cookbook

A Unique Collection of Easy-to-Prepare, Appetizing, Black American, Creole, Caribbean, and African Cuisine

MADEMOISELLES NOIRES

....

St. Paul, Minnesota: Mademoiselles Noires, 1987
76 pages

I DON'T KNOW WHAT compelled *les dames* to publish their romp through four African American cooking styles, or even who the women were, for that matter. All I can tell you is that I am convinced that their upscale masterpieces should assure everyone once and for all that classic methods, regional foods, and ancestral knowledge were the canvas upon which African American cuisine was created and maintained. All the presumed trademarks of soul, Louisiana, island, and African food are here, but you might not recognize them. They appear with detailed instructions unseen so far—napped in rich sauces, laced with liqueurs, and sophisticated, frenchified techniques. The recipes are grouped according to the following themes:

Black American—green onions and chitlins baked into quiche; barbecued spareribs marinated overnight in herbs, crushed red pepper, wine vinegar, garlic, and onion; baked raccoon with sweet potatoes in a red wine sauce; roast duck with apricot stuffing and plum sauce spiked with ginger and chili sauce; and, from Africa, mixed greens garnished with cornmeal dumplings.

Creole-Cajun—Creole Baked Tongue stuffed with vegetables and served with rice and gravy, Quail in Sherry Sauce over Scrambled Eggs, Cajun Fried Frog Legs served on a bed of crisp fried parsley, Bread Pudding with Rum Sauce and whipped cream spiked with Frangelico and cognac.

Caribbean—fried chicken marinated in dark rum, roast chicken with banana stuffing, Edam cheese with shrimp stuffing, lobster crowned smoky tomato-ham *sofrito* sauce, red bean soup with dumplings, and a polenta-like porridge, Fungi.

African—Braised Chicken in Coconut Cream Sauce, with directions for making coconut milk from fresh coconut; Lemon Chicken with Olives, which includes instructions for a thirty-day process for making Preserved Lemons; greens made savory with sautéed tomatoes and crushed peanuts rather than fatty pork. ❧

African Cookery

A Black Heritage

ANNETTE MERSON

....

Nashville, Tennessee: Wilson-Derek, 1987
68 pages

UNLIKE PREVIOUSLY published works on the subject, which presented a more scholarly look at the culinary habits of Africans, this book is a lightweight that will be remembered primarily for its artistic elements. But like the others, it presents a social history that investigates the point at which Africa and the American South intersect, using images to extend an invitation to cook the way Africans do.

The opening pages explain the sources of the geometric designs that surround the pages dividing each chapter: carvings found on an African musical instrument, a South African stone building, a cloth pattern showing the significance of tribal dances, a heavy woven floor mat from Sudan, or a fabric popular in Equatorial Africa. What follows is a brief discussion of African ingenuity in working with limited resources, plus the medical aspects of food, vegetarian practices among certain tribes, and few random statements labeled "Of Interest Regarding Food and Drink in Africa."

More than sixty choice recipes from all over the continent, interspersed with a bit of background, ensure that readers will be able to distinguish a Dutch-influenced dish from one that originated in Malay. The recipes include South African stew; Zanzibar duck; a version of *boontjie bredie*, a one-dish braise of beef, pork, and lamb cubes; and dishes so common that their ethnology is a mere afterthought—*berbere* (an Ethiopian spice mix), *injera* (sourdough flatbread), banana fritters, *fufu* (yam paste balls), *doro wat* (stewed chicken in red pepper sauce), chicken–peanut butter stew, and spiced meat pastries (samosas). ❧

Aspects of Afro-American Cookery

HOWARD PAIGE

....

Lanthrup Village, Michigan: Aspects, 1987
256 pages

As an independent foodways scholar, Paige had a hard time being taken seriously in established food media circles. It didn't help that he was promoting the idea that black cooking was something everyone, everywhere—not just black folks—could value and respect, be proud of. So he did what passionate African Americans had done for generations before and after him: self-published his study. We should all be very glad that he did.

Paige's footnoted work may seem both novel and familiar to those familiar with modern food studies, but at a time when few mainstream authors were making the case, this book presented an impressive chronology of the "Afro-American cook as an active partner in the development of America's foodways, rather than as a separate entity" responsible only for "soul food."

Paige examined a wide range of sources and then concluded his extensive investigation with reviews of more than a dozen regionally diverse cookbooks (all of them included in *The Jemima Code*) and a handful of recipes from family and friends. The accompanying biographical sketches of each author, along with his or her recipes, serve as a permanent attestation of culinary range and creative skill.

The exploration of black culinary history begins at the beginning, introducing readers to African foods and revisiting Middle Passage practices and New World experiences that turned competent slave cooks into those advertised for sale because of their "outstanding credentials in the culinary arts." Sukey Hamilton, he wrote, cooked for Governor Francis Fauquier (1703–1768) of Virginia; a New York City

The Jemima Code

newspaper notice in 1734 advertised for sale a twenty-year-old slave woman: "She dos all sorts of House work; she can Brew, Bake, boyle soaft soap, Wash, Iron & Starch; and is a good Darey Women [dairywoman] . . . She can Cook pretty well for Rost and Boyld [roast and boiled]." An early American Thanksgiving menu links native African foodways and slave experiences to colonial dishes such as spoon bread, hot molasses cake, and beaten biscuits.

From here, Paige traces the African American experience to Washington, D.C., unearthing black participation in the culinary occupations of the region. He names fifteen entrepreneurs who owned oyster houses, fruit stores, taverns, hotels, and restaurants, or were cooks, bakers, and gardeners. He introduces readers to the "excellent service, good food, and hospitality" at James Wormley's hotel through illustrations and recipes.

He theorizes that the work of household managers, plantation big-house cooks, and field-hand cooks influenced the foodways of their time with their ingenuity in using basic plantation food allowances. Their preparations lifted squirrel, rabbit, and other small game from edible to delicious. He uses travel journals to identify and commend black vendors. As part of his research, he excavated a wide variety of food preparation techniques and tools from unspecified archaeological sources, explored plantation Christmas traditions, uncovered the contributions of Civil War cooks from army task records, and discovered the world-class chefs responsible for fine dining on America's railroads.

In my book, his work goes down as an instrument of historical significance. ❧

Caribbean and African Cookery

ROSAMUND GRANT

....

London: Grub Street, 1988
160 pages

THIS IS A GRACEFULLY WRITTEN and artfully illustrated introduction to tropical black cookery. The author, a cook, demonstrator, teacher, and restaurateur invites readers to experiment with the fresh flavors of West African, Caribbean, and black American cooking. In the foreword, Maya Angelou accepted the invitation. So do I.

Growing up in Guyana, Grant learned that the essence of good cooking meant using fresh vegetables and fruits and seasoning meat and fish with herbs and spices so that they were "full of pepper." Her narratives give an overview of each chapter, providing history and relevance and interjecting short bursts of memory like anecdotes told off script. We travel with her to West Africa to learn about the village traditions, street festivities, and maternal influences that shape her menus.

She acknowledges the challenge she set for herself: "It has been a formidable task trying to encapsulate the feelings of movement, individuality, colour, struggle and loving care that have been essential ingredients in our traditional cooking." But she does it. Some dishes are traditional. Others were created out of her imagination with ingredients and styles borrowed from other cultures: an Asian backdrop is reflected in a vegetarian version of Caribbean black pudding rolled in Japanese nori and served with mango and apple sour, and in Prawn Low-Mein. She sweetens banana bread with demerara sugar and spices cornbread with a hint of cinnamon.

A few color photographs capture the delightful array of dishes from each chapter, and illustrations transplant readers into tropical scenes— a veranda where a table is set with an elaborate feast; a view from the Demerara River in Guyana of an island peeking through coconut trees, with mountains on the horizon.

The detailed and thoughtfully illustrated glossary of Caribbean and African foods and cooking techniques is painstakingly useful. Line drawings are an amazing asset. These pictorial aides help cooks distinguish between fish types; end confusion about two types of taro, *eddoe* and *coco*; show what ackee, cassava, *corilla* (bitter gourd), *egusi*, *jingy*, sorrel, soursop, sugar cane, and tamarind look like; amplify a series of how-tos, including ways to clean and prepare fresh fish, peel fresh pineapple, and prepare and cook plantains. Other snapshots into the island kitchen show steamy soup bowls, handwoven baskets, and jars of relishes and preserves.

Grant concludes with a rare and enchanting tale of the *Que Que* ceremony, a premarital practice of song and dance found primarily in the Berbice region of Guyana. It survived slavery and descends from the Ibo peoples of Nigeria. The *Que Que* queen leads the ritual, which is performed on the night or on a series of nights before the church ceremony, and involves the couples' families, friends, and neighbors—and free-flowing rum. ❧

The Que-Que Ceremony

143

PREPARING AND COOKING PLANTAINS

TO PEEL A PLANTAIN (OR GREEN BANANA)

Using a small sharp vegetable knife, top and tail the plantain and cut in half. Make three or four slits lengthwise in the skin, without cutting the flesh. Lift off the edge of a slit and run the tip of your thumb under the edge, lengthwise, peeling back and removing all of the skin.

TO BOIL

Put the peeled plantains into a saucepan of boiling, salted water, to which 5 ml (1 tsp) of cooking oil has been added (this helps to stop them discolouring). Alternatively, boil the plantains in their skins (after slitting them) until tender.

TO PREPARE RIPE PLANTAINS

Ripe plantains are easier to peel. Follow the method above. They can be boiled (better when firm) or sliced and fried. Over-ripe plantains make a delicious snack — try Tatale, for example (see p. 28).

TO MAKE FUFU

Fufu is usually made by pounding cooked root vegetables in a mortar. There are many types of fufu — this one is made with boiled green plantains. I used a food processor and 'like magic' the plantain was rolled into the perfect oval shape, without any effort from me.

Boil the green plantain until just cooked, then put into the bowl of a blender or food processor. Sprinkle with water and blend. Keep hot in foil, until ready for use, then slice and serve. Serve with soups or stews.

TO MAKE PLANTAIN CHIPS FROM GREEN PLANTAINS

Peel then slice with a sharp knife into thin rounds, or use a slicer for potato crisps and then fry the plantains in hot oil until golden brown and crisp, then drain on kitchen paper. Sprinkle with salt, if desired and store in an airtight tin. Serve as a snack or appetizer, separately or mixed with nuts.

Viola's Favorite Recipes

VIOLA LAMPKIN

....

Olathe, Kansas: Cookbook Publishers, 1988
74 pages

**Barbara Clagett and Viola Lampkin
The Perpetrators of this Cookbook**

Ａnother cook, another monument. This narrative of a faithful servant, loving member of the family, and great cook sharing her "magic" with a beloved white woman gives the impression that little had changed in cookbooks from the Old South during the preceding hundred years. As Barbara Clagett puts it in the introduction: "Now I can stand in my kitchen . . . and muster up some of the best country cooking imaginable . . . and have Viola right there with me." Its just over 160 standard-issue southern dishes don't include a single recipe for scarcity cooking.

Lampkin was the cook on Springfield Farm, the Clagett family home in Berryville, Virginia.

At the age of nineteen, after years of observing, absorbing, and practicing her mother's techniques, she "became an artist in the kitchen," celebrated in Clarke County for her "famous culinary creations."

Brown Edge Vanilla Wafer, Iced Green Tomato Pickles that are crisp and glasslike, baked dove breasts, and Jellied Meat Loaf stand out among recipes that are easy to follow and come with complete instructions and a few tips.

There are no headnotes to tell more about the relationship between Viola and her charges. But a warm familial photograph of the two serves as the book's back cover. The caption reads: "The Perpetrators of this Cookbook." ❧

In Pursuit of Flavor

EDNA LEWIS

....

New York: Knopf, 1988
323 pages

*T*HE ROMANTIC MEMORIES and just over two hundred glamorous adaptations of southern masterpieces presented here are like an invitation requesting the pleasure of one's company at a special occasion. In six nontraditional chapters, Lewis entreats readers to follow the example established by her mother, a country cook who fed family and guests on her farm in Freetown, Virginia. Seasonal menus employ methods designed to preserve original flavors and seductive aromas, "a welcome introduction to good food simply and lovingly prepared."

We learn the value of organic and local produce, and the way to get the best out of vegetables, in the chapter "From the Gardens and Orchards." In "From the Farmyard," we are taught to keep a bit of ham around as a complement to a wide array of dishes, to season with a variety of fresh herbs and spices, to braise in clay pots, and to roast bones in order to create intensely flavored stocks. In "From the Lakes, Streams, and Oceans," we develop an appreciation for cooking in parchment. In "From the Cupboard," we discover how to make baking powder at home, how to listen for signs that a cake is finished baking, and when to use butter in place of lard in pastry. She pleads for purity in "From the Bread Oven and Griddle," recalling the taste of wheat berries in freshly milled flour made from grain that her family threshed themselves. She encourages us to bake in winter in order to bring back the tastes and smells of summer, in "The Good Taste of Old Fashioned Desserts."

Throughout, her imaginative recipes are a sheer delight. She bakes sweet potatoes with lemon flavoring, grates fresh coconut into rice, laces headcheese (souse) with port or sherry, stuffs roast duck with oysters, and sweetens roast Peking duck with an orange sauce of fresh orange juice and brandy. Red snapper is one of her favorite fish, and she serves it with a homemade garlic mayonnaise that is flecked with pureed Mediterranean olives. Her oyster stew is garnished with salsify and finely cut parsley. She made Chocolate Soufflé famous at New York's Cafe Nicholson, and here reveals its secrets, along with those for Wild Persimmon Tarts and two types of pralines.

Amazingly detailed and accurate line drawings of Lewis at work accent all of this—her hair swept back into a classic bun away from her face, dangling earrings, and her signature dress, an African caftan. She is shown shaping biscuits, setting the luncheon table, and selecting game birds at the butcher's shop. In the appendix, she tells us her favorite mail-order sources for open-pollinated seeds, plants, fruit trees, and berries; shops that carry game and wild turkey; and where in the Union Square Greenmarket to find the most exquisite wild greens, white peaches, and organically grown lettuce. ❧

Cooking the African Way

CONSTANCE NABWIRE AND
BERTHA VINING MONTGOMERY

....

Minneapolis: Lerner, 1988
46 pages

THIS BOOK IS PART OF the series Easy Menu Ethnic Cookbooks. After a brief introduction to the land, climate, people, and village life of Africa, the authors discuss important tools, techniques, and food traditions. Thirty-six Americanized recipes paint a picture of the cooking of eastern and western Africa. The volume concludes with a list of safety rules for careful cooks (including the proper handling of chiles), a metric conversion chart, and table of measures and equivalents. Attractive color photographs show cooks exactly how the dishes should look.

The authors show off updated versions of dishes that were unfamiliar at the beginning of the 1980s: *fufu* combines Cream of Wheat cereal and instant potato flakes; rice pancakes are cardamom scented; fried egg roll wrappers encase a mildly seasoned ground-meat mixture in samosas; the cakes made of ground black-eyed peas known as *akara* sport optional chopped cooked shrimp; drained oysters and chicken are recommended substitutes for crab and beef in *egusi* soup; East African Meat Curry calls for chicken but approves of lamb or goat substitutions. Sweet Balls, little doughnuts from Ghana served warm, remind me of the New Orleans cala, the women known as cala women, and their marketplace call, "Calas Tous Chaud!" meaning, "Get 'em while they're hot!" ❧

Barbeque'n with Bobby

Righteous, Down-Home Barbecue
Recipes by Bobby Seale

BOBBY SEALE

....

Berkley, California: Ten Speed, 1988
142 pages

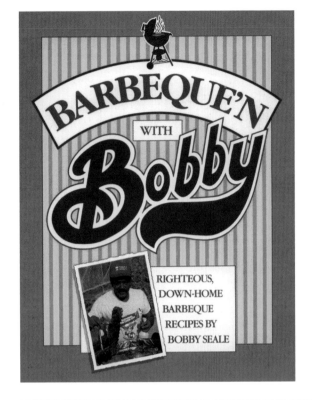

THE FOUNDING CHAIRMAN of the Black Panther Party, comedian, actor, jazz drummer, and "griller extraordinaire" provides tips for everything barbecue related. He starts with building the fire and moves on to making stews, side dishes, and even meat loaf over hot coals. All this is a throwback to the spirit of improvisation and soul cookery he picked up as a youngster in East Texas. In his world, barbecuing, or "bobbyque'n," is "truly an act of soulful hospitality" that "doesn't have to be an isolated festive occasion set aside only for holidays and summer days." With his book, the activist and air force veteran hopes that barbecuing will become the reader's "own savory, mouthwatering regular dining event."

It would have been so cool to learn the inside scoop about the people and places connected to "bobbyque." Instead, we must be satisfied with a great selection of bastes and marinades that he fashioned, which are strikingly creative, incorporating orange and apple juice, pineapple juice, wine, tomato juice, V-8 Vegetable Juice Cocktail, aromatic vegetables, fresh herbs, and a secret ingredient—a splash of liquid hickory smoke.

DECLARATION: BARBEQUE BILL OF RIGHTS

WHEN IN THE COURSE OF HUMAN DEVELOPMENT it becomes necessary for us, the citizens of the earth, to creatively improve the culinary art of barbe-que'n in our opposition to the overly commercialized bondage of "cue-be-rab" (barbecuing backwards); and to assume, within the realm of palatable biological reactions to which the laws of nature and nature's God entitle us, a decent respect for all the billions of human taste buds and savory barbeque desires; we the people declare a basic barbeque bill of rights which impels us to help halt, eradicate, and ultimately stamp out "cue-be-rab!"

As the commercialized backwards "bottle-back" recipe methods pursue and invariably evince a design to reduce our backyard-picnics into burnt, half done, bland, badly seasoned, improperly pit-qued entrees, then it is the right of we the barbeque lovers of the world, to alter the cue-be-rab phenomenon and creatively change our recipe process for a more righteous saucy, down-home, wood-smoking, delectable, baste-marinating, barbeque'n methodology.

The mixtures douse all the usual cuts of meat, fish, and poultry plus hot dogs, sausages, and a stuffed beef concoction he calls "Rice Burgers." On occasion, and for added flavor, wood chips are bathed in the brew before being tossed onto the glowing coals.

Moreover, his baste-marinades figure prominently in out-of-the-ordinary side dishes like honeyed greens, macaroni and cheese with bacon, and an outrageous salad composed of thirty ingredients, including leftover smoked meat. The book wraps up with a selection of low-sodium and no-sugar versions of southern standbys, a nod to health-conscious times.

And don't even get him started on the uninspired meat offered in restaurants that spell the word "barbe*cue*." He sounds off: "In the Black community the word was always spelled 'Bar Be Que' or 'Bar B Que' or shortened to BBQ and accompanied with that special hickory aroma. I began to feel that the 'cue' spelling represented something drab, or even 'square.'" To explain the difference, Seale quotes his pit master and mentor, Uncle Tom: "When you bobbyque, you don't put no sauce on it till it's done. Da base makes it tender." ꙮ

Colorful Louisiana Cuisine in Black and White

BIBBY TATE AND ETHEL DIXON

....

Gretna, Louisiana: Pelican, 1988
351 pages

NEARLY FIFTEEN YEARS before invaluable research by the food history scholar Susan Tucker into the lives of domestic workers and their employers in the South inspired the best-selling novel and award-winning film *The Help*, these authors designed their cookbook by telling the Creole/Cajun cooking story literally in black-and-white. Here, credit is given where credit is due, with a *B* to identify a dish of black origin and a *W* for white. The two-sides-of-the-story format is admirable for its effort to make up for all the times that the publishing world passed over black cooks when exalting Louisiana cuisine. But in another strange sort of way, the concept seems stuck on the same old narrative: that white cooking has more moxie than black cooking. Here is how it happened.

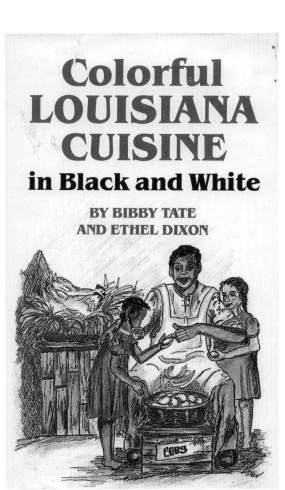

TEA CAKES - W

1 cup margarine or butter, melted	1 tsp vanilla
2 cups sugar	3 tsps baking powder
3 eggs	2 3/4 cups flour
4 tbsps milk	

Mix first five ingredients together; then stir in flour and baking powder. Drop by teaspoonfuls. Pat down to form cake. They may be cooked on ungreased cookie sheet. Cook at 350°.

OLD FASHIONED TEACAKES - B

1 cup sugar	2 1/3 cups all purpose flour, sifted before measuring
1/3 cup shortening or lard	
1 egg	1/4 tsp salt
1/2 tsp nutmeg	1/3 tsp soda
1/2 tsp vanilla	1/3 cup buttermilk

Grease baking sheet lightly. Start oven ten minutes before baking. Set to moderately hot (425°F). Measure sugar and shortening into mixing bowl and grease well. Add egg and beat until smooth and fluffy. Stir in nutmeg, vanilla, and salt. Stir soda into buttermilk and add flour and buttermilk, alternating in 2 or 3 portions, beginning and ending with flour. Stir gently until just smooth between additions. Remove 1/3 of dough at a time to a floured pastry cloth and roll out about 1/8 inch thick. Sprinkle lightly with sugar and cut with 1/2 inch cutter. Lift out with pancake turner onto baking sheet. Bake for 8 to 10 minutes. Makes 36 teacakes.

281

Tate, a white woman, was an "ardent cook and party giver"; Dixon was an African American artist and the author of *Big Mama's Old Black Pot* (described above). In a dozen chapters, the Louisiana natives record recipes that were handed down through generations, modernizing some and retaining the original charm of others. The chapters are set off by Dixon's paintings, which depict two little girls—one clad in a pinafore, her two long braids festooned with ribbons; the other, a barefoot pickaninny in a smock. The pair dance, picnic, play dress-up and hide-and-seek and jacks, have potato-sack races, and take it easy under a tall oak tree.

In the first chapter, "Morning Bells Are Ringing: Breakfast and Brunch Foods," the girls hold hands as they ring the plantation work bell to alert workers that it is "quittin' time." Tate's recipes—grillades, baked grits, fresh ham, pork chop casserole, company omelet, creamed chicken on toast, brunch chicken wings, eggs Benedict, and quiche lorraine—are identified by a *W*. A *B* marks Dixon's contributions: toast, bacon and cheese, shortenin' bread, country crackling shortenin' bread, hoecakes, syrup bread, drop biscuits, Plain Old Country Doughnuts, French toast, buckwheat pancakes, old-fashioned rice cake, old-fashioned country syrup pancakes, and Watermelon Delight.

And the book goes on like this, chapter after chapter, with the little girls scampering about in sentimental scenes that recall youth in Dixieland. More than six hundred segregated recipes and vignettes provide commentary about events in "old Louisiana days" and the foods and cultures that shaped them.

Naturally, some recipes simply refuse to accept discriminatory labels: Refrigerator Rolls, Mexican Cornbread, Country Fried Cakes, Meringue, Divinity Icing, Sour Cream Lemon Pecan Cake, Country Lemonade Cream Cake, Coffee Cake, Fig Cake, and a multitude of pies—Pecan, Sweet Potato, Sour Cream, Chess, and Molasses—plus Brownies and Bread Pudding. 🐝

Black Pioneer Cookbook

ALTON MUSEUM OF HISTORY
AND ART

....

Alton, Illinois, 1989
116 pages

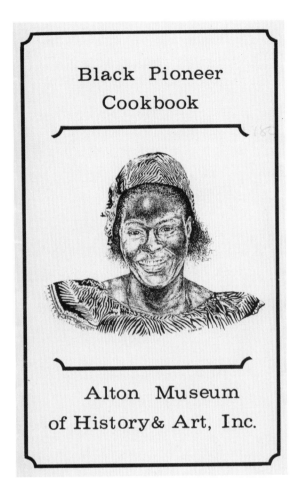

THE ALTON MUSEUM OF History and Art is dedicated to preserving Illinois's black past, with a particular focus on collecting the historiography of blacks in the River Bend region. This gift-shop keepsake collects community recipes from a half-dozen women, probably committee members, for southern favorites plus one or two outlandish mixtures, such as Seven-Up Meat Casserole and Veggie Bars.

Most notable, in addition to the hot yeast breads, cornbreads, and homely entrees made with pig parts, cabbage, beans, and greens, are a few recipes that teach basic cooking methods and illustrate knowledge of complex techniques. Fresh Roast Picnic Ham, How to Boil a Ham, To Clean and Dress Chicken for Frying, and To Smother-Broil Chickens are examples.

The book is also valuable for its documentation of historic landmarks and important people of the region. Photographs and artifacts tell the stories of pioneering African Americans who settled in the area and worked as farmers, teachers, and businessmen, including the world-renowned jazz musician Miles Davis. Line drawings and poor-quality black-and-white photos depict farms where migrating black southerners found work, "bottleboys" handling hot bottle molds for the glassblowers at Owens-Illinois, and the Reverend Augustine Toldton, the first black Catholic priest in the United States, who was ordained in Rome in 1886. ❧

Heart and Soul

Facts and Foods for Your Heart

....

Cleveland: MetroHealth System, 1989
33 pages

W HEN THE HEALTH CARE professionals behind this brightly colored handout (the American Heart Association Northeast Ohio Affiliate Inc., the St. Ann's Foundation, and the Diabetes Association of Greater Cleveland) joined forces, they had one goal in mind: to get black families "to care about the foods they eat and the health of their hearts," and to understand that their beloved "soul food" was the problem. Too bad they forgot to include food that tastes like home.

"Fried chicken, greens with salt pork, macaroni and cheese—soul food. Foods that bring back good memories and make you hungry just thinking about them . . . have large amounts of fat, cholesterol and salt," the introduction reminds readers. "These can cause heart disease, the leading cause of death in America."

The opening page prominently displays a frightening graph analyzing the rates of black mortality from heart disease. An annotated illustration of the inside of a blood vessel spells out how cholesterol causes hardening of the arteries (atherosclerosis). Six pages of cooking and shopping tips put into words the simple steps that people should take to reduce their risk from death and disease. All this enlightenment is reinforced by a chart featuring a week's worth of menu suggestions for breakfast, lunch, and dinner, plus nineteen restrictive recipes that lower the fat, cholesterol, and sodium content of black culinary standards. Some of those recipes—especially No-Salt Barbecue Sauce and Eggless Sweet Potato Pie—seem too pedantic to have held much appeal.

No wonder African Americans still suffer disproportionately from diseases with diet as a risk factor. 🐦

Soul Food

Classic Cuisine from the Deep South

SHEILA FERGUSON

....

New York: Grove, 1989
161 pages

JUST WHEN YOU THINK the soul trend has become passé, its authors having invoked everything from "gumption" to "voodoo magic" to explain the seductive thumbprint that black cooks left on every pot they stirred, Ferguson sashays onto the scene with an interpretation of soul pizzazz that goes well beyond highbrow discussions of African American foodways. It is food cooked with the senses and intended for young, hip cooks like her daughters.

She writes in a fast-talking, jive style that is complete with snappy expressions and memories of cooking and eating at home with family and friends in order to demonstrate cooking the soul food way: "You must use all of your senses. You cook by instinct, but you also use smell, taste, touch, sight, and particularly, sound . . . These skills are hard to teach quickly. They must be felt, loving, and come straight from the heart and soul."

SWEET POTATO MOUNDS

SERVES 4

3 medium sweet potatoes (total about 1 lb, 500 g), boiled and still hot
2 tablespoons butter
2 tablespoons light brown sugar, or to taste
1 large egg yolk
pinch of salt

$\frac{1}{8}$ teaspoon ground nutmeg
1 teaspoon rum (or pure vanilla extract)
$\frac{1}{4}$ cup (2 fl oz, 60 ml) heavy (double) cream
1 large egg white, stiffly beaten
1 cup (4 oz, 120 g) crushed walnuts (or pecans)

Preheat your oven to 450°F (230°C, gas 8). Peel and mash your sweet potatoes, and beat in the butter, brown sugar, egg yolk, salt, nutmeg, rum, and cream. Fold in your stiffly beaten egg white.

Divide the mixture into 8 individual lumps and pat them until firm. Spread the nuts out on a plate and roll the lumps in the nuts to coat them. Form them into

Wondering which American staples arrived from Africa with the slaves? Eggplant (guinea squash), okra, black-eyed peas, sesame, and yams, she says. Curious to know the sweeping history of black cookery in the cabin, the big house, the White House, on railroad cars, in restaurants, and as the heart of the community? She expounds on that too, providing dozens and dozens of cooking tips. Then she esteems black soul cooks from previous generations, writing about their brilliant dishes of animal guts smothered with rich cream gravy in such a colorful rhythm you will want to run out and trap a possum. For real.

Ferguson, the lead singer of the R&B singing group the Three Degrees, grew up in Philadelphia and learned to cook from relatives, whom she honors with words, pictures, and recipes for more than two hundred predictable African American dishes. There are also a few eye-openers from southern cookbook writers, such as crispy crawfish, known as Cajun popcorn, which is attributed to Terry Thompson-Anderson and Paul Prudhomme, and John Egerton's Sausage Biscuits. She adds parsley and a splash of Worcestershire sauce to spruce up home fries; recommends onion pancakes as a side dish for gumbo or creamed sweetbreads; ornaments Red Kidney Beans with Rice and Sausages with several taste variations, including coconut cream and beer; and concocts a dish she calls Sweet Potato Mounds, a sort of pone without all the peeling and grating.

She wrote the book as a gift to her twin daughters, one that would preserve part of their cultural and culinary heritage while the family lived in England. In addition to the women who were her kinfolk, Ferguson's writing embraces the "big black mammy" in the Tom and Jerry cartoons, who "typifies all that we hold dear about the wealth of spirit and strength of character of the black soul food cook." The author explains why this is so: "We don't even see her face . . . but we presume that she can cook up one mighty fine storm and that the blackberry pies she puts out on the ledge to cool will taste some kinda good. We can feel her strength and we can almost smell the aromas coming from her kitchen. Now that's one helluva strong faceless image!"

Instead of the usual chapter headings, Ferguson's recipe categories are snazzy: "The High and Mighty Breakfast"; "Down-Home Breads"; "Grits, Grits, Grits"; "Fine Feathered Fowl"; "Critters That Swim"; "The Almighty Pig"; "If You See It, Shoot It"; "Beans 'n' Rice"; "Kissin' Cousins"; "Soulful Salads"; "God's Green Acres"; "The Glorious Sweet Potato"; "Sweet Thangs"; "Cakes and Cookies"; and "Pickles and Drinks." The book concludes with a reading list of classic and soul cookbooks and scholarly works that cover slavery, southern studies, and culinary history. ❧

Iron Pots and Wooden Spoons

Africa's Gifts to New World Cooking

JESSICA B. HARRIS

....

New York: Atheneum, 1989
195 pages

The Negro is a born cook. He could neither read nor write, and therefore he could not learn from books. He was simply inspired; the god of the spit and the saucepan had breathed into him; that was enough.

—Charles Gayarre, *Harper's Magazine*, 1880

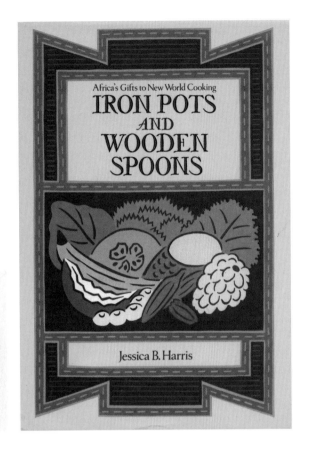

Africa's Gifts to New World Cooking
IRON POTS
AND
WOODEN
SPOONS

Jessica B. Harris

FOUR YEARS AFTER publishing *Hot Stuff: A Cookbook in Praise of the Piquant* (described above), Harris expanded on the linkages between African and Caribbean culinary traditions and African American foodways. She presents a thorough history of African foods before the Middle Passage and their transformation in the New World, pointing to the "'genius' of the African cooks" who substituted local ingredients for original ones and infused European recipes with techniques formerly practiced in their homeland.

Harris presents a comprehensive glossary of ingredients and utensils and then provides nearly two hundred recipes for African dishes that "transformed the eating habits of planters in the American South," not least by introducing spices, peppers, and okra. Exhaustive headnotes accompanying virtually every recipe explain regional lore, suggest adaptations, make serving suggestions, and provide testimonies that connect dishes to places, friends, family, and special occasions.

Among the foods and combinations that were major components of the African diet before the slave trade are beans consumed with a kind of millet known as dukhn; grains such as sorghum, wheat, and rice made into thick porridges, pancakes, fritters, and breads; particular kinds of puddings; yams, green leafy vegetables; boiled or roasted meat; vibrant seasonings; aromatic spices; and hotter-than-hell peppers. They were accompanied by highly seasoned stews served with a starch. Drinks included water plain or sweetened with honey, milk, millet beer, mead, and palm wine. All these practices were adapted to indigenous foods in America. ❧

The Soul of Southern Cooking

KATHY STARR

....

Jackson: University Press of Mississippi, 1989
Reprint edition, Montgomery, Alabama: NewSouth, 1989
192 pages

STARR WROTE TO EASE the anxiety associated with cooking, to teach readers how to cook fresh food the way her family cooked it in the old days—vegetables from the garden, chickens from the yard, hogs raised and killed at home—and to share the secrets of soul cooking. Like her grandmama, she turned her back on the professional world and devoted herself to the love of cooking.

She embellishes her collection of recipes for winter, spring, summer, and fall with entertaining narratives that record traditions and foodways of the Mississippi Delta. Abstract line drawings provide visual cues for such interesting subjects as preparations for a whole hog, men and women casting fishing lines at a river's edge, dinner on the grounds outside a church, and a kitchen scene where a woman, presumably her grandmama, has her hands on steaming cauldrons on the stove.

The recipes reflect the consumption of foods available seasonally, in the natural environment. The section "Pork Preparations Straight from the Hog" includes subsections labeled "How to Kill a Hog at Home" and "How to Fry Out Fat for Cracklins" (a snack made from fried pig skin). Starr identifies the best time of year for slaughter so that the meat is not "rubbery"; provides a recipe for hot pepper sauce to serve with Battered Hog Maw and Homemade Hog Head Souse; explains why "jecking" (boiling) ribs before barbecuing is important; and gives "The Ingenuity Test," the perfect way to make sure that Homemade Mixed Sausage is well-seasoned. ❧

The Dooky Chase Cookbook

LEAH CHASE

....

Gretna, Louisiana: Pelican, 1990
224 pages

Untitled by M. Bengu

Leah Chase

LEAH CHASE is a spirited woman who speaks candidly about how she transformed her husband's family restaurant, Dooky Chase's, from a small sandwich shop and lottery ticket purveyor into a pulsating hub of political activism, fine black art, and delicious Creole home cooking. Her meditation goes on to demonstrate the ways that love, humor, wisdom, and French flair spur on cooks who are new to the world of Creole cooking. "You have to love that pot and love what you are doing," she enjoins. "Talk to almost any black Creole person about their food and you will hear all the love in the world as they speak. You get hungry just listening to how they put that food together. They really enjoy doing it."

Southern-style sweet potato pone, biscuits, and rolls stand with Creole dishes such as Breakfast Shrimp (Louisiana Shrimp and Grits) and Eggs New Orleans in the "Breads and Breakfasts" chapter, which opens the book. The Giblet Stew, Mirliton Soup, Stewed Eggs, Okra Gumbo, and B.L.T. Soup (made by braising the bruised outer leaves of iceberg lettuce in bacon

drippings) in the chapter "Soups, Stews, and Gumbos" reveal her imaginative use of leftovers.

Health conscious cooks may find comfort in low-sodium, low-cholesterol versions of jambalaya, potato salad, red kidney beans, Bean Cakes with Hot Chili Sauce, Crowder Peas with Okra, Sweet Potato Dressing, and Leah's Cole Slaw (sweetened with pineapple juice and dotted with pineapple chunks). And although Chase explains that she doesn't like desserts and doesn't make them, she offers a few simple recipes for familiar treats so that there is "something for everyone, from fruits to pies to cakes."

Cooking in Magnalite cookware "is like religion" to the Chase family, which explains the treatise on keeping stockpots, Dutch ovens, and chicken fryers "shiny, shiny, shiny, both inside and out."

A cautionary note: The book contains a significant typo in Crab Soup: 3 cups of all-purpose flour instead of 3 tablespoons, so watch out. The author personally corrected my edition. ❧

Living High on the Hog

Updated African-American Recipes

Charla Draper and Robin Kline for the
National Pork Producers Council, 1990
32 pages

TWO OF MY FRIENDS, the registered dietitian Robin Kline and the food writer Charla Draper, personified the synergistic relationship between white "ladies" and slave "wenches" working together in plantation kitchens to create what we now know as southern cuisine and southern hospitality when they joined forces to produce this free pamphlet as a celebration of Black History Month. Their collaboration preserved African American cultural heritage while demonstrating how traditional African American dishes could be made with all the usual flavor but with less fat and fewer calories, and in less time. "One major change was to use lean, fresh pork, and whenever possible we replaced butter with low-fat yogurt and used egg whites instead of whole eggs," Draper said in the press release that accompanied the booklet.

Traditional African American cooking springs from many sources and regions, the duo explains, so the updated recipes combine familiar ingredients and techniques from around the globe. Cajun spices and garlic flavor pork roast, Caribbean jerk seasoning perks up the profile of pork loin, and the taste of spareribs is made bright with a splash of citrus. And just in case versatility and streamlined dishes are not enough to convince critics of black culinary aptitude, famous African American inventors and their advancements are included as part of the collection. ❧

Cookin' with Queen Ida

"Bon Temps" Creole Recipes (and Stories) from the Queen of Zydeco Music

QUEEN IDA GUILLORY
WITH NAOMI WISE

....

Rocklin, California: Prima, 1990
Second revised edition, 1996
240 pages

Q UEEN IDA GUILLORY was the queen of reinvention. She transformed herself from a school bus driver to a Grammy Award–winning leader of a hot zydeco band. So when food began to creep into her concerts, few were surprised. In this informative and educational diary, Guillory shares the intimate details of how favorite dishes were developed, recalling life on a farm just outside Lake Charles, Louisiana. The book is organized around delightful stories of special times with family, and menus and recipes based loosely on those memories.

"Early on we realized the wisdom of skipping lunch when we had a business meeting at Queen Ida's," wrote John Ullman and Irene Namkung, members of the creative team that put this project together. "After several hours of discussing tour logistics, and promotional materials, Ida would step over to the stove, lift the lid off a large pot, and say 'John and Irene, sit down and try just a little of this!' 'A little of this' usually turned out to be boudin, neck bone stew, okra and tomatoes, gumbo, catfish courtbouillon, hog's head cheese, or another of the marvelous recipes contained in the following pages . . . It was everyday cooking for Ida, but it was a whole new culinary world for us."

Guillory's culinary training began in the family's truck gardens and on the large rice farm that her father managed near Beaumont, Texas, where, as a young apprentice, she recalled playing with the pigs, eating the rock candy that was leftover in the sugarcane press, fetching water from the well, pulling taffy, making toys out of old brooms and straw and ribbons, and watching her mother make cottage cheese and caramel-flavored milk (café au lait).

Guillory's memory for details is profound. She describes chores and tasks associated with cooking meals for the many hired hands working the fields, and then relates these experiences to family recipes. Grandma's Crepes, Mama's Homemade Syrup, *maque choux* (the Creole version of fried corn, with tomatoes), several unusual types of étouffée (made with beets, turnips, and okra), and Sweet Patty Pan Squash (cymling) Dessert are part of Guillory's sweet talk.

We learn that jambalaya, fried chicken, and sweet potatoes complement the menu at a *fais-dodo* (a dance party) in the chapter "Creole Courtship." Turnips Étouffée and Grillades aux Tomates illustrate the survival skills every family needed in order to begin again in a new town. The section "A Country *Boucherie*" (a party to celebrate butchering time) makes recipes for swine entrails sound enticing.

The appendix contains a thorough listing of Creole ingredients, cooking techniques, and sources. "Required Reading" includes a primer on roux and miscellaneous resources for additional study. A few line drawings of ingredients such as rice, vegetables, and the components of pie pastry beautify some pages. Devotees will love the part about zydeco. ❧

Family of the Spirit Cookbook

Recipes and Remembrances from African-American Kitchens

JOHN PINDERHUGHES

....

New York: Simon and Schuster, 1990
Reprint edition, New York: Amistad, 2001
320 pages

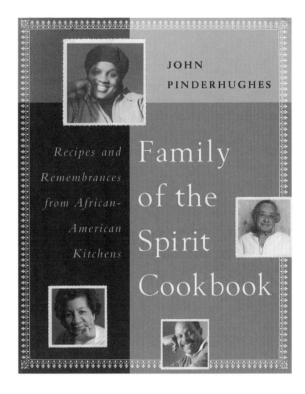

THE AUTHOR'S GRATITUDE, his love of the kitchen, and the joy he gained from helping his grandmother peel potatoes, shuck oysters, and pick tomatoes—or from "just sitting with her"—is revealed in this volume, which honors ten cooks who inspired his passion. Each had his or her own way of doing things, which they divulge in a half-dozen recipes each and brief narratives that tell us a little something about the time and place in which their talent bloomed.

The folk wisdom begins with Pinderhughes himself and the recipes he crafted from memories of making biscuits, browning the flour for chipped beef, and then "laughing, talking, and being together around a wonderful meal." He teaches about the southern summertime habit of eating tomatoes with almost every meal, and the penchant for fish he discovered while cooking seafood dishes with family and friends on

Martha's Vineyard: Grilled Stuffed Bluefish, Striped Bass Sauteed in Garlic Butter, swordfish, and spring scallops.

The remaining text and black-and-white photographs introduce the cooks who served as his culinary mentors: Gum Gum, his paternal grandmother, known for crab cakes, seafood casserole, and deviled crab. She "never had pigtails, and we never had—what do you call those things?—chitlins . . . We had oysters, crabs, and lots of fish—sea trout and those little flat fish. We called them diamonds"; Gram T, remembered for "the smells of pies, cakes, and cookies coming from her kitchen," including a vanilla-wafer-type treat; and Aunt C, whose dishes recall the days when families "put down eggs in a big crock with water to keep over the winter when the hens didn't lay." 🌸

Jerk

Barbecue from Jamaica

HELEN WILLINSKY

....

Berkeley, California: Crossing Press, 1990
173 pages

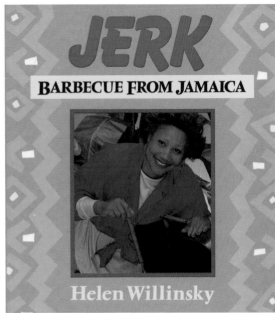

THE EXOTIC SMELLS and tastes of the Jamaican jerk hut wash right into the home kitchen when foods are spiced Willinsky's way and cooked over an open fire. In addition to jerking history, the author tutors on jerking basics, such as grill types, controlling the heat, and determining when the jerk is done, followed by more than a hundred recipes for jerked meats and vegetables and a grand selection of accompaniments in chapters delightfully entitled "Pork Tails and Tales," "Feathered Friends," "Seafood Sampler," "Here's the Beef," and "Lamb and Goat."

"The taste of jerked foods is hot with peppers," the author writes, "but, as you savor it, the variety of spices catches up with you, and it is like a carnival where all the elements come together in your mouth. The combination of spices tastes as if they were quarreling and dancing and mingling in your mouth all at the same time." That combination of onion, thyme, salt, ground allspice, nutmeg, cinnamon, and peppers is rubbed onto meat, poultry, seafood, or vegetables, whirred into a paste in the food processor, or blended into a marinade when soy sauce and a bit of cider vinegar are stirred into the mix.

African slave hunters adapted the seasoning methods of Jamaica's native Arawak Indians as a seasoning for food cooked in a pit. Escaped ex-slaves, known as Maroons, trapped wild boars, spiced the meat as a means of preservation, wrapped it in leaves, and buried the marinated pig in a hole in the ground filled with hot stones so that the pork steamed slowly in its own juices. The meat also was cooked slowly over a fire of green pimiento wood.

Its improvisational character is inherent, according to the author: "It is not a predictable flavor, but rather a hot, spicy, uncontrolled festival that engages all your senses."

To return your temperature to normal, the chapter "Wid It" offers bland and palate-cooling side dishes such as Festival, a sweetened version of hush puppies spiked with nutmeg; gungo peas (like pigeon peas) and rice; Grilled Pineapple with Passion Fruit Sauce; and a few vegetables enlivened with jerk seasoning, such as Jamaican Cole Slaw and Steamed Callaloo.

In "Tropical Sweet Tooth," Willinsky shows off home-style desserts such as Gizadas (chewy coconut filling wrapped in pastry), Honey Pineapple Bread, and a long list of refreshing coffee, alcoholic, and exotic fruit drinks, including Rum Punch, Ginger Beer, Sorrel Drink, Tamarind-Ade, and Bloody Mary à la Jerk. ❧

Sweet to the
SOUL

The Hope of
Jemima

Ef oona ent kno weh oona da gwine,
oona should kno weh oona come from.

GULLAH PROVERB

If you don't know where you are going,
you should know where you come from.

ENGLISH TRANSLATION

I N 1994, Mrs. Wilkes' Boarding House was world renowned; its owner, Sema M. Wilkes, a living legend. That year, a whopping 165,000 copies of her updated classic, *Famous Recipes from Mrs. Wilkes' Boarding House in Historic Savannah*, were in circulation. The new edition of the spiral-bound book added fifty-three recipes, reprints of news articles, celebrity fan letters, and photographs of Mrs. Wilkes posed with her husband, Mr. Lolis H. Wilkes, along with her famous dishes and various awards. But it was a grainy, sepia-toned picture of Mrs. Wilkes that caught my attention.

Mrs. Wilkes stands in the foreground, dressed simply in a button-down sweater, her arms crossed behind her back. Three black women are posed at her heels, their street clothes barely visible underneath the standard-issue housekeeper's uniforms. Crisp white aprons are tied around their generous waists. All the women bear the same stoic glare. It is not clear where the picture was taken. Nothing suggests the kitchen or the dining room. Naked walls surround them.

I am not sure what the publisher intended to convey with this snapshot. An unbiased reading says that even in modern times, black women are the soul behind this successful southern food enterprise. In an era when mainstream cookbooks with titles such as *The Opinionated Palate*, *The Artful Eater*, and *Great Cooks and Their Recipes* signaled a growing "foodie" culture, and the title of chef was broadened to include skilled cooks who managed the kitchen—or not—it is hard for me not to think that it is the black women who belong out in front. Let me explain.

Mrs. Wilkes was admired for her brand of southern hospitality at home and abroad. The food and travel writers Jane and Michael Stern described the home-style cooking they enjoyed there as "filling, not fancy, tantalizing, not trendy"—huge dishes of Boiled Rice with Hot Peppers, Homemade Spiced Pork Sausages with Brown Gravy, Southern Fried Chicken with Cornbread Dressing and Georgia Cane Syrup,

Hoppin' John, Fresh Okra with Tomatoes, Candied Yams with Raisins and Lemon, coleslaw, pickles, corn muffins and biscuits, and "an entirely outstanding Sweet Potato Pie." A Brussels audience gave Mrs. Wilkes and her daughters a standing ovation for their *Gone with the Wind* dinner, the *Savannah News-Press* reported in 1986. The Japanese discovered Mrs. Wilkes three years later when Brunswick Stew and Savannah Red Rice took center stage at a special food fair called "Georgia on My Mind." *Condé Nast Traveler* magazine named Mrs. Wilkes's dining establishment, an icon of southern cooking, one of the fifty most distinguished restaurants in the United States.

Commingling in the kitchen built this empire, and it is the same cultural blending that melded European and African techniques with the indigenous ingredients of the Americas into something hallowed: southern cuisine. Scholars have described the synergy that took place in early American kitchens as "African grammar," "wok presence," and "creolization." Chefs in the 1990s applied arts and music terminology to the rich exchange, giving it a label that stuck. They called it "fusion cuisine."

In their *Fusion Food Cookbook* (1994), the chef Hugh Carpenter and the photographer Teri Sandison presented 150 recipes and more than 100 photographs of vividly flavored dishes so intricately woven it is hard to tell where one culture begins and another ends. The culinary historian Jessica Harris went a bold step further, declaring that creolized cooking predated fusion cuisine, in *Beyond Gumbo: Creole Fusion Food from the Atlantic Rim* (2003).

The fusion trend made it possible for African Americans to reclaim disrespected dishes in their own, unique way. The restaurant and catering chef Jeanette Holley, for example, wore her African American fusion sensibilities like a culinary badge of honor. Born to a Japanese mother and a black father, she built her reputation on the best of what each culture had to offer. Ginger and rum spiced sweet potato pie. Asian spices such

as star anise, coriander, and Szechwan peppercorns dusted barbecued pork spareribs. In a 1994 article for the *Los Angeles Times* Syndicate, she described it as a style in which "dishes borrowed parts from each other to develop a new language of their own."

Other examples of this "great flavor revolution," as Carpenter characterized it, sprang from the pages of black cookbooks published during the 1990s. As handcrafted, artisanal, and exotic ingredients became readily available in the marketplace, a coterie of authors wriggled free from the labels that had once tethered them to cabin cooking and the soul food of migrants. This was the decade when historians, chefs, church ladies, health agencies, vegetarians, musicians, barbecue pit masters, a magazine editor, a supermodel, and a former boxer adapted familial tastes to the latest trends for a broader readership. For them, blending different elements as an artistic, creative expression was a pleasure, making the Wilkes's perspective seem all the more outdated.

The cookbook author Dori Sanders esteemed the old ways as new in a collection of fabulous country-cooking recipes adorned with endearing reminiscences from her family's farm stand. Taking cues from the oral tradition of her ancestors, she proposed a return to the South, embraced community traditions and family values, and rejoiced in a heritage of seasonal eating that was neither homogenized nor mongrel—one that merged present-day appetites with the flavors of the farm. "Down home healthy" books embraced the low-fat and low-sodium ingredients popular among the health conscious in order to make cultural favorites like macaroni and cheese more wholesome. Soul food aficionados ensured permanency for their cookery with precise instructions that put fixed actions to inner culinary thoughts so that novices could throw down in the kitchen with a soul cook's state of mind. I even joined in the reformation, coauthoring a cookbook that integrated essential elements of the black past with the classic techniques of schooled African American chefs.

The mainstream couldn't help noticing. In a 1993 report, the *New York Times* food columnist Florence Fabricant observed the sophistication of African American fusion cooking. From interviews with black head chefs at fine restaurants in San Francisco, New York, and Washington, D.C., she determined that blacks were ascending to the top ranks of restaurants in nonracialized kitchens and were cooking culturally neutral food. Black *cooks* were still preparing the soul food and barbecue that epitomize cultural-heritage cooking, she wrote. Black *chefs* took cues from heritage cooking *and* from classical French dishes and techniques, such as blancmange and making good stock. "For hundreds of years there have been black cooks in America. Now there are also black chefs. In the past few years, more blacks have begun achieving prominence and recognition as professionals in fine restaurants, diversifying a field that was once almost exclusively white, male and, in the most prestigious restaurants, European," she observed. "At the same time, this generation of chefs is also turning out food that tends to be colorblind."

In that same year, a committee of food, wine, and restaurant experts partnered with the 100 Black Men of Sonoma County to honor the "talent, inspiration and accomplishments" of great chefs at a chic wine country dinner. Matanzas Creek Winery hosted "Celebrating America's Top Black Chefs," a fête that honored, among others, the author and restaurateur Leah Chase. In the following year, a young award-winning chef named Patrick Clark, who had been tickling palates in New York and Los Angeles with silky and seductive sauces and exotic vegetables such as fiddlehead ferns, joined the honorees.

I met Clark in 1990 while writing a story for the *Los Angeles Times*. Our paths crossed again when I wrote his profile for *A Taste of Heritage: The New African-American Cuisine* (2002). Sadly, he passed away suddenly while we were working on a cookbook proposal for his harmonization of haute and southern cuisines (Roasted Saddle of Rabbit, Wild Mushrooms and Parsnips, and Chilean Sea Bass with Zucchini, Chanterelles, and Curry Oil). Clark wanted to show the world the myriad ways his creative gait raced forward, but did so without treading on his African American past. The Patrick Clark Family Trust and the chef Charlie Trotter published *Cooking with Patrick Clark: A Tribute to the Man and His Cuisine* in 1999.

For the last twenty years, cultural culinary dignity has enriched black cookbooks with reasoning that riffs on the well-known philosophy of the great French food writer Jean-Anthelme Brillat-Savarin: "Tell me what you cook and I'll tell you who you are." Modern authors publish in a climate where fresh ingredients and innovative approaches appeal to new audiences, and at a time when nostalgia for old-fashioned practices looks smart and the color-blind are politically correct—a time when our collective palates think home-cooked anything tastes good again.

Society has once again found a common denominator in the soul foods of the South. Integrating black cultural foods into trendy restaurant menus is now chic. The foods that represent modern eating (local, organic, sustainably and ethically produced) are the victuals of yesterday's poor with a newly hip personality. The nation's young hot chefs have discovered greens, fried chicken, watermelon, and swine. Homemade pickled okra appears on menus. Pork belly and cheeks, pig tails and pig ear sandwiches, fascinate the uninitiated—so much so that trend watchers announced a tongue-in-cheek threat of a hog shortage: "aporkalypse."

But the times are not yet postracial. Black female food industry workers are still disparaged. Celebrity chefs and prominent authors are mostly men.

In 2002, Texas A&M University's student newspaper, the *Battalion*, published a political cartoon that resembled the kind of degrading Jim Crow–era imagery that appeared routinely on manufacturer's labels and in advertising, magazines, and southern daily newspapers. Only worse. The illustration depicted a large black woman wearing an apron, holding a spatula, and chastising her son at test time. Testing is serious business for politicians, school districts, and parents in the Lone Star State. Evidently, black boys performed pretty poorly that year.

Neither the student, nor his or her editor, nor the journalism advisor questioned the suitability of using a bigoted turn-of-the-century image to portray a modern mother's concern for her son's poor academic performance. The black students did. They brought the lapse to the attention of school officials and, in the words of the newspaper's faculty adviser, Ronald E. George, "commenced fax warfare alleging racism where there was none."

In an op-ed commentary that ran in newspapers all over the state, George told of a particularly racist outburst that a Houston television reporter had made against African Americans (off camera) thirty-two years earlier. George's point, in providing such a stark example of unmistakable prejudice, was to defend his editors, students, and their staffs against accusations of racism. He invoked the vulgar language and debasing images used by his colleague in hopes of making clear to readers that he understood the difference between "ignorance, bigotry and hate" and an "insensitive," "unfortunate" mistake.

I'm not so sure.

It is true that we live in a society that values diversity, abhors "pulling the race card," and promotes "no color line" policies, but the A&M cartoon experience says that even with redoubled efforts, our best and brightest technology-saturated children cannot see beyond Jemima's narrow cliché. In the absence of a written history that defies—or at least counterbalances—the stereotype, the picture of an African American woman in our national mind's eye still resembles an insensitive exaggeration. At least for some.

I know that we can not take back three hundred years of harsh words and pictures, but I believe it is possible to undo some of the damage just by looking at the vast diversity of talents and abilities displayed by African American food professionals through the cookbooks they left behind. And thereby seeing ourselves.

Today, African Americans are just as likely to engage in catering, food service, and retail as we are to explore food writing, food studies, or food archaeology. Restaurant architecture and design intrigue us. Creative entrepreneurs develop hog maw shops, chitlin delivery services, and their own private labels of canned and packaged southern or soul food. African American "foodies" host wine dinners, book clubs, and couples classes. We spice up cocktail parties and health with diasporic dishes. We believe in sustainability and in knowing your farmer. We are importers of free-trade coffee and chocolate. We make wine.

The insightful Persian poet and theologian Rumi brought it all together this way: "Fresh, perfect fruit is the last thing to come into existence, but it is in fact the first, for it was the goal." ❧

Titles

The African American Educational Center
Kwanzaa Cookbook Journal

Compiled by Brenda Allen and Rosa Bland
Teaneck, New Jersey: AAEC of Northern New
    Jersey, 1991
104 pages

....

My Kwanzaa Book

Carolyn Cockfield
Third edition
Beltsville, Maryland: Sea Island Information
    Group, 1991
Previous editions, 1986, 1990
44 pages

....

Kwanzaa
An African-American Celebration
of Culture and Cooking

Eric V. Copage
New York: Quill, 1991
Reprint, *Fruits of the Harvest: Recipes to
    Celebrate Kwanzaa and Other Holidays*
New York: Amistad, 2005
356 pages

....

Louis Evans' Creole Cookbook

Louis Evans
Gretna, Louisiana: Pelican, 1991
Paperback edition, 2006
239 pages

....

Sky Juice and Flying Fish
Traditional Caribbean Cooking

Jessica Harris
New York: Fireside, 1991
242 pages

The Black Family Reunion Cookbook
Recipes and Food Memories

National Council of Negro Women
New York: Fireside, 1991
212 pages

....

Louisiana Creole and Cajun Cooking
at Its Best

Tyrone A. Willis
Olathe, Kansas: Cookbook Publishers, 1991
93 pages

....

Bittle en' T'ing'
Gullah Cooking with Maum Chrish'

Virginia Mixson Geraty
Orangeburg, South Carolina: Sandlapper, 1992
78 pages

....

The McClellanville Coast Cookbook

Edited by Susan Williams
McClellanville, South Carolina: McClellanville
    Arts Council, 1992
254 pages
Note: This is not a book by or about African
    Americans, though it is often associated with
    black cooking.

....

Sylvia's Soul Food
Recipes from Harlem's World-Famous Restaurant

Sylvia Woods and Christopher Styler
New York: Morrow, 1992
144 pages

Jazz Cooks
Portraits and Recipes of the Greats

Bob Young and Al Stankus
New York: Stewart, Tabori and Chang, 1992
216 pages

....

Curtis Aikens' Guide to the Harvest

Curtis George Aikens
Atlanta: Peachtree, 1993
221 pages

....

Soul Cookin' Southern Style
A Collection of Old-Time Southern Recipes

Melvett Chambers
Denver, 1993
Reprint, 2002
96 pages

....

Down Home Healthy
Family Recipes of Black American Chefs

Leah Chase and Johnny Rivers
Publication of the National Institutes of Health
Washington, D.C.: Government Printing Office,
   1993
44 pages

....

Bill Hall's Land and Lakes Cookbook

Bill Hall
Nashville: Favorite Recipes Press, 1993
174 pages

....

The Black Family Dinner Quilt Cookbook
Health Conscious Recipes and Memories

Dorothy Height and the National Council of
   Negro Women
Memphis, Tennessee: Wimmer, 1993
222 pages

Cookin' Up the Blues with
Tabasco Brand Pepper Sauce

Paul McIlhenny
Avery Island, Louisiana: McIlhenny Company,
   1993
42 pages

....

The African-American Child's
Heritage Cookbook

Vanessa Roberts Parham
South Pasadena, California: Sandcastle, 1993
289 pages

....

Our Family Table
Recipes and Food Memories from
African-American Life Models

Thelma Williams
Memphis, Tennessee: Wimmer, 1993
95 pages

....

The Joy of Not Cooking
Vegetarian Cuisine Cooked Only by the Sun

Delights of the Garden [restaurant]
Edited by Imar Hutchins
Washington, D.C.: Delights of the Garden
   Press, 1994
200 pages

....

Addy's Cook Book
A Peek at Dining in the Past with
Meals You Can Cook Today

Edited by Jodi Evert
American Girls Collection
Middleton, Wisconsin: Pleasant Company, 1994
43 pages

A Traveler's Collection of Black Cooking

Yvonne M. Jenkins
New York: Carlton, 1994
128 pages

....

The African-American Kitchen
Cooking from Our Heritage

Angela Shelf Medearis
New York: Dutton, 1994
258 pages

....

"Essence" Brings You Great Cooking

Jonell Nash
New York: Amistad, 1994
465 pages

....

Celebrating Our Mothers' Kitchens
Treasured Memories and Tested Recipes

National Council of Negro Women
Memphis, Tennessee: Wimmer, 1994
222 pages

....

Meals and Memoirs
Recipes and Recollections of African Americans
in Tucson, Arizona

Compiled by Tani Sanchez
Tucson: African American Historical and
   Genealogical Society, Tucson Chapter, 1994
95 pages

....

Curtis Cooks with Heart and Soul
Quick, Healthy Cooking from the Host of TV's
"From My Garden"

Curtis G. Aikens
New York: Hearst, 1995
225 pages

Kwanzaa Karamu
Cooking and Crafts for a Kwanzaa Feast

April Brady
Minneapolis: Carolrhoda, 1995
64 pages

....

Down-Home Wholesome
300 Low-Fat Recipes from a New Soul Kitchen

Danella Carter
New York: Dutton, 1995
283 pages

....

Soul and Spice
African Cooking in the Americas

Heidi Haughy Cusick
San Francisco: Chronicle, 1995
303 pages

....

Food From the Soul
A Collection of Recipes That Provides a Brief
History of Their Origin and Their Modern
Day Rendition

Louise Goggans
Indianapolis, 1995
88 pages

....

The Welcome Table
African-American Heritage Cooking

Jessica B. Harris
New York: Simon and Schuster, 1995
285 pages

....

A Kwanzaa Keepsake
Celebrating the Holiday with New Traditions
and Feasts

Jessica Harris
New York: Simon and Schuster, 1995
176 pages

Food and Our History

Kibbi Mack-Williams
African American Life series
Vero Beach, Florida: Rourke, 1995
48 pages

··········

A Kwanzaa Celebration
Festive Recipe and Homemade Gifts from
An African-American Kitchen

Angela Shelf Medearis
New York: Dutton, 1995
194 pages

··········

African American Family Cookery
Healthy Eating; Low Fat, Low Sugar, Low Salt

Howard Paige
Southfield, Michigan: Aspects, 1995
195 pages

··········

Cookin' Up a Storm
The Life and Recipes of Annie Johnson

Jane Lee Rankin
South Fallsburg, New York: Grace, 1995
165 pages

··········

Dori Sanders' Country Cooking
Recipes and Stories from the Family Farm Stand

Dori Sanders
Chapel Hill, North Carolina: Algonquin, 1995
224 pages

··········

B. Smith's Entertaining and Cooking for Friends

Barbara Smith
New York: Artisan, 1995
176 pages

Ruby's Low-Fat Soul Food Cookbook

Ruby Banks-Payne
Chicago: Contemporary, 1996
175 pages

··········

Smokestack Lightning
Adventures in the Heart of Barbecue Country

Lolis Eric Elie
New York: Farrar, Straus and Giroux, 1996
225 pages

··········

George Foreman's Knock-Out-the-Fat
Barbecue and Grilling Cookbook

George Foreman
New York: Villard, 1996
175 pages

··········

Vertamae Cooks in the Americas'
Family Kitchen

Vertamae Grosvenor
San Francisco: KQED Books, 1996
192 pages

··········

In the Kitchen with Ainsley Harriott
Over 100 Deliciously Simple Recipes

Ainsley Harriott
London: BBC Books, 1996
128 pages

··········

The New Soul Food Cookbook
Healthier Recipes for Traditional Favorites

Wilbert Jones
New York: Birch Lane, 1996, New York
125 pages

Low-Fat Soul

Jonell Nash
New York: Ballantine, 1996
213 pages

....

The African-American Heritage Cookbook
Traditional Recipes and Fond Remembrances
from Alabama's Renowned Tuskegee Institute

Carolyn Quick Tillery
New York: Citadel, 1996
210 pages

....

Cooking

Angela Shelf Medearis and Michael R. Medearis
African American Arts series
New York: Twenty-first Century Books, 1997
80 pages

....

The Lost Art of Scratch Cooking
Recipes from the Kitchen of Natha Adkins Parker

Curtis Parker
Elk Grove, California, 1997
93 pages

....

Grace the Table
Stories and Recipes from My Southern Revival

Alexander Smalls
New York: HarperCollins, 1997
298 pages

....

Heart-Healthy Home Cooking
African American Style
With Every Heartbeat Is Life

U.S. Department of Health and Human
    Services, National Institutes of Health
Washington, D.C.: Government Printing
    Office, 1997
Revised edition, 2008
47 pages

The Africa Cookbook
Tastes of a Continent

Jessica Harris
New York: Simon and Schuster, 1998
383 pages

....

Mother Africa's Table
A Collection of West African and African
American Recipes and Cultural Traditions

Compiled by Cassandra Hughes-Webster for
    the National Council of Negro Women
New York: Main Street Books, 1998
210 pages

....

Mama's Tea Cakes
101 Delicious Soul Food Desserts

Wilbert Jones
New York: Birch Lane, 1998
122 pages

....

Ideas for Entertaining from the
African-American Kitchen
Recipes and Traditions for Holidays
throughout the Year

Angela Medearis
New York: Dutton, 1998
307 pages

....

Rappers' Delights
African American Cookin' with Soul

Al Pereira
New York: Universe, 1998
95 pages

....

If I Can Cook / You Know God Can

Ntozake Shange
Boston: Beacon, 1998
113 pages

Soul Food
Recipes and Reflections from African-American Churches

Joyce White
New York: HarperCollins, 1998
355 pages

....

A Healthy Foods and Spiritual Nutrition Handbook
A Comprehensive Guide to Good Food and a Healthy Lifestyle

Keith Wright
New York: A&B, 1998
127 pages

....

Mama Dip's Kitchen

Mildred Council
Chapel Hill: University of North Carolina Press, 1999
230 pages

....

The African American Kitchen
Food for Body and Soul

George Erdosh
New York: Rosen, 1999
64 pages

....

The New Soul Food Cookbook for People with Diabetes

Fabiola Demps Gaines and Roniece Weaver
Alexandria, Virginia: American Diabetes Association, 1999
201 pages

....

Vertamae Cooks Again
More Recipes from the Americas' Family Kitchen

Vertamae Grosvenor
San Francisco: Bay Books, 1999
160 pages

LaBelle Cuisine
Recipes to Sing About

Patti LaBelle, with Laura B. Randolph
New York: Broadway, 1999
216 pages

....

Rituals and Celebrations

Barbara Smith
New York: Random House, 1999
241 pages

....

The Peppers, Cracklings, and Knots of Wool Cookbook
The Global Migration of African Cuisine

Diane M. Spivey
Albany: State University of New York Press, 1999
422 pages

....

Food in Grandma's Day

Valerie Weber and Jeraldine Jackson
Minneapolis: Carolrhoda, 1999
32 pages

....

Sylvia's Family Soul Food Cookbook
From Hemingway, South Carolina, to Harlem

Sylvia Woods and Family
New York: Morrow, 1999, New York
275 pages

....

African-American Holiday Traditions
Celebrating with Passion, Style, and Grace

Antoinette Broussard
New York: Citadel, 2000, New York
244 pages

The George Foreman Lean, Mean,
Fat-Reducing Grilling Machine Cookbook

George Foreman and Connie Merydith
Rocklin, California: Pascoe, 2000
236 pages

....

George Foreman's Big Book of Grilling,
Barbecue, and Rotisserie
More Than 75 Recipes for Family and Friends

George Foreman, with Barbara Witt
New York: Simon and Schuster, 2000
224 pages

....

Cooking with Heart and Soul
Making Music in the Kitchen with
Family and Friends

Isaac Hayes
New York: Putnam, 2000
222 pages

....

Food for the Soul
A Texas Expatriate Nurtures her
Culinary Roots in Paris

Monique Y. Wells
Seattle: Elton-Wolf, 2000
French version, *La Cuisine Noire Americaine*
Geneva: Editions Minerva, 1999
191 pages

....

The New Low-Country Cooking
125 Recipes for Coastal Southern Cooking
with Innovative Style

Marvin Woods
New York: Morrow, 2000
224 pages

John Henry's Backyard Grilling
and Barbecuing

John Henry Abercrombie
Houston: John Henry's Press, 2001
128 pages

....

Leah Chase
Listen, I Say like This

Carol Allen
Gretna, Louisiana: Pelican, 2001
189 pages

....

Larissa's BreadBook
Baking Bread and Telling Tales with
Women of the American South

Lorraine Johnson-Coleman
Nashville: Rutledge Hill, 2001
245 pages

....

At Home with Gladys Knight
Her Personal Recipe for Living Well,
Eating Right, and Loving Life

Gladys Knight
Alexandria, Virginia: American Diabetes
    Association, 2001
193 pages

....

Real Men Cook
Tips, Quips, & Recipes

K. Kofi Moyo
2001
129 pages

....

The Church Ladies' Divine Desserts
Heavenly Recipes and Sweet Recollections

Brenda Rhodes Miller
New York: Putnam, 2001
196 pages

A Taste of Heritage
The New African-American Cuisine

Joe Randall and Toni Tipton-Martin
New York: Macmillan, 2002
352 pages

....

A Taste of Freedom
*A Cookbook with Recipes and Remembrances
from the Hampton Institute*

Carolyn Quick Tillery
New York: Citadel, 2002
260 pages

....

And Still I Cook

Leah Chase
Gretna, Louisiana: Pelican, 2003
152 pages

....

Coming Together
Celebrations for African American Families

Harriette Cole and John Pinderhughes
New York: Jump at the Sun, 2003
121 pages

....

*50 Great George Foreman Recipes! Lean,
Mean, Fat-Reducing Grilling Machine*

*50 Great George Foreman Recipes! Lean,
Mean, Contact Roasting Machine*

George Foreman
Rocklin, California: Pascoe, 2003
64 pages

....

Beyond Gumbo
Creole Fusion Food from the Atlantic Rim

Jessica B. Harris
New York: Simon and Schuster, 2003
384 pages

New Soul Cooking
*Updating a Cuisine Rich in Flavor and
Tradition (Melting Pot)*

Tanya Holland
New York: Stewart, Tabori & Chang, 2003
152 pages

....

The Gift of Southern Cooking
*Recipes and Revelations from Two Great
American Cooks*

Edna Lewis and Scott Peacock
New York: Knopf, 2003
332 pages

....

The Kitchen House
*How Yesterday's Black Women Created
Today's American Foods*

Carole Marsh (author not African American)
Our Black Heritage series
Decatur, Georgia: Gallopade, 2003
36 pages

....

Gullah Home Cooking the Daufuskie Way
*Smokin' Joe Butter Beans, Ol' 'Fuskie Fried Crab
Rice, Sticky-Bush Blackberry Dumpling, and
Other Sea Island Favorites*

Sallie Ann Robinson
Chapel Hill: University of North Carolina Press,
2003
170 pages

....

Celebrating Our Equality
*A Cookbook with Recipes and Remembrances
from Howard University*

Carolyn Quick Tillery
New York: Citadel, 2003
262 pages

Brown Sugar
Soul Food Desserts from Family and Friends

Joyce White
New York: Morrow, 2003
297 pages

....

Hallelujah! The Welcome Table
A Lifetime of Memories with Recipes

Maya Angelou
New York: Random House, 2004
218 pages

....

Occasions to Savor
Our Meals, Menus, and Remembrances

Delta Sigma Theta Sorority
Text by Edna Lee Long-Green
New York: Putnam, 2004
288 pages

....

George Foreman's Indoor Grilling Made Easy
*More than 100 Simple, Healthy Ways to
Feed Family and Friends*

George Foreman
New York: Simon and Schuster, 2004
230 pages

....

Patti LaBelle's Lite Cuisine
*Over 100 Dishes with To-Die-For Taste
Made with To-Live-For Recipes*

Patti LaBelle
New York: Gotham, 2004
227 pages

....

A Little Bit of Soul Food

Amy Wilson Sanger
Berkeley, California: Tricycle, 2004
18 pages

African American

Compiled by Ellyn Sanna
Recipes contributed by Rosa Waters
American Regional Cooking Library series
Broomall, Pennsylvania: Mason Crest, 2004
72 pages

....

Home Plate Cooking
Everyday Southern Cuisine with a Fresh Twist

Marvin Woods and Virginia Willis
Nashville: Rutledge Hill, 2004
226 pages

....

Food for the Soul
*Recipes and Stories from the Congregation of
Harlem's Abyssinian Baptist Church*

Abyssinian Baptist Church
New York: One World, 2005
268 pages

....

Ainsley Harriott's Feel-Good Cookbook
150 Brand-New Recipes for Body and Soul

Ainsley Harriott
London: BBC Books, 2006
240 pages

....

Smothered Southern Foods

Wilbert Jones
New York: Citadel, 2006
178 pages

....

Grub
Ideas for an Urban Organic Kitchen

Anna Lappe and Bryant Terry
New York: Tarcher, 2006
352 pages

Harlem Really Cooks
The Nouvelle Soul Food of Harlem

Sandra Lawrence
Lanham, Maryland: Lake Isle, 2006
152 pages

....

Sweets
Soul Food, Desserts, and Memories

Patty Pinner
Berkeley, California: Ten Speed, 2006
176 pages

....

The Soul of a New Cuisine
A Discovery of the Foods and Flavors of Africa

Marcus Samuelsson
Hoboken, New Jersey: Wiley, 2006
344 pages

....

Neo Soul
Taking Soul Food to a Whole 'Nutha Level

Lindsey Williams
London: Penguin, 2006
176 pages

....

Delilah's Everyday Soul
Southern Cooking with Style

Delilah Winder
Philadelphia: Running Press, 2006
280 pages

....

45 Healthy Soul Food Recipes

American Heart Association
Lincolnwood, Illinois: Publications
    International, 2007
95 pages

Cooked
From the Streets to the Stove,
from Cocaine to Foie Gras

Jeff Henderson
New York: Morrow, 2007
275 pages

....

Sweety Pies
An Uncommon Collection of Womanish
Observations, with Pie

Patty Pinner
Newtown, Connecticut: Taunton, 2007
171 pages

....

Dining In
150 Special Dishes Easy Enough to
Make Everyday

Gerry Garvin
Des Moines, Iowa: Meredith, 2008
224 pages

....

Chef Jeff Cooks
In the Kitchen with America's Inspirational
New Culinary Star

Jeff Henderson
New York: Scribner, 2008
264 pages

....

Recipes for the Good Life
Patti LaBelle
New York: Gallery, 2008
224 pages

....

The New African American Kitchen

Angela Shelf Medearis
New York: Lake Isle, 2008
272 pages

Cooking with Rhythm

Kariem Abdulassamad
Xlibris, 2009
250 pages

....

Authentic Southern Cooking
Four Generations of Black Culinary Tradition

Lamont Burns
Minocqua, Wisconsin: Willow Creek, 2009
Originally published as *Down Home Southern
    Cooking*, 1987
179 pages

....

The Princess and the Frog
Tiana's Cookbook; Recipes for Kids

Deanna F. Cook and Cindy Littlefield (authors
    not African American)
New York: Disney, 2009
64 pages

....

The Black Farmer Cookbook
Flavors without Frontiers

Wilfred Emmanuel-Jones
London: Simon and Schuster, 2009
192 pages

....

New American Table

Marcus Samuelsson, with Heidi Sacko Walters
Hoboken, New Jersey: Wiley, 2009
356 pages

....

B. Smith Cooks Southern-Style

Barbara Smith
New York: Scribner, 2009
326 pages

Vegan Soul Kitchen
*Fresh, Healthy, and Creative
African American Cuisine*

Bryant Terry
Cambridge, Massachusetts: Da Capo, 2009
222 pages

....

The Soul Food Restaurant Cookbook

Delbert Washington
Saint George, Utah: Solar-Vision, 2009
40 pages

....

Great Food, All Day Long
Cook Splendidly, Eat Smart

Maya Angelou
New York: Random House, 2010
156 pages

....

Art Blakey Cookin' and Jammin'
Recipes and Remembrances from a Jazz Life

Sandra Warren
Donaldsonville, Louisiana: Margaret Media,
    2010
187 pages

....

America I Am
*Pass It Down Cookbook; Over 130
Soul-Filled Recipes*

Edited by Jeff Henderson and Ramin
    Ganeshram
New York: SmileyBooks, 2011
307 pages

Bon Soir

Bon Appetit!

Page from *Colorful Louisiana Cuisine
in Black and White*.

ACKNOWLEDGMENTS

AN ELEGANT new southern cuisine luncheon wowed members of the Association of Food Journalists in the dining room at the Ritz-Carlton Buckhead—Fried Green Tomato with Crabmeat Salad, Pecans and Basil, Quail Chop in Collard Greens with Acorn Squash Risotto, and Marinated Figs in Parchment Paper with Butternut Sorbet—but it was John Egerton's remarks that captured my attention. After regaling the audience with a brief history of southern food that demystified its treasures as more than just "six food groups: sugar, cream, salt, butter, eggs and bacon grease," he turned to the role that African American cooks had played in creating this storied cuisine. The year was 1994, and I was still finding my way as a curious student of African American and southern culinary history. John was the first white person I ever heard pay any attention at all to my ancestors. I was spellbound. "Without the contribution of black cooks it [southern cuisine] might have been as boring and bland as British food," he declared boldly. "They were not all

culinary geniuses, but without them, southern food would never have soared."

I waited for the after-lunch gaggle surrounding him to disperse, then plied him with questions of my own. I don't remember everything he said, but I do know that he responded to my curious enthusiasm in true Egertonian fashion: thoughtfully and attentively, in a way that made you feel as if you were the only person in the room. In the few minutes we had together, he described the mystery of a rare black cookbook he had just discovered at the Library of Congress, suggesting that we meet in the hotel pressroom so that I could make a copy. He rummaged through his brief case and generously gifted me with a small stack of blurry recipes written in 1912 by Mrs. W. T. Hayes and gathered under the title, *The Kentucky Cook Book: Easy and Simple for Any Cook*, by "a Colored Woman." And off we went.

John and I talked often after that about our shared passion for the African American cooks who had simply disappeared from the pages of southern history. He challenged me to think seriously about how best to reclaim their heritage while at the same time spurring racial reconciliation at the table. Over time, I began to think that John should share credit for this project. We had tossed thoughts around the table so many times and for so long that it seemed impossible to tell his from mine. (Thank you, John T. Edge, for admitting this first!) But John was adamant, saying, "I may have helped steer you to a few resources, but you have made this book your own . . . That's my story and I'm sticking to it."

When I think about John's way of *not* helping, the clichéd expression "words cannot express" feels just about right. Many people contributed to the completion of this book, some directly through their scholarship, others with research assistance, including Angela Gooden, Noel Harris Freeze, and the University of Texas students Valerie Lopez, Genna Wade, Annie Boggs, Shakila Powell, Merriah Wilhite, Spencer Iwatuje, Caley Burton, Lauren White, and Jaime Daiman. Many more simply listened or held my hand.

I want to thank Ann, Brooks, March, Allison, and Lila Pearl for unselfishly sharing John with the world; Jan Longone, Barbara Ketchum Wheaton, Barbara Haber, Psyche Williams-Forson, Bill and Marcie Cohen Ferris, Rebecca Sharpless, and Elizabeth Engelhardt for their encouragement as academics and friends; Adrian Miller, for telling me about obscure book titles he discovered while researching and reimagining soul food; Damon Lee Fowler, who opened his heart with emotional reflections of a revered family cook; John T. Edge and members of the Southern Foodways Alliance, especially Ronni Lundy, Nathalie Dupree, Elizabeth Sims, Martha Johnston, Donna Pierce, Scott Barton, Hoover Alexander, and Ari Weinzweig for their tough love and friendship, particularly during the early years; and the writers Molly O'Neil, Virginia Wood, Addie Broyles, and Nancie McDermott, whose generous words kept this work in the public's eye.

I am indebted to family and friends who cared for my children when I was head down, or who asked hard questions that challenged my ideas. Thank you to Heather Hutt for hours on the telephone; to Ellen Sweets and Mary Margaret Pack, for nudging me back to the keyboard when staying focused writing was a struggle—and for keeping me well fed.

I am grateful to my brother Derrick Hamilton, my sister-in-law LaTanya, and my niece Aliya for concert interventions; to my husband Bruce and our children, Brandon, Jade, Christian, and Austin, who never once complained when *The Jemima Code* stood between them and a home-cooked meal. And to Mom—for everything.

Most importantly, I deeply appreciate the University of Texas Press staff and my editor, Casey Kittrell, for preserving this important legacy. This book would not exist without your vision and direction. You believed in "the ladies and a few gentlemen" from day one, and fit perfectly in the space created when I lost my partner, mentor, and friend. ❧

INDEX

Note: Page numbers in **bold** indicate recipes
contained within illustrations.